**Books are to be returned on or before
the last date below.**

What did you do in the War, Auntie ?

What did you do in the War, Auntie ?

BBC BOOKS

TEXT AND PICTURE CREDITS

BBC Books would like to thank the following for providing photographs and for permission to reproduce copyright material. While every effort has been made to trace and acknowledge all copyright holders, we apologize for any errors or omissions and, if informed, would be glad to make corrections in future editions.

Photographs
Associated Press 10, 12, 24, 27; BBC Picture Archive 21, 26, 40, 46, 49, 51, 53, 56, 60, 71, 72, 76, 83, 93, 94, 101, 103, 109, 113, 115, 125, 131, 132, 136, 137, 139, 140, 144, 145, 149, 151, 154, 175, 180, 183, 185, 190, 194; Camera Press 192; Hulton Deutsch Collection 2–3, 6, 13, 17, 18, 29, 30, 32, 34, 35, 38, 48, 54, 58, 62, 68, 69, 77, 79, 86, 97, 98, 99, 104, 106, 107, 112, 116, 118, 121, 122, 124, 129, 134, 146, 148, 170, 173, 196, 209, 210; Illustrated London News 153; Imperial War Museum 22, 85, 157, 160, 168; Courtesy Dame Vera Lynn 91; Popperfoto 15, 36, 64–65, 66, 73, 78, 89, 156, 159, 163, 179, 198–99, 212; Topham Picture Source 201

Text
We'll Meet Again (by Ross Parker, Hugh Charles)
Copyright © 1939 Dash Music Co. Ltd, 89 Frith Street, London W1V 5TZ. Used by permission.
All rights reserved.
Don't Let's be Beastly to the Germans by Noel Coward.
© 1945 Chappell Music Ltd, London W1Y 3FA.
Reproduced by permission of International Publications Ltd.

Frontispiece: newsreader Frank Phillips looks for somewhere to sit in the Broadcasting House canteen. In the pre-war BBC he would not have been able to have a pint – BH was 'dry'.

Published by BBC Books, a division of BBC Worldwide Publishing
BBC Worldwide Limited, Woodlands,
80 Wood Lane, London W12 0TT

First published 1995

© Tom Hickman 1995

ISBN 0 563 37116 1

Set in Minion by BBC Books
Printed and bound in Great Britain by Clays, St Ives plc
Jacket printed by Lawrence Allen Ltd, Weston-super-Mare

CONTENTS

ACKNOWLEDGEMENTS

No one trying to write a popular history of the BBC during the Second World War could do so without consulting *The War of Words,* volume three in Asa Briggs's massive history of broadcasting in the United Kingdom, which was published in 1970. I acknowledge my debt to Lord Briggs; to the many broadcasters and others who lived through the period and wrote about it; and to Jeremy Bennett, producer of the BBC1 series, *What did you do in the War, Auntie?*, who gave me access to confidential documents and to the transcripts of all the interviews he and his team conducted.

Two points. It seemed not to worry the BBC of fifty years ago that calling a radio service a programme resulted in programmes going out on a programme. I have obviously referred to such services (i.e. the Forces Programme) by their proper titles when necessary, but wherever possible have substituted the more familiar 'network', both for clarity and my own sanity. I have also used the word 'radio' rather than 'wireless', although at the time the latter was still in much commoner usage.

Searchlights pick out the dome of St Paul's Cathedral. When German bombers set the City of London ablaze on the night of 29 December 1940, Robin Duff reported: St Paul's Cathedral was the pivot of the main fire. All round it, the flames were leaping into the sky. but there the Cathedral stood, magnificently firm, untouched...'

HITLER DECLINES TO READ THE SCRIPT

War broke out on the crystal-clear morning of Sunday 3 September 1939, but the BBC had moved to a war footing thirty-six hours earlier. On Friday 1 September – the day on which Hitler invaded Poland, the evacuation from London of over one million children began at sunrise and the black-out was imposed at sunset – the BBC merged its National and Regional radio networks.

The first warning that this was about to happen was given in the six o'clock evening news. Less than thirty minutes earlier Whitehall had informed the BBC that the change-over was to take place and the message was flashed to every transmitter station and studio in the country, telling engineers to open their sealed orders and act on them. For the next two hours the announcer, Robert MacDermot, played records, every few minutes repeating the warning and urging listeners to tune in either on 391 or 449 metres, the wavelengths which, until then, had belonged to the Scottish and North regions. At 8.15 p.m. Britain, for the first time, heard the words: 'This is the BBC Home Service'. The infant television service operating from Alexandra Palace had already been unceremoniously taken off the air, ten minutes after noon, leaving 20 000 households staring at their blank 10-inch screens.

WAR IS DECLARED

The announcement that everyone had expected for two days came at ten o'clock on Sunday morning: the Prime Minister would speak to the nation at 11.15 a.m. Most of the BBC's staff had been dispersed out of London during the previous week but those who were left in Broadcasting House – engineers, newsroom people and members of the foreign language sections – gathered in the concert hall to hear Chamberlain's broadcast over the big loudspeakers:

I am speaking to you from the Cabinet Room at Number Ten Downing Street. This morning the British Ambassador in Berlin handed the German Government a final note, stating that, unless the British Government heard from them by 11 o'clock that they were prepared at once to withdraw their troops from Poland, a state of war would exist between us. I have to tell you now that no such undertaking has been received and that consequently this country is at war with Germany…

You may be taking your part in the fighting Services or as a volunteer in one of the branches of Civil Defence. If so, you will report for duty in accordance with the instructions you have received. You may be engaged in work essential to the prosecution of war for the maintenance of the life of the people – in factories, in transport, in public utility concerns, or in the supply of other necessaries of life. If so, it is of vital importance that you should carry on with your jobs…

Godfrey Talbot, a news sub-editor who was to become a household name as a war correspondent, listened to the 'sepulchral tones of poor Chamberlain' (who was seventy and already terminally ill with the cancer that would kill him little more than a year later) and felt he heard a sense of doom in the 'terrible, brief statement'. The national anthem was played. Everyone stood, an inviolate mark of respect until a later age; in the thirties, people even stood for the national anthem in their own homes. A peal of bells followed and then, suddenly, eight minutes after Chamberlain had stopped speaking, at 11.28 a.m., the air-raid sirens resonated through Broadcasting House. There had been a few practices, but this was the first continuous wailing that had been heard and it went on and on like a great cry of pain which was erupting across the country. Talbot remembers the chill in the pit of his stomach as the lights flickered and someone said, 'My God, Godfrey, my wife's out in the street,' and people, including the commentator John Snagge, rushed for gas masks and tin hats and made for the roof to spot where the bombs were falling.

'It was absurd, Hitler wasn't expecting us to declare war on him precisely at that moment, it was a false alarm,' Talbot says. 'But it gave everybody a sinking feeling that war was here.' He went back to the newsroom on the second floor to write the one o'clock news: the air-raid sirens had been a false alarm; a war agriculture committee had been appointed in each county; the hospitals needed more midwives; any firm in the London area could have free sand for sandbags if they were prepared to collect it.

Tension mounted a little with the 4 p.m. bulletin: a War Cabinet had been formed. The other news affected people's lives more directly: all places of entertainment were to close until further notice and members of the public were to carry their gas masks and their addresses (clearly written on an envelope or

Newspapers did a roaring trade at the beginning of the war, but quickly lost ground to the BBC. After Norway was overrun in 1940 paper was strictly rationed. By 1941 broadsheets had as few as four pages, the tabloids eight.

Within eight minutes of Chamberlain's declaration the air-raid sirens wailed in earnest for the first time – a false alarm. Caught in St James's Park, these Londoners troop down into a shelter in orderly fashion.

luggage label) at all times. They were advised to acquaint themselves with the location of air-raid shelters and first-aid posts.

The 6 p.m. bulletin sagged – 'There is little fresh news from the war zone' – but it did feature King

George VI, shy and hesitant, speaking from his heart:

> In this grave hour, perhaps the most fateful in our history, I send to every household of
> my peoples, both at home and overseas, this message, spoken with the same depth of
> feeling for each one of you as if I were able to cross your threshold and speak to you
> myself.
>
> For the second time in the lives of most of us, we are at war ... and war can no longer
> be confined to the battlefield ...

The 7 p.m. news did nothing to inspire confidence that Britain's main ally was ready
for the fight: 'It is the official view that, since five o'clock, France has been at war with
Germany.' But at 9 p.m. came the news that Australia had thrown its bush-hat into the ring; and at 10.30 p.m. that Lord Gort had become Commander of the British Field Force. It is unlikely that J.B. Priestley's gruff, kindly voice reading the first of seventeen instalments of his novel, *Let the People Sing* (the first unpublished novel to be serialized by the BBC and one of the very few peacetime projects to survive the transition to war) sent many to a restful bed. Outside their windows the searchlights nervously fingered the starry sky, probing for Hitler's bombers. The black-out enveloped the land. In his diary, the newsreader Stuart Hibberd noted that London was 'strange and eerie, yet with an unsuspected beauty, the buildings on either side of Portland Place rising like the steep sides of a Norwegian fiord.'

THE RUN-UP TO WAR

The BBC had played its part in readying the nation during the long drift to war. After Germany overran Austria in March 1938, it broadcast appeals to recruit men and women for the jobs that war would necessitate – as air-raid wardens, auxiliary firemen, special constables, ambulance drivers – and it did everything it could to help launch the new Women's Voluntary Reserve. It broadcast talks on the use and care of gas masks, on ways of implementing the black-out, on

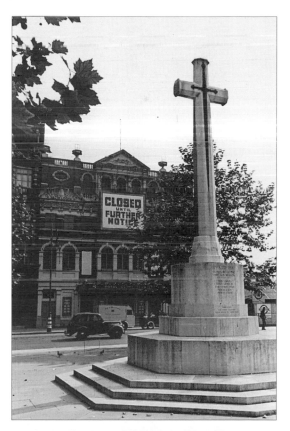

Like all places of entertainment, the London Royal Court Theatre shut on the declaration of war on 3 September 1939. Cinemas began to open again from 9 September. By December all the West End was back in business.

protecting the home from aerial attack. It even transmitted the sound of an air-raid siren so that people would recognize it. In January 1939 Chamberlain spoke about national service in the regular and reserve Forces – 'A scheme to make us ready for war' – and at the end of March, when Hitler marched into Czechoslovakia and Britain formally guaranteed Poland's independence, the BBC carried broadcasts about the call-up.

On 21 August 1939, Stuart Hibberd noted in his diary, 'a bombshell': he had just read the bulletin telling the nation that Russia had entered a non-aggression pact with Germany. The next day, for the first time, Parliament was recalled by radio, as were, two days later, tens of thousands of school-teachers who were about to be affected by the evacuation of children from London and the other big cities.

On 25 August, the BBC, which had not previously broadcast a news bulletin before six in the evening (because of a long-standing agreement with the newspapers), introduced one at 10.30 a.m. and another at 1 p.m. On 31 August, the Government issued orders that the evacuation should begin the next morning, although the one o'clock news added, rather hollowly, that 'no one should conclude that this decision means that war is now regarded as inevitable'. At six o'clock came the news that the fleet was mobilized. The 10.30 a.m. bulletin on the following day announced Poland's fate.

The British Government anticipated an immediate blitzkrieg, followed by air and sea invasion. In the light of that, and by agreement, the BBC stripped down its schedule to what in such circumstances was essential: news. The two announced wavelengths were kept open by light music which could be interrupted at any moment for declarations by the nation's leaders and for whatever instructions to the population became necessary. Other than the bulletins, the only fixed points were the *Daily Service*, for spiritual comfort ('requests to the Almighty for his support', one commentator has written), and *Children's Hour*. In a schedule shaped for a period during which people might have been fighting in the streets for their lives, the importance attached to *Children's Hour* seems faintly bizarre and wholly Reithian, even though the BBC's founding father had departed in June the previous year to become chairman of Imperial Airways.

THE PHONEY WAR

But where was the war? In 1939, some nine million radio licences were in issue, seventy-three for every hundred households, and all of them were permanently tuned for the news that everyone anticipated and dreaded. On the day after Chamberlain's declaration, the passenger liner *Athenia* was sunk by a U-boat in the Irish Sea, heightening the sense of impending danger (and heralding the ability of enemy submarines to blockade food shipments). Yet very little else was happening, and there simply was not enough news to fill the ten daily bulletins which the BBC had mounted. The seven-month period which was to be known as 'the phoney war' had begun. Richard Dimbleby, who went to France with the British Expeditionary Force, was able to provide colour, but not much in the way of content:

> We are standing in the pouring rain at the side of a French road, a road squelching with mud and lined right away over the plain to the far sky-line with the inevitable double row of poplars. It's a grey, cold, dismal day. A few lorries only are splashing by to and from the forward areas. But coming down the road towards us is a battalion that I know to be of a famous Irish regiment. (*Bagpipes.*) They are marching in threes, and in their full battledress and kit they blend with the dripping green grass of the roadside and the brown of the haystacks. (*Bagpipes.*) As they passed us on that road, with their brown capes glistening and their tin hats perched on their heads, I thought how similar this must be to pictures of the last war: the road, the trees, the rain, and the ever-lasting beat of feet.

November 1939: a column of smiling British troops march past the Paris Opera House. Six months later the Germans had driven the British Expeditionary Force on to the beaches of Dunkirk.

What frustrated a public deprived of cinemas, sporting venues, concert-halls, dance-halls and theatres, and consequently driven back indoors (if a high state of anxiety had not already kept them there, listening to the radio) was that the only entertainment provided by the BBC consisted of endless records and Sandy Macpherson at the theatre organ – and there was now no second network to which to escape. It did not help the BBC's position that much of what else was being broadcast was trivial and officious. Ministers of the Crown came to the microphone to describe the plans of their departments; an endless flood of directions and regulations on everything from private cars and food prices to conscription and blood transfusions took up at least an hour a day; and the interminable talks on such subjects as the evacuation, black-out problems, first-aid and, somewhat precipitately, on *Making the Most of a Wartime Larde*r, drove the public to distraction. The radio did not inform: it hectored and, like a spinster aunt, it fussed. The BBC had never been called Auntie before the war, despite the number of aunties who, with rather more uncles, kept children occupied on its National and Regional networks. Now the sobriquet began to enter the language and it was not born of the affection it later engendered.

PLAYING FOR TIME

The BBC had moved the bulk of its programme-makers out of London on 1 September so that, if saturation bombing knocked out the capital, broadcasting could continue from elsewhere; the 'sustaining service' was meant to last only until they could set up shop again. But while this was the reality, the BBC was foolishly congratulating itself, in the first emergency issue of *Radio Times*, on the splendid service it would continue to provide in wartime – this during a fortnight when the country's nerve-ends were being rubbed raw by forty-five sessions of Sandy Macpherson. Frank Gillard, a programme-maker who was later a war correspondent like Godfrey Talbot and ultimately a managing director of BBC Radio, had some sympathy for the organist, who played until his toes and fingers were numb: 'Poor man, he really did seem chained to his instrument because he had to go on playing, playing, playing to fill up time. It seemed to me he was playing without musical scores, because it wasn't the usual polished performance, I can tell you.' He is less sympathetic about the BBC's performance at this time: 'What I remember is the boredom of it.'

People wrote in, saying they would rather face the German guns than more Macpherson. The Press was no more charitable. The BBC's war effort was described as 'puerile' by the *Sunday Chronicle*, and the *Sunday Pictorial* thundered: 'For God's sake, how long is the BBC to be allowed to broadcast its travesty of a programme which goes under the name of entertainment?' The *Daily Mail* described 'its disappearing trick to two refuges "somewhere in England" 'as a scandal. In the House of Commons, the

Leader of the Opposition, Clement Attlee, retorted that listening to the BBC depressed him and a Labour MP suggested that, as the Government was determined 'to make the life of everybody as miserable as possible, it would be as well if we could have some brighter entertainment from the BBC.' A Conservative back-bencher insisted that 'the BBC wants a thorough clearing out of ... its present personnel and the substitution of men attuned as few of them are to the needs of war, with new ideas and a fresh outlook.'

As the BBC's head of Drama, Val Gielgud, said with sarcastic truth, the corporation had planned with great efficiency but for the wrong war. Properly, the Government, which had made the projections on which the BBC based its strategy, should have come to its defence. Even a brief statement to the House to explain that the National and seven Regional services had been reduced to the single Home Service for reasons of national security (for which reasons television had been taken off the air) could have absolved the BBC in the public's eyes. Indeed, the Government should have gone further and explained that, unless these measures had been taken, the transmitters would have offered a navigational guide to enemy aircraft. But the Government preferred to maintain a perverse silence and was evasive when questioned about the quality of what was being broadcast.

9 January 1940: Neville Chamberlain makes his first public speech since the outbreak of war, at the Mansion House. Four months later, after the British defeat in Norway, he lost a vote of confidence in the Government and was replaced by Churchill.

Finally, Chamberlain, who did not really see a wartime role for the BBC, because, he believed, no one would have the time to listen, told the Commons that 'conditions are very different from what they were' and added that 'in present circumstances to maintain quite the same standard as before the war' was not possible. This elliptical declaration raised more questions than it answered. The simple truth was that the Government was not prepared to acknowledge its part in the broadcasting build-up. Hitler had, apparently, declined to read the script, the predicted consequences of the declaration of war had failed to materialize and, for its part, the Government was content to leave the BBC looking foolish, prematurely guarding the perimeter fence.

Tʜᴇ ꜰɪɢʜᴛ ꜰᴏʀ ɪɴᴅᴇᴘᴇɴᴅᴇɴᴄᴇ

The BBC might have expected some support from the newly formed Ministry of Information, to which it was now accountable, but it already knew that such help would not be forthcoming; whatever references the Minister, Lord Macmillan, made to the BBC were 'inaccurate or derogatory or lukewarm'. When it became known at the end of September that five of the BBC's board of governors had effectively been dismissed at the beginning of the month, leaving only the chairman and his deputy, Macmillan happily fuelled speculation that the Government had taken over the corporation. He told the House of Lords that he 'believed' the board had 'been more or less suspended' but that he did not know 'exactly what the control was'. The BBC was independent, he added, but only 'shall I say, in the lighter parts of its programmes'.

Whatever the Minister implied, the BBC had not been taken over. What was interesting was not that five governors had gone but that two remained. The Government had intended to remove them all and annexe the corporation to the Ministry, but it had lost its nerve; the BBC's constitutional independence made it a spiky fish to swallow whole.

Why did the Government want to try? The reasons are complex and laced with ambiguities. Certainly there were those who had no faith in the BBC's ability to conduct itself in war. 'The Government was responsible for running the war, for fighting the war ... and here was this very important instrument of communication being organized and commanded by those who were not by training or background fitted for this,' said Harman Grisewood, the assistant controller of the BBC's European Service during the war and later the corporation's director of the Spoken Word, in an interview conducted in 1987 for the BBC's official archives. 'It's scarcely to be wondered at that the Government felt that the BBC was not up to the job.'

There was also the view that the BBC was a wilful organization. That was certainly the opinion of the Foreign Office, which remembered the start of Arabic broadcasting, at the Government's request, in January 1938. The Foreign Office had thought that it should organize broadcasts to the Arab world, where Mussolini was undermining British interests; the BBC had argued that no one else had the necessary expertise. The Foreign Office had thought that news items should be entirely in British interests, omitting those 'to which broadcasting by wireless would give undue emphasis'; the BBC had insisted on the same freedom from Government control which was enjoyed by the domestic services, and on the first day carried an item that reported the execution of a Palestinian Arab who had been found in possession of arms. The Foreign Office complained. The BBC's reply was tart: 'The omission of unwelcome facts of news and the consequent suppression of truth runs counter to the corporation's policy laid down by appropriate authority.'

It was precisely this policy that continued to make the Government, in control of every other aspect of national life by virtue of its emergency powers, consider why the broadcasters should escape its direct authority. As some saw it, the BBC was potentially a loose cannon on deck.

'There was no doubt that there was a strong body of opinion within the Government, within Parliament and in influential circles outside, that the BBC should cease to be independent, that it should be openly recognized as the voice of the Government,' says Gillard. 'Indeed, the Ministry announced that it had appointed a director of radio, and there was a tremendous outcry in Parliament about this. What business had the Ministry of Information to create a director of radio? Radio was an independent institution. And they had to change the title and call him the director of Radio Relations.' Other people, 'wiser people', who urged that the constitutional position should not be infringed, prevailed. Had they not, Gillard maintains, 'that would have been the ultimate end of the BBC. Never again would the BBC have been seen by the world and by people here at home as free and trustworthy. It would have been a propaganda instrument for all time, in the hands of the government in power. And thank God it never happened, but it was a near thing, and it had to be fought most resolutely.'

After the first days of national panic, Britain's sense of balance returned and so did the BBC's. A tougher line was taken with the politicians, the civil servants and the administrators who felt they had a right to shoulder their way into the studio and sit at the microphone in the interests of national concern. The outpouring of officialese was stemmed, making room for what Gillard describes as 'proper programmes – because one of the BBC's functions was to keep proper programmes going, to provide people with entertainment, with relaxation, with enjoyment. God knows there wasn't much pleasure to be had in life at that time, but the BBC could bring a bit, and a degree of normality, and a sense of stability.'

NORMAL SERVICE IS RESUMED

With hindsight, the corporation had been guilty of not having an alternative policy to meet the scenario that actually unfolded; now it had to get on with putting matters to rights. Within three days the scattered departments began to produce live programmes, led by Variety.

During the slide from peace, while the Government clung to a policy of appeasement, jokes about Hitler had been banned everywhere. Now they were officially encouraged and the entertainers – and the public – needed no prompting. On the evening of Wednesday 6 September, the first live revue of the war was on the air, with Tommy Handley singing a topical lampoon that immediately became popular: *Who is this man who looks like Charlie Chaplin?* Ten days later a skit entitled *Adolf in*

Blunderland had Maurice Denham as Hitler playing Alice, and Jack Train as Goering playing the Duchess. Meanwhile, a new series of *Band Waggon*, the best of the pre-war shows, was being hammered out and was back on the air on 16 September. Even Parliament noted its reappearance and commended it as a national pick-me-up.

By mid-October, drama and serious music had returned. There was innovative output to meet the needs of the times. And there were fewer records: indeed, there were fewer than there had been pre-war. By the end of the month, with cinemas and theatres reopened and sport back on the agenda, the outside broadcast units were making the rounds of their familiar haunts. They were at the camp concerts, too, at home and abroad, where the laughter of men who were forcibly absent made those listening at their firesides realize that the war was not a thing of unrelieved despair.

Band Waggon teamed Arthur Askey (right) with Richard Murdoch, a light comedian who was working in revue. It was the first BBC variety show to go out in a fixed weekly slot with a fixed cast.

Evacuation from the danger zones produced much unhappiness. By January 1940, of the 1½ million people who moved away, almost two-thirds had gone back home. Even when the Blitz began, only one family in five registered children for another evacuation.

Quietly, the BBC reduced the ten daily news bulletins to seven and then to six, the arrangement that was to last throughout the war, and began to include eye-witness reports in them. This was something entirely new, although a start had been made even before war was declared. Early on the morning of Friday, 1 September, twelve hours before the Home Service began broadcasting, S.J. de Lotbinière was at Waterloo Station:

> We're on number twelve platform at Waterloo, one of the ten big metropolitan stations that are engaged today on the evacuation of London's schoolchildren.... The train's in and the children are just arriving, coming along in their school groups, with a banner in front saying what school they are - this lot is St John's, Walworth …

It may have been banal, but the BBC was moving tentatively towards its wartime idiom. At the same time, it was well aware that it remained under the Government's watchful eye.

2

FIRST, THE BAD NEWS

The BBC's attitude to news was expressed quite simply by R.T. Clark, the Home Service's news editor, in an internal memo:

> It seems to me that the only way to strengthen the morale of the people whose morale is worth strengthening, is to tell them the truth, and nothing but the truth, even if the truth is horrible.

The Government would hardly have disagreed in principle. The alternative would have been a Goebbels-style propaganda machine.

The news was horrible. And it remained so, with setback after setback, until Hitler opened up the second front in June 1941, thereby bringing Russia into the war, and Japan's raid on Pearl Harbour six months later brought in the Americans. (Churchill heard the news of Pearl Harbour on his small radio at Chequers. 'So we have won after all!' he wrote. 'Our history would not come to an end.... I went to bed and slept the sleep of the saved and thankful.')

The noose tightened slowly in the early months, with the Navy bearing the brunt of what fighting there was. On 17 September 1939 the aircraft carrier *Courageous* was torpedoed in the Bristol Channel; on 14 October a U-boat daringly entered Scapa Flow and sunk the battleship *Royal Oak*. In the first fortnight of the war, Britain lost twenty-seven merchant ships. Even the weather was at the nation's throat. The winter of 1939-40 was the bitterest in living memory. Roads were impassable. Trains arrived not hours late, but days.

Then, in the beautiful spring of 1940, Hitler attacked Norway and Denmark and swept through Holland, Belgium and Luxembourg towards France and the Channel. The British Expeditionary Force was driven back and trapped on the beaches of Dunkirk. On 14 June the Germans marched into Paris. Three days later, the vast and vaunted armies of France threw up their hands and asked Germany for an armistice. Britain was alone.

In June 1940, in the Forest of Compiègne, the delegates of Pétain's French Government signed the armistice with Germany – in the very railway carriage in which, twenty-two years before, the Germans had signed the terms that ended the First World War.

FRANCE SURRENDERS

Godfrey Talbot was on duty in the newsroom when the final act of French humiliation took place on 17 June 1940. He sat at his desk with the news agency tapes in front of him and dictated the story to a typist. 'The word got around Broadcasting House that this terrible thing had happened, the French had given up. I was conscious of people coming and standing behind my shoulder and you could hear the swift intake of breath as they read what I was dictating.' The story took up almost the entire one o'clock news. Charles Gardner, who had become the BBC's second war correspondent, took Talbot for a drink. 'All great empires go down with a wallop and a drink,' he said.

Accusations that the BBC had been falsely optimistic in earlier reports from France were levelled by the Government, though the BBC could hardly be blamed. Bulletins had been based on the communiqués of the French military authorities which spoke of strategic withdrawals to prepared positions, heavy enemy losses, brilliant counterattacks. The Government's censors had passed the bulletins for broadcast. No one knew that the military might of France was on the run and, in Godfrey Talbot's phrase, 'the Maginot Line and all its bunkers – there might just as well have been a pink ribbon across Europe for all the good it was.'

THE BBC IS TAKEN TO TASK

The BBC already had a black mark against its name. During the Norwegian campaign it unknowingly carried false reports of British successes, emanating from neutral Sweden, which had helped to create a general feeling that Hitler had bitten off more than he could chew. These reports had also been passed for broadcast. Yet the Lord Privy Seal, Sir Kingsley Wood, criticized the BBC and raised the question of whether its officials 'were sufficiently charged with patriotism and wisdom …'

This was a bit rich, to say the least. When the Supreme War Command had decided to pull out of Norway, editors of the national newspapers had been taken into the Government's confidence, but the BBC had not. Left to dangle in the wind, the BBC had continued to buoy up the hopes of listeners who were all the more shaken when the withdrawal took place. The BBC complained bitterly, feeling with probable justification that it had been deliberately used by the Government 'to throw dust in the eyes of the enemy'.

There was also a running conflict with the Admiralty which had levelled a charge, not of optimism but of pessimism – 'unrelieved pessimism' – over the BBC's reports of Britain's losses at sea (which at the end of the first eleven months amounted to one-and-a-half million tons). If the Admiralty had had its way, it would have revealed nothing; indeed, in February 1940 it attempted to block news of the sinking of the *Daring*. The BBC argued that it was futile not to report what the enemy already knew and had reported on its own airwaves – and on which it taunted Britain for delays in making such announcements. 'If the enemy said that a battleship had been sunk – HMS *Hood*, for example – there was no point in concealing that, because the Germans had seen the blessed ship go down,' says Frank Gillard. 'But we told it in a way which made us proud that she'd fought and fought…. It was a heroic story and it was told that way.'

It was not as though the BBC alone was responsible for what was broadcast. The BBC amassed information from official sources, news agencies (which were, of course, also censored), its own expanding journalistic activities and the trawl of other nation's broadcasts by its monitoring unit. From this mountain of material it compiled its summaries and interpretations. But it was 'officially guided' by the Ministry of Information which had its headquarters in the University of London in Bloomsbury. There were open telephone lines between the Ministry and the Broadcasting House newsroom. There were teams of BBC men seconded as liaison officers within the Ministry and 'vigilants' (they did not call themselves 'censors') from the Ministry, and often from the Services, were ever-present in the newsroom. Depending on the story in question, there were others with the right of veto or sanction at the Home Office, the Foreign Office, the Ministry of Defence, the War Office, the Air Ministry, the

The **BBC** newsroom (with news editor R.T.Clark, standing) in February 1941. The newsroom had moved from the second floor of Broadcasting House to the basement once the Blitz began.

Admiralty and the three Armed Forces. The BBC's foreign language broadcasters had yet other 'guides'.

THE QUESTION OF CENSORSHIP

There were two kinds of censorship: one of security, which related to the activities of the Services and the Defence Forces; and one of policy, which related to the morale of the nation. No script could be broadcast unless it bore both stamps. Among the ground rules of censorship were that the names of regiments, the numbers of troops or planes and precise geographic locations were never given, nor were the whereabouts of members of the Cabinet and the Royal Family. The weather was never mentioned either, in case it revealed the conditions for bombing. This sensible precaution, however, had some faintly ludicrous results. John Snagge covered one wartime Boat Race without mentioning that he could not see how far ahead Cambridge was because the sun was in his eyes.

When the Battle of Britain began in the summer of 1940, and was swiftly followed by the Blitz, the BBC reported the damage caused by enemy action. But it did so within the dictates of giving nothing to the enemy that would be of help. The phrases used in bulletins were vague: 'heavy enemy raids were directed upon the East Coast last night';

'a district in North London'; 'considerable damage to house property'; 'many casualties, some fatal'. Says Talbot: 'What we didn't say was "Birmingham was heavily hit last night and the town hall is now in ruins"; or "the casualties filled all the hospitals in Bristol"; or "a bomb went down into the Tube and killed people sheltering in the station". But what we reported was true. It had to be. It would have been silly to pretend to people who were there in their ruined houses that there hadn't been a raid.'

Gillard was visiting his parents near Exeter when a night raid on the city caused massive destruction and a bomb exploded inside the cathedral. He wrote a piece, dashed to Bristol and dictated it up the line to London where it was recorded for the nine o'clock news. At five minutes to nine the duty editor rang back to say that the Air Ministry had refused to allow its broadcast – because it would have told the enemy that he had found his target.

Gillard was disappointed, because 'I was much moved by Exeter, the ever-faithful city, being treated in this way,' but he accepted the reasoning. However, he did not accept the reasoning for the censorship to which his report of the disastrous combined operations raid on Dieppe in August 1942 was subjected, and more than half a century later it still fills him with moral outrage.

Desperate after nearly three years of war, the Allies staged a rehearsal for D-Day. The plan was to seize the town of Dieppe, destroy the enemy positions and harbour installations and return, towing back forty-two small craft that Hitler might have used in an invasion. Five thousand men, mainly Canadians, tried to get

> The 'reconnaissance in force' on Dieppe on 19 August 1942 ended in disaster, although it provided lessons on how to invade a well-defended coast, which the Allies put into practice on D-Day. Censorship prevented BBC correspondent Frank Gillard from reporting the full story.

ashore in France. Only one-quarter of them came home. Gillard remembers the sea red with blood and his uniform caked with the blood of men he pulled from the water.

> There was an immediate 'stop' put on all reports about the action on the beaches. We were not allowed, for twenty-four hours, to say a word about that. 'Deferred another six hours', 'deferred another six hours'. Finally the report I was allowed to go on-air with concerned almost entirely the air action that was going on above our heads. Everything else was heavily censored and I was not able to tell the true story of Dieppe.
>
> I read in BBC literature about my 'memorable report' from Dieppe. To me it's memorable in all the wrong ways. It's memorable with shame and disgrace that I was there as the BBC's one and only eyewitness and I couldn't tell that story as I ought to have told it.

What was necessary censorship, what was bloody-mindedness and what was crass stupidity was always a matter of viewpoint. Most of the BBC's problems lay with the Ministry of Information and some were shared by the Press. When the British Expeditionary Force landed in France a 'stop' was put on broadcasting and bundles of newspapers, which carried a report, were dragged off the night trains by police. When an RAF pilot was awarded a medal, the Ministry's statement refused to confirm that he had been the leader of the raid on Kiel on 4 September 1940, although 'any newspaper which assumed that he was would not be inaccurate'. (There was no mention of the BBC.) The Ministry found reasons for killing or delaying such uplifting stories as the visit of the young princesses to evacuees in Scotland and the King's inspection of the fleet. It even found security grounds for refusing to release the text of the eighteen million leaflets that were dropped on Germany to inform the population (with commendable pugnacity but, at the time, scant credibility) that Hitler had started a war he could not win.

Another of the BBC's problems was not shared by the Press but was caused by it. The powerful newspaper lobby was attempting to regain some of the ascendancy it had lost with the outbreak of war and it was using the Ministry to these ends.

In the early years, unable to afford a newsgathering service of its own, the BBC had been forced to subscribe to the news agencies. The price, exacted by the Newspaper Proprietors' Society, was that the corporation could not broadcast news bulletins before 6 p.m. or carry live descriptions of news events. War had swept these restrictions away, but repeatedly the BBC found its reports held up by the embargo 'not to appear before tomorrow morning's papers'. This occurred on the evening in January 1940 when Hore-Belisha resigned as War Minister – although German radio had already broadcast the news. Of the daytime bulletins, the 4 p.m. one especially infuriated the newspapers because it stole a march on their evening editions. The Ministry, unbelievably, agreed with them. The BBC protested national interest. In fact, the BBC did remove the bulletin, as part of the scaling-down it initiated on a reassessment of the requirements of war; it was not, as the Minister of Information claimed, because he had ordered it. But the BBC flatly refused to concede a demand that Richard Dimbleby's dispatches from France should be held over each night.

CHURCHILL STEPS IN

At 6 p.m. on 10 May 1940, the day that Hitler invaded the Low Countries, Winston Churchill became Prime Minister of a National Government. Within a week of taking office he was contemplating a take over of the BBC.

Churchill was no lover of the corporation. It had defied Baldwin's Government during the General Strike of 1926 by carrying statements from the strike leaders when Churchill, then Chancellor of the Exchequer, believed it should carry only the Government's views; he had belonged to the minority of the Cabinet which wanted to annexe the BBC for propaganda purposes. During his wilderness years in the thirties, the BBC had kept him off the air (he broadcast only four times between 1934 and the outbreak of war) largely because of the mutual loathing which he and Sir John Reith, the corporation's aloof and autocratic director-general, felt for each other.

Ironically, Reith ('Old Wuthering Heights', Churchill called him) had become the second Minister of Information at the beginning of 1940. Churchill sacked him. It was not just a settling of old scores. The truth was that Reith, who had been appointed unwillingly and who was not enjoying being referred to as 'Dr Goebbels' opposite number', was not the right man for the job. It needed someone less confrontational to sort out the Ministry, not only in regard to the BBC but also in its wider public role. The Ministry, which had quickly established itself as the great national joke of the war (it was the place where the Crazy Gang went in the daytime, someone cracked), continued to be held in public contempt.

At the time of sacking him, Churchill told Reith that the BBC 'was the enemy within the gates, doing

Reith (left), former BBC director-general sacked as Minister of Information by Churchill, became Minister of Works and Public Buildings. It was in this capacity that he inspected bomb damage in a number of South Coast towns in March 1941.

more harm than good'. He never lost a feeling of hostility towards the organization. Later he referred to it as 'one of the major neutrals', an ambiguous description that could be taken to mean he felt the BBC lacked patriotism or that, however grudgingly, he respected its integrity in trying to report the truth. In any event he decided against take-over, finding a compromise instead, in early 1941, which left the BBC's constitution intact but gave the Government a tolerable control. The Ministry of Information appointed two 'advisers' to oversee all programme output; as a kind of counter-weight, the BBC's board of governors was brought back to its pre-war level.

Gillard regarded the home adviser, Patrick Ryan, a former BBC man who had helped to set up the Ministry, as 'well qualified both to meet the requirements of broadcasting and to meet the requirements of Government regulation.' He goes on: 'His main function, as he saw it, was to oversee all the BBC's journalism: the news, the topical talks, the discussions, the interviews, all the way down the line even to the sermons – the churches were having a hell of a time. How on earth do you promote the gospel of peace inside a nation that's at war? And Ryan took all this under his command. And he was first-class.'

Gillard remembers how Ryan used to disappear to the Ministry every morning: 'He was a civil servant from ten o'clock until noon – and a BBC person for the rest of the day. When he got back he held an informal meeting of all the heads of his news departments in his office. He was a low-profile sort of chap, unostentatious. He'd sit with his feet up on the desk, reaching back in his chair and smoking his pipe and gazing at the ceiling. But he clearly knew everything that was going on within Government, within the military operations, what was happening on the Russian front and so on, and he would talk to us very freely. A good deal of this was highly confidential information, but it was the sort of thing that good newspeople needed to have as background.... Ryan was able to make a knowledgeable, informed input into the BBC's news machine that couldn't have come from any other source.'

Brendan Bracken, leaving No.10 with Churchill, sorted out the Ministry of Information, which had been regarded as one of the jokes of the war. After his arrival there was no more question of the Government taking over the BBC.

In the summer of 1941, Churchill sacked Duff Cooper, who had replaced Reith, and brought in Brendan Bracken, whom he trusted implicitly. Here at last was someone who could inspire Information in the way of Beaverbrook at Aircraft Production, Woolton at Food, Bevin at Labour. And Bracken believed in the independence of the BBC. After his appointment there was no more talk of take-over.

The public, for the most part, was unaware of the BBC's problems. Few people would have seen a difference between the loss of constitutional freedom and the imposition of controlling 'advisers'. What people were interested in was the news, not the rows that had occurred in producing it.

It is impossible to exaggerate the impact of the BBC's wartime news. Newspapers were thin because, like everything else, paper was rationed, and they could not match radio's fast reflexes. Listening to the news, which quickly settled into a fixed pattern of broadcasts at 7 a.m., 8 a.m., 1 p.m., 6 p.m., 9 p.m. and midnight, became a ritual. Sixteen million people – half the adult population – listened to the nine o'clock news, but even more tuned in when Churchill's lisping, growling declarations followed it. Pitt, in the years of the French Wars, spoke to a handful of men in the Commons; Gladstone's addresses on the Bulgarian massacres, when the public meeting was in its heyday, were delivered to a few thousand; Churchill was heard by nearly seven out of every ten of his countrymen. There was a great deal of public listening during the war and, Talbot comments: 'In public houses people didn't order a drink, or take a drink, but huddled to the end of the bar where the loudspeaker was. In millions of homes up and down these islands, and elsewhere too, nothing happened. The records of the water companies, telephone companies, gas suppliers, electricity suppliers show the demand going down, down to nothing. Nobody went to spend a penny, nobody put the kettle on, nobody did anything but listen to this man who was so confident that confidence somehow oozed out of the loudspeakers.'

CHURCHILL'S SPEECHES

By any sober reckoning, Britain should have been doomed, and would have been, if it had not been for Churchill – and for the radio which let his words shake a fist at 'the beastly gang', as he himself is said to have shaken his fist at the *Luftwaffe* from the step at Number Ten. 'Churchill made a dream come true', says Talbot. 'It was an impossible dream, but not to him. And the very fact that he was saying "we are going to do this" or "we are going to do that" made people, people who were in despair, think again. If Churchill said it, and believed it, then perhaps it was possible after all.'

Even today, merely reading the text of Churchill's wartime speeches, one can feel the emotional charge. His first as Prime Minister was given on 19 May 1940, six days after he told Parliament: 'I have nothing to offer but blood, toil, tears and sweat.'

No lover of the BBC, Churchill none the less understood the power of radio and used it to broadcast to the nation. After the war he recorded a number of the speeches he had delivered only in the House.

I speak to you for the first time as Prime Minister in a solemn hour of the life of our country, of our empire, of our allies, and above all, of the cause of freedom.… I have formed an administration of men and women of every party, and of almost every point of view. We have differed and quarrelled in the past, but now one bond unites us all: to wage war until victory is won and never to surrender ourselves to servitude and shame, whatever the cost and the agony may be … the long night of barbarism will descend … unless we conquer, as conquer we must, as conquer we shall …

There were many more like it, ringing with phrases that have entered the language. Four days after the Germans entered Paris on 14 June 1940, this:

What General de Gaulle called the Battle of France is over. I expect that the Battle of Britain is about to begin. Upon this battle depends the survival of Christian civilization. Upon it depends our own British life.… Though the fury and might of the enemy must very soon be turned on us, Hitler knows that he will have to break us in this island or lose the war. If we can stand up to him, all Europe may be free and the life of the world may move forward into broad, sunlit uplands. And if we fail then the whole world … will sink into the abyss of a new dark age.… Let us therefore brace ourselves to our duties and so bear ourselves that if the British Empire and its Commonwealth last for a thousand years men will still say: 'This was their finest hour.'

And this on 14 July, when the large-scale daylight raids had begun, criss-crossing the skies with vapour trails, and the sirens were being heard for the first time since the previous September:

Wherever he may appear, should the invader come to Britain there will be no placid lying down of the people in submission before him as we have seen in other countries. We shall defend every village, every town and every city. The vast mass of London itself, fought street by street, could easily devour an entire hostile army, and we would rather see London laid in ruins and ashes than that it should be tamely and abjectly enslaved.

And this on 20 August, when the RAF had driven the *Luftwaffe* back across the Channel:

> Never in the field of human conflict was so much owed by so many to so few. All our hearts go out to the fighter pilots whose brilliant actions we see with our own eyes day after day. But we must never forget that … night after night, month after month, our bomber squadrons travel far into Germany to find their targets in the darkness by the highest navigational skill, aim their attacks, often under the heaviest fire, often with serious loss, with deliberate, careful discrimination, and inflict shattering blows upon the whole of the technical and war-making structure of the Nazi power.

Many have tried to analyse the appeal of Churchill's style. His arrival at the microphone, someone said, was as good as a new battleship. For the writer and broadcaster Desmond Hawkins, the fascination lay in the manner in which Churchill salted the flights of 'high Augustan prose with touches of sudden slang'. He gives as an example a speech to the Canadian Parliament at the end of 1941 during which Churchill said: 'When I warned them [the French Government] that Britain would fight on alone, whatever they did, their generals told their Prime Minister and his divided Cabinet: "In three weeks England will have her neck wrung like a chicken."' At which point Churchill interjected: 'Some chicken! Some neck!'

'It was irresistible,' Hawkins says. 'He knew exactly how to get a response from the audience. That's why he was careful always to talk about the Nazis with a soft "z", because ordinary people didn't know that the "z" was hard.'

Robin Scott, later the controller of BBC2 but then working in the BBC French section, remembers a speech to the people of France in October 1940 'which was full of Churchill things like "tomorrow the dawn will rise" and "the glorious days of France will return"' and which was to have ended with the line: 'We are waiting for the long-promised invasion.' Churchill added: 'So are the fishes.'

That broadcast was made from the bunker beneath Whitehall. A member of the French section, Michel Saint-Denis, had spent most of the day helping to make a colloquial translation of what the Prime Minister had written ('I want to be understood as I am,' Churchill said), and by the time they finished they had demolished a bottle of brandy. When it was time for the transmission ('*Français! prenez garde, c'est moi, Churchill, qui vous parle*'), Churchill insisted that Saint-Denis stay, to guide him through the text. Because the room was so small he did so sitting on Churchill's knee.

Altogether, Churchill went on-air to deliver thirty-three major wartime speeches. Some were original; others had first been heard in the Commons. He attached no historical importance to 'the broadcasts' (he never spoke of the radio, or 'the wireless' as it was still most commonly called) and wrote nothing about them in his epic account of

Parliament installed radio sets for the first time after war was declared. So did many public places. Communal listening – particularly of the nine o'clock evening news – was a feature of the times.

the war. 'The people's will was resolute and remorseless. I only expressed it', he contented himself in saying. 'They had the lion's heart. I had the luck to be called upon to give the roar.'

Usually, Churchill spoke from his own study in Downing Street or at Chequers, reading from untidy pieces of paper covered with large typescript and his pencilled impromptus. But he did come into Broadcasting House to record what he had told Parliament after the evacuation from Dunkirk was completed. The address contained the passage that everyone knows, even if they misquote it:

> We shall go on to the end … we shall fight on the seas and oceans, we shall fight with growing confidence and growing strength in the air, we shall defend our island whatever the cost may be. We shall fight on the beaches, we shall fight on the landing grounds, we shall fight in the fields and in the streets.… We shall never surrender.

When he came off the air he is supposed to have added: 'And we'll fight them with the butt-ends of broken glass bottles, because that's all we'll bloody well have left.' Dennis Main Wilson, a wartime programme assistant who became the head of Television Light Entertainment, adds: 'It's probably apocryphal. I choose to want it to be true.'

THE COUNTER-OFFENSIVE AGAINST LORD HAW-HAW

The five-minute talks slot which directly followed the nine o'clock news became a strikingly popular innovation from February 1940, which was the soonest the BBC could mount an offensive against the traitor William Joyce who was broadcasting Nazi propaganda from Hamburg as Lord Haw-Haw. Until the opening of the Forces Programme as a second network in January 1940, there was not the air-time to spare for counter-measures.

Right from the first panicky month of war, Haw-Haw (whose unfortunate brother worked in the BBC's Civil Engineering department before joining the Army) attracted a big following in Britain. As many as six million people tuned in to him once the nine o'clock news was finished. There were many reasons: a desire for more details than the BBC was giving (the German High Command was very much faster than the British defence ministries in putting out communiqués); a guilty desire to listen to the enemy; perhaps, most of all, boredom with the restricted output of the Home Service. There was also Haw-Haw's entertainment value. For a start, his sneering tones were a parody of upper-class condescension (he introduced himself with the tripartite 'Germany calling, Germany calling, Germany calling', pronouncing Germany as if the first syllable were 'chair') and the claims he made bordered on the comical: 'Famine stalks side by side with Winston Churchill today. England will become a land of skeletons by the wayside' is a typical example. On another occasion he claimed that British women and girls, frightened of being injured by splintering from German bombs, were 'requesting their milliners to

Lord Haw-Haw, the chief German broadcaster in English, was William Joyce, a British citizen of Irish-American birth, who fled to Germany in 1939 at the age of thirty-three. After the war, he was executed as a traitor.

shape the spring and summer hats out of very thin tin plate which is covered with silk, velvet or other draping material.' Britain adopted him as a kind of music-hall act. Sometimes, however, he had snippets of local knowledge ('Lewisham town clock is three minutes slow') which made some people worry that a network of fifth columnists worked for him; and it worried the Government that some of his distortions inevitably contained elements of truth. Clearly, Haw-Haw had to be refuted.

The BBC resisted calls from the Ministry of Information to do so directly. Its answer, until the Forces Programme doubled its options, was to schedule its most popular output after the news; later, while it kept variety shows going on the Forces, it created on the Home Service what became the five-minute *Postscripts*. Many speakers, including the actors Robert Donat and Leslie Howard, came to jolly the nation along during the course of the war. Some were very popular, including Duff Cooper, Sir Harold Mackintosh of Halifax, the chairman of National Savings, and a American journalist named Quentin Reynolds who insulted Hitler in open letters using what was alleged to be the Führer's family name as he began: 'Dear Mr Schicklgruber …'

The pick of the bunch was the Yorkshire novelist J.B. Priestley, whose voice had become familiar to the public in the first months of war, reading the instalments of his novel *Let the People Sing*. He came to the *Post-script* microphone for the first time on 5 June 1940. The disaster – and the triumph – of Dunkirk was still vivid in people's minds; the bravery and the improvisation of the 300 warships and 400 other craft which had brought back 338 000 British, French, Dutch and Belgian troops. Churchill had spoken of 'a miracle of deliverance'. Priestley spoke of the little pleasure steamers, 'so characteristically English, so

The most popular broadcaster after Churchill himself, the novelist J.B.Priestley, was too political for some Conservative MPs and was taken off the air.

typical of us, so absurd and yet so grand and gallant, that you hardly know whether to laugh or to cry when you read about them':

> Yes, those *Brighton Belles* and *Brighton Queens* left that innocent foolish world of theirs to sail into the inferno, to defy bombs, shells, magnetic mines, torpedoes, machine-gun fire, to rescue our soldiers. Some of them – alas – will never return. Among those paddle-steamers that'll never return was one that I knew well, for it was the pride of our ferry service to the Isle of Wight, none other than the good ship *Gracie Fields*. I tell you we were proud of the *Gracie Fields*. She was the glittering queen of our local line and instead of taking an hour over her voyage, she used to do it, churning like mad, in forty five minutes. And now, never again will we board her and go down into her dining saloon for a fine breakfast of bacon and eggs. She has paddled and churned away for ever. But now – look – this little steamer, like all her brave and battered sisters, is immortal. She'll go sailing proudly down the years in the epic of Dunkirk. And our great grandchildren, when they learn how we began this war by snatching glory out of defeat, and then swept on to victory, may also learn how the little holiday steamers made an excursion to hell and came back glorious.

Priestley's language was robust and simple. He left the fire and brimstone to Churchill and talked about practical things: about the day when Britain would be a springboard to defeat the Germans, about the necessity of keeping alive 'the bright little thread of our common humanity that still runs through these iron days and black nights'. For nineteen weeks he spoke his mind and the nation identified with what Desmond Hawkins describes as his 'north country dourness and stubbornness … and the kind of hard core that the English do have when they're finding life a bit difficult.' An audience of ten million listened weekly. People talked to Priestley in shops and bars and touched him in the streets.

In January 1941 Priestley began a second *Postscript* series for which he was given more air-time. He began to introduce more critical comment (those who had left Britain should have their property confiscated, he said), which some Conservative MPs protested amounted to an exposition of political socialism. The Tory Press turned hostile and Priestley, the war's best-loved straight broadcaster after Churchill himself, was taken off the air on instruction from the Ministry of Information (though he received a letter from the Ministry blaming the BBC). However, he continued to broadcast in the BBC's overseas services; by 1942 he was a household name in America. At various stages of the war the BBC was accused of being wholly left-wing in its choice of speakers but, as Harold Nicolson, at the time Parliamentary Secretary to the Ministry of Information, wrote: 'Most of the right-wing people make bad broadcasters. Let them find their own Priestley.'

'HERE IS THE NEWS, READ BY …'

Between them, Churchill and Priestley were heard on fewer than a hundred occasions during the war. The men who read the home news were heard over 13 000 times. And they acquired celebrity status from the day in June 1940 when they began to give their names as an introduction to each bulletin. One, Alvar Lidell, whose unusual name was due to his Swedish parentage and caused particular interest, even appeared in a film with Vera Lynn.

In peacetime, newsreaders had remained unidentified on-air, although the *Daily Express* in 1932 revealed 'The Secret Five' – Stuart Hibberd, T.C. Farrar, John Snagge, Godfrey Adams and Freddie Grisewood. The wartime change happened quite casually. Snagge, who had been in Outside Broadcasts but was now in charge of presentation after the break-up of his old department, remarked one day to the assistant controller of Programmes, S.J. de Lotbinière, that it

Newsreader Alvar Lidell in an underground studio – complete with bunk beds.

was farcical that the newsreaders, who were drawing vast audiences, did not put their names to their voices. Lotbinière agreed and told him to organize it. The following day the nation heard: 'Here is the news, read by Alvar Lidell.'

It was only now that Snagge and his boss thought they should cover themselves and drew senior management's attention to what had happened in Poland, where the Germans had added to the confusion of invasion by imitating Polish broadcasts. The explanation was accepted without demur, the only comment being that it would have been better for the newsreader to have said: 'Here is the news and this is Alvar Lidell reading it' – the construction of the original introduction being open to the interpretation that a second voice would actually read the news. The newsreaders adopted the modification.

Explaining why they now identified themselves, the *BBC Handbook* of 1941 stated: 'The reason for this is not a hankering after self-advertisement – although at first some listeners unfairly took it to be so; in wartime listeners must be able to recognize instantly the authentic voice of British broadcasting and then, in any possible emergency, they will be on their guard against some lying imitation by the voice of the enemy.' In fact, in October 1944, it came to light in liberated Belgium that, during the period when the invasion of Britain was likely, the German Secret Service had run a special school to train impostors.

WILFRED PICKLES JOINS THE TEAM

The possibility of counterfeit news was raised in the House of Commons in 1941. Was it not a potential danger that the team of Lidell, Snagge, Frank Phillips, Alan Howland, Joseph McLeod, Freddy Allen and Bruce Belfrage all sounded too much alike? All, of course, spoke in the style on which Reith had founded the BBC and which he defined as 'educated Southern English', more accurately termed Received Pronunciation. Churchill passed the buck to Brendan Bracken, who told Snagge (without evidence) that people were growing tired of the tones of Oxbridge and that a regional voice would be less easy for the Germans to copy. Priestley suggested Wilfred Pickles, a Yorkshire character actor who had done a bit of announcing in Manchester but who was best-known for a regional series called *Billy Welcome* (the predecessor of the post-war *Have a Go!*) He arrived in November 1941 – and found himself pitched into a national controversy. The papers carried eeh-bah-gum headlines and cloth-cap-and-muffler cartoons.

Pickles made his début on the six o'clock news on 17 November. He recalled in his autobiography, *Between You and Me,* that, on his way to studio S1 with the bulletin in his hand, he showed his pass to a man sitting by one of the big iron gas-doors and he remembered a story about Freddy Allen:

Yorkshireman Wilfred Pickles briefly broke the monopoly of Home Counties' voices reading the news. In wishing listeners 'good neet', he caused a sensation.

When Broadcasting House got a bomb … the terrific explosion caused a rush of air which blew Freddy beyond the door and its keeper and up along the passage. As he scrambled to his feet, his grey hair powdered with soot and his eyes filled with dust, he called out: 'Well, that's the first time I've got through that door without showing my pass!'

The memory steadied Pickles' nerves as he entered the studio:

…a cramped airless basement room equipped with a desk, high stools like those against a bar and two bunks for the Home Guards who stayed on all night. Straight in front of the announcer's position was a window which might have been a car windscreen and which gave a view over part of a control room…. With consideration, somebody had supplied a blind which could be pulled down by the announcer to shut out the engineers. I had made up my mind about that. I would pull down the blind as soon as I got inside. Alan Howland not only left it up, but pulled faces and made rude gestures at the engineers as he read the news.'

The bulletin went well. Pickles did not know that his wife Mabel, who was listening in the lounge of their London hotel, had exchanged angry words with another woman who jumped to her feet when he came on-air, saying: 'Can't we switch this dreadful man off?' He was more relaxed when he read the midnight bulletin and rounded off by bidding listeners: 'Good night to you all – and to all Northerners, wherever you may be, good neet.' That caused a sensation. The fan mail poured in. Listener research confirmed Pickles' popularity which, interestingly, was heavily tilted towards the South. But after five months Pickles felt that his presence had added nothing and he chose to return to Manchester and his programme work.

In his autobiography, Pickles gave a few glimpses of his fellow newsreaders. It fascinated him that McLeod chose to deliver the news standing up and not sitting on a stool like everyone else, and that Lidell rubbed his stomach throughout a bulletin. The way Lidell read, which 'was perfect according to BBC standards', Pickles found 'cold, detached and impersonal', though he added 'he was a stickler for accuracy'.

In a much less amiable autobiography, *One Man in His Time*, Bruce Belfrage's only comment about Lidell was that he 'dwelt with astonishing concentration on the satisfying of the inner man'. He described Howland as 'tetchy and irritable', McLeod as 'morose and perpetually immersed in a Russian grammar' and Phillips as 'given to excessive personal reminiscence'. He blamed his own 'totally unreasoning resentment of authority' to a digestion that kept him in 'perpetual discomfort'.

CONTINUITY ANNOUNCERS ARRIVE

Sent to Manchester as Pickles' replacement (muttering 'What am I supposed to do, play *Billy Welcome?*'), Belfrage returned to London in the late spring of 1942, eager to get back to newsreading and to his duties as a special constable – when not in Broadcasting House, he and Howland directed traffic in the neighbourhood of Whitehall and Trafalgar Square. What greeted him did not make him happy. From June, every programme was to be covered by a fully-manned shadow studio ready to take over in any emergency. This meant a bigger announcing staff and newsreaders had to perform other announcing duties. Belfrage, who had been the BBC's drama booking manager before becoming a newsreader and who had never been an announcer in the wider sense, hated it. He wrote:

> The Home and Forces programmes were now conducted each from a separate underground studio known as Continuity. The continuity announcer sits for hours in this small room linking up the programmes and filling in gaps with merry quips or carefully selected (more or less appropriate) chunks of gramophone records.

This occupation was varied by occasional visits to outside studios, often to announce dance-bands, which depressed Belfrage even more. And more newsreaders were added to the team which had seen the BBC through the first half of the war. The new recruits included a young actor, Robert Robinson, who had been invalided out of the Army after Dunkirk, and the pre-war veteran Stuart Hibberd, who had spent most of the war until now announcing music programmes. There was still no place for another newsreading veteran, Franklin Engelmann; the Germanic sound of his name confined him to unnamed general announcing.

Hibberd, the most popular pre-war newsreader, remembered affectionately for the way he paused in saying 'Good night, everybody … good night', did not understand Belfrage's attitude. He wrote in his diary that he thought presenting talks, plays and recitals and mixing with the artists in the studio was just as important as reading the news. 'I am quite certain, too, that if I went on doing nothing else but reading the news

I should get very stale, and the public would at once recognize it.' Hibberd's heart was in the old BBC, when announcers wore dinner jackets after 6 p.m. to present programmes performed before an audience and as a courtesy to distinguished visitors. That practice had ended in September 1939 but he still felt that newsreaders in sweaters and flannels (one was even seen in shorts) rather let down the side.

Belfrage, who achieved fame as the man who carried on reading the nine o'clock news when a bomb exploded inside Broadcasting House in October 1940, eventually resigned and joined the RNVR. Many listeners were disappointed by his departure, including, no doubt, the man who came up to Godfrey Talbot in a Yorkshire pub, when he was home on leave from reporting the Desert War, and told him that Belfrage was his favourite newsreader. Asked why, the man replied: 'Well, you know all them communics from the Air Force about Dorniers shot down by Spitfires, and how many bombers we've brought down? Well, you know, yon Belfrage – he reads it as though he shot all t'buggers down himself.'

Belfrage handed in his notice on 4 November 1942 – the day on which the Germans were in full retreat from El Alamein and Lidell broke the ruling that bulletins were to be read formally and impersonally by beginning: 'I'm going to read you the news – and there's some cracking good news coming.'

It was another two-and-a-half years before Germany surrendered. From that day, 4 May 1945, newsreaders ceased to give their names. The practice had served its purpose in wartime. But the BBC was not going to allow what it saw as a personality cult to stand in the way of a return to peacetime standards.

3

LAUGHTER BECOMES A MUNITION OF WAR

The attacks on the BBC at the outbreak of war were so furious that the corporation wagons were quickly arranged in a defensive circle. It was the Variety department which came over the hill like the cavalry to its rescue.

The announcement on the 6 p.m. news on Friday 1 September 1939 about the merging of the National and Regional networks was the pre-arranged signal which sent three entire programme-making departments, including Variety (*sans* Sandy Macpherson, who stayed with his theatre organ at St George's Hall), on their way to Bristol, where the influx swamped the small West Region headquarters. On the Sunday morning those who had already arrived listened in the town hall to Chamberlain's broadcast. Then, while engineers got on with wiring up Clifton College, which was to be the department's base, and kitted out three parish halls with apparatus hastily stripped from the London studios, the director of Variety, John Watt, called a meeting of about fifteen producers, accompanists, scriptwriters and the conductor of the BBC Variety Orchestra. How was the department going to meet the situation? The lurch into war meant that many existing scripts were useless, others needed to be reworked and new shows created from scratch: all this while living and working accommodation was being sorted out, missing personnel and band parts tracked down and every new performer vetted by the Ministry of Information. And what would censorship prevent them from broadcasting?

OLD FAVOURITES RETURN

Variety got stuck in. Old favourites like *Songs from the Shows*, *The White Coons Concert Party* and *The Kentucky Minstrels* were given a fresh lick of greasepaint. On 19

Radio Times, October 20, 1939   Vol. 65   No. 838   Registered at the G.P.O. as a Newspaper

PRICE TWOPENCE

PROGRAMMES FOR
October 22—28

RADIO ✶ TIMES

JOURNAL OF THE BRITISH BROADCASTING CORPORATION

(INCORPORATING WORLD-RADIO)

A new 'Radio Times' picture of 'Big-Hearted' Arthur Askey and 'Stinker' Richard Murdoch

'Band Waggon, perhaps the most popular programme of all...' Sir Samuel Hoare in the House of Commons, October 11, 1939

ALSO THIS WEEK	Jessie Matthews and Sonnie Hale in 'Songs from the Shows'	Harvest of the Sea the story of how Britain gets her fish	The Pickwickians Set Out the first of a new Pickwick series
	Jack Jackson every weekday except Tuesday	Mid-Week Music-Hall with Phyllis Robins, Flotsam and Jetsam, Stainless Stephen, and Claude Dampier	George Graves in person, in another 'Star-Gazing' programme

44

September, three days after *Band Waggon* reappeared, *It's That Man Again* (it was not yet known as *ITMA*) was brought back. In the first month, Variety produced 118 flesh-and-blood shows, an average of four a day. By then transport had improved and radio artists from all parts of Britain were finding their way to Bristol – 'Variety Town', as the *BBC Handbook* of 1941 called it.

None of this could have been achieved without the twenty-two members of the Variety Repertory Company whom the BBC had had the foresight to sign up against the eventuality of war. The BBC had given them sealed envelopes of instructions stamped (theatrically, one cannot resist saying) 'Top Secret'. A phrase about the change of wavelengths delivered in the 6 p.m. Friday news was the pre-arranged signal for the envelopes to be opened and their addressees to join the trek to Bristol. Maurice Denham heard the coded message when he came up from the basement in Broadcasting House where he had been recording a play.

The beginning of the war was an extraordinary period for the Variety Rep. The actors took part in nine or ten programmes a week, with no more than three hours' rehearsal. A feature of wartime variety was the early-morning broadcasts to brighten the breakfasting family's day; some of these entailed a run-through before 7 a.m. By the end of November 1939, Denham, a first-class mimic, had played 225 parts in 100 shows, appearing variously as a French peasant, a child of four, a Cockney bus driver, a dude, a dustman, numerous animals, Alf Perkins in *At the Billet Doux* and, in *It's That Man Again*, the Russian inventor Vodkin, the charlady Lola Tickle and the Radio Fakenburg announcer. He also did a little announcing, sang solo with the BBC's Men's Chorus and read the epilogue. Denham was paid seven pounds a week. A newspaper at the time called him 'the BBC's best bargain'.

'I kid myself that listeners didn't always recognize my voice,' he says. He had joined the Army before the heavy bombing of Bristol drove Variety to Bangor in mid Wales in the spring of 1941. 'I did once show up there when I came on leave. I can't remember what it was. They were funny times.'

The Variety department must have thought so too. Before the war its programmes had appeared rather in the margins of the schedule; now they practically blanketed peak hours.

Why peacetime entertainment had been held in low esteem had much to do with Reith. His dictum, 'He who prides himself on giving what he thinks the public wants is often creating a fictitious demand for lower standards which he will then satisfy', applied to all programme output. But it mitigated particularly against entertainment and, thinks Dennis Main Wilson, who produced countless post-war television sitcoms, it made the BBC 'élitist and toffee-nosed'.

Pre-war research showed that three-quarters of

Arthur Askey and Richard Murdoch front the 20 October 1939 edition of the *Radio Times*.

all listeners spent one-sixth of their listening-time tuned to dance-band programmes, half tuned in to all studio variety and even more to broadcasts from variety theatres: and *Music Hall*, which the BBC itself mounted in full costume, attracted sixty-one per cent of the potential audience. But 'if you were a listener looking for comedy during the week, generally speaking, hard luck,' says Main Wilson. 'It was only on Saturday nights that the BBC let its hair down and allowed the masses their hour of music-hall.' Even then the broader performances were considerably less broad than in the theatre, and polished but near-the-knuckle entertainers like Noel Coward and Ronald Frankau made all too few appearances.

And yet, within days of the declaration of war, the BBC unhesitatingly gave entertainment a role of equal importance to the news. It was a remarkable volte-face, displaying an instinct for the time which those MPs who continued to demand 'stirring music' and less 'loose and debased' comedy were sadly lacking. It was a sad irony that, on 16 April 1940, while an MP was on his feet in the Commons railing about 'the badness of BBC programmes', Gracie Fields was singing to the troops at an all-star Franco-British concert at the Paris Opera House, the first great broadcasting occasion of the war and one so moving that for many people it

Garrison Theatre, **devised by BBC producer Harry S. Pepper (extreme right) and the conductor Charles Shadwell (back) brought Jack Warner (second from left) instant fame. Joan Winters, his 'little gurl', is on his immediate left.**

remained the wartime memory which outlasted all others. One-third of the adult population – eleven million people – listened to *Band Waggon* on Saturday nights. And on Thursdays during 1942, sixteen million – a listening figure previously reached only by the nine o'clock news – were glued to *ITMA*'s fifth series. Laughter was as much a munition of war as shells and aircraft engines.

Arthur Askey, a moderately successful comedian who became an overnight star after a single series of *Band Waggon* in the summer before the war, bounced back for his second run, saying: 'Well, Playmates … I think it's a stroke of genius putting *Band Waggon* on the air. It'll make old Nasty realize what the British public will put up with.' He was affectionately received. But the public was not asked to put up with a third series from 'Big-Hearted' Arthur and 'Stinker' Murdoch as the supposed caretakers of the Greenwich time-pips in the imaginary flat on top of Broadcasting House. Why, considering *Band Waggon*'s pedigree, remains a puzzle; however, Askey continued to appear in numerous other shows.

Garrison Theatre replaced *Band Waggon* and took over not only its slot but its popularity. A copy of the type of revue put on for troops in a large garrison town, it was performed in front of an audience of men and women in uniform and it ran for a year. And it made a star of Jack Warner who played the compère and who arrived on a bicycle which he abandoned somewhere in the theatre, punctuating proceedings thereafter with cries of 'Mind my bike!' Every week, he was spurned by his 'little gurl' (Joan Winters) who ignored his advances, merely repeating her refrain of 'Programmes, chocolates, cigarettes'. Warner's recitations from the heavily censored letters of his brother Sid somewhere in France brought the house down: 'Yesterday the colonel caught his thumb in a tank. His only remark was twenty-four blue pencils.'

THE BIRTH OF *ITMA*

It's That Man Again had begun because the BBC wanted another series like *Band Waggon*, which had broken new ground by being the first series planned for a thirteen-week run. The BBC also wanted a starring vehicle for Tommy Handley, who was firmly established as a 'handyman' of BBC comedy but who had had his own show. At first, the producer Francis Worsley toyed with the idea of creating an English version of the American Burns and Allen show, teaming Handley with the Canadian actress Celia Eddy. The flaw in this was that Gracie Allen was the comic of the team and George Burns the feed: for Handley it was the wrong way round. At his suggestion, the gag-writer Ted Kavanagh was hired to come up with something else and on 12 July 1939, with a title appropriated from a *Daily Express* headline relating to Hitler, the show went on-air from one of the BBC's studios at Maida Vale.

The germ of possibilities was apparent in the show, which had Handley as an

The one and only Tommy Handley, rehearsing *ITMA* in May 1942, with Dorothy Summers, who played Mrs Mopp ('Can I do yer now, Sir?') and Jack Train. Handley carried *ITMA*, the war's most popular programme, into the post-war period.

entertainments officer on a cruise liner with Celia Eddy as his secretary, Cilly. But no one liked the first episode or, for that matter, the following three. There was talk of ending the series. Then the run was interrupted by broadcasts from the Radiolympia, where manufacturers were exhibiting cheaper television sets and predicting sales of 80 000 by Christmas. The outbreak of war dashed such hopes but revived *It's That Man Again*: in Bristol the Variety department was grabbing at anything half-way decent to fill the schedule. A new format was devised, with Handley as the Minister of Aggravation and Mysteries, housed next to the Office of Twerps. Any assumption on the part of the Ministry of Information that it was the butt of this joke would not have been inaccurate. Handley was supported by a new cast: the original one was not in the group that had been vetted by the Ministry (of Information, that is).

It was not until the second wartime series that the title was shortened to *ITMA*, but the show had already found its niche. Handley's war opened like this:

TOMMY   Heil folks, it's *Mein Kampf* again. Sorry, I should say 'Hello, folks, it's that man again.' That was a Goebbled version, a bit doctored. I usually go all goosey when I can't follow my proper-gander.... (*Phone rings.*) Hello – yes ... no, sorry, the pigeon post is late today, the postman ate the express messenger, feathers and all. I haven't had a word from any of my spies. When I get those spies [*those pies*] here I won't mince my words, I can tell you. Ring me up again when I'm out. Goodbye or, as they say in Pomerania, 'arf window-screen. Now where's my new secretary?

VERA LENNOX   Here I am, Mr Handtorch.
TOMMY   Well, puncture me with a portfolio. Are you my new secretary?
VERA LENNOX   Yes, I'm Dotty.
TOMMY   I'm balmy myself. My last secretary was Cilly and you're Dotty.
VERA LENNOX   Cilly was my sister.
TOMMY   Well, splash my spats. Cilly was your sister? I'll have to see a silly-sister – a lawyer – about this.

After Dunkirk, when jokes at the expense of Government departments became less popular, *ITMA* moved to Foaming-at-the-Mouth, a seaside resort of appalling dinginess, where Handley was in turn mayor, factory manager, squire of Much-Fiddling, farmer, schoolmaster, hotel-keeper and prospective MP. The position was nominal and unimportant because he was endlessly interrupted by the telephone or by visitors who came and went with the speed of imagination via the *ITMA* prop door.

Tommy Handley (centre) with Jack Train, who used a tumbler to create the voice of Funf the Spy, and Fred Yule (left).

The characters tumbled over each other: Funf the spy (Jack Train speaking into a glass tumbler), Ali Oop the saucy postcard vendor, Lefty the Gangster and his side-kick Sam Scam, the bibulous Colonel Chinstrap, the hoarse-voiced Diver, the polite Commercial Traveller, the even more polite handymen Claude and Cecil, and countless more. Public conversation was stitched together by their catch phrases.

There had been others, earlier. In *Monday Night at Eight*, the Cockney comic Syd Walker, who played a wandering junkman, each week ended the telling of a tale that illustrated some human problem with the words, 'What would you do, chums?', which had become common coinage. So had Askey's 'I theng-yew' from *Band Waggon*. Warner's 'Mind my bike!', 'blue pencil' (for anything banned or forbidden) and 'di-da-di-da' (meaning 'and so on'), picked up from *Garrison Theatre*, were also doing the rounds. But *ITMA* contributed a veritable lexicon.

People found excuses to ring each other up just so they could say, 'This is Funf speaking'. They left each other's company with either a 'Ta-ta for now' or a 'TTFN', like *ITMA*'s second char, Mrs Mopp, whose very name passed into the language as a synonym. Pub barmen served customers with her 'Can I do you now, sir?' Virtually everyone invited to have a drink would accept with Chinstrap's 'I don't mind if I do'. 'Don't forget the Diver,' taxi drivers and waiters pointedly remarked. Those in lifts or seeking shelter in the London Underground (and, it was claimed, pilots on bombing raids) quoted the same source when they said, 'I'm going down now, sir'. Anyone who bumped into someone else in the black-out invariably said, 'After you, Claude'; to which the rejoinder was, inevitably, 'No, after *you*, Cecil'.

No one missed *ITMA* if they could help it. Desmond Hawkins remembers a summer's evening when his train made him late getting home but he missed hardly a word because all the windows were open and he was able to listen as he walked from the station. Newspapers suggested that if Hitler was going to invade, 8.30 on Thursday evenings was the time when Britain would be taken unawares. It became known that *ITMA* was the King's favourite programme and in 1942 a private performance was given at Windsor Castle for Princess Elizabeth's sixteenth birthday. The cast toured factories and Service bases, and went to Scapa Flow in June 1944 to entertain the sailors who ran the convoys over the perilous Arctic route to Russia. It was so cold there that the brass instruments could not be tuned properly and the violin strings snapped, but the reception was rapturous. In that year, recorded repeats of *ITMA* began to be played around the world. Handley was reaching more listeners than any British comedian in history.

ITMA found a place in people's hearts because it punctured pomposity, it tapped the British delight in simple wordplay, schoolboy slang and execrable puns and, in its cartoon fashion, it was a commentary on the war. Kavanagh would often add something to a script after listening to the six o'clock news on a Thursday night. And there was the presence of Handley himself, the sane, genial Liverpudlian who twisted his tongue around some of the most convoluted sentences ever written for broadcast and who never made a mistake. 'The best script-reader ever. There's never been anyone to touch him,' says fellow comic Charlie Chester.

OTHER POPULAR SHOWS

There was not another variety show to touch *ITMA*, either. *Hi, Gang!* and *Happidrome* were popular, but they did not run *ITMA* even close.

Hi, Gang! starred the American husband and wife team of Bebe Daniels and Ben Lyon, plus Vic Oliver. It had the speed that characterized American comedy (which *ITMA* imitated) and a friendliness that people liked. Daniels and Lyon were well known as film stars and were appreciated for having chosen to stay in Britain while some British stars, at the outbreak of war, had found pressing reasons to go to America. The Vienna-born Oliver, a violinist-turned-comic and a naturalized American, was Churchill's son-in-law.

Harry Korris (standing, right, behind the pianist), star of *Happidrome*, with producer Ernest Longstaffe (spectacles), and Cecil Frederick (left) and Robbie Vincent (centre) who played his dim-witted assistants. The *Happidrome* trio motored hundreds of miles to Bangor every week to broadcast.

Happidrome was typically British provincial, the setting a palace of delights kept going by Harry Korris as Mr Lovejoy. He would try to instil a little sense into two dim-witted young helpers, Ramsbottom and Enoch, whose response, 'Eh, I don't know', triggered Korris's despairing 'Take him away, Ramsbottom' – another catch phrase. Everyone knew the *We Three* song:

> We three, in Happidrome,
> Working for the BBC,
> Ramsbottom, and Enoch – and me!

Early in the war, the BBC invited parties of munition workers to theatre-studios as the audience for broadcast programmes of the make-'em-laugh sort; on one occasion Labour Minister Ernest Bevin was at a *Music Hall* watched by five thousand workers. It occurred to John Watt that, rather than bring the workers to a show, it might be better to bring a show to the workers and he suggested taking *Garrison Theatre* on the road. That idea did not get off the ground, but out of it were born *Workers' Playtime* and *Music While You Work.*

Music While You Work was first broadcast in June 1940 to aid the war effort by relieving the monotony of the production line. It played at 10.30 a.m. and 3 p.m., the times of day when workers' concentration dipped. At first, vocal numbers were popular, but they were dropped when it was realized that many women stopped work to write down the words. Almost every famous band toured the factories at some time, serving up light, rhythmical dance music. Other types of music proved unsatisfactory: anything dreamy or with a marked beat clashed with the rhythm of production. In five years, *Music While You Work* visited hundreds of factories, which between 1940 and 1945 increased at the rate of over 1000 a year to more than 8000, with four-and-a-half million workers. In 1942, after Russia came into the war and Churchill diverted armaments to help on the Second Front, *Music While You Work* also played at 10.30 p.m. for the night-shift.

Its companion programme, the lunchtime variety show, *Workers' Playtime*, started to do the rounds of factory canteens in May 1941, and was so successful that the initial six weeks became six months. After a break, the show went out thrice weekly for the rest of the war. Bevin gave it a launch and called the BBC 'a factory of entertainment and education'. The third edition of the week was recorded for broadcast to America at midnight and for home consumption on Sunday mornings.

The comics who plied their trade in *Workers' Playtime* tried to send workers back from their lunchtime fish and chips with a spring in their step; it was the comics who stripped down the nation's defiance to simple expression and the nation loved them for it. Says Dennis Main Wilson: 'All the comics felt in their own hearts, in their guts,

The comics who appeared in *Workers' Playtime* helped the war effort by sending people back to the production line laughing. Syd ('What would you do, chums?') Walker, is seen here at an aircraft factory in May 1942.

that it was a fight and their weapon was wit. There weren't many clever topical comedians like Tommy Handley and Leonard Henry, but even if most could only manage fairly crude, simplistic jokes, they all came out with an anti-Hitler joke or an anti-Nazi joke, or they'd mock little dwarf Goebbels or fatty Goering.'

Hitler had never been called Schicklgruber (the name was almost certainly the invention of British Government propaganda), but that did not stop a song by The Two Leslies from being wildly popular:

What a race, what a choice, what a face, what a voice
Rake's moustache, snaky eyes,
Wicked old Hun you've had your fun
Now comes your great surprise

53

Chorus
Old Man Schicklgruber
You're going to lose the rubber
Your doom is coming, you know that it's true
Old man Schicklgruber
We're going to make you blubber
You've got something that's coming to you

One night after Bristol and the docks at Avonmouth were bombed and Haw-Haw was gloating at Britain's misfortune, Leonard Henry told the audience that the German bombers had hit Haw-Haw's parents' home in Dulwich. 'And that,' Main Wilson says with relish, 'was true.'

Wartime broadcasting revived the careers of a number of fading troopers like Marie Lloyd, Little Titch and Dan Leno. And it made a new reputation for the established patterman Robb Wilton, who for years had delighted audiences as Mr Muddlecombe JP. Wilton soon had the character entangled in problems of ration

Robb Wilton (centre), whose monologues echoed so many people's sense of helplessness, rehearses a broadcast in Bangor. Wearing sergeant's stripes is the BBC producer Max Kester.

books and ARP posts. Yet it was as a confused but patriotic citizen determined to do his bit that his popularity soared. His monologues always began, 'The day war broke out,' and they recounted his failures in such roles as a would-be fire-watcher, special constable or – his classic turn, constantly repeated, and performed at Windsor Castle when he was part of the cast that supported *ITMA* – as a member of the Home Guard.

> The day war broke out, my missus looked at me and she said, 'What good are you?' I said, 'How do you mean, what good am I?' She said, 'Well, you're too old for the Army, you couldn't get into the Navy and they wouldn't have you in the Air Force, so what good are you?' I said, 'How do I know, I'll have to think.' [*He joined the Home Guard.*] The first day I got my uniform I went home and put it on – and the missus looked at me and said, 'What are you supposed to be?' I said, 'Supposed to be? I'm one of the Home Guards.' She said, 'One of the Home Guards? What are the others like?' She said, 'What are you supposed to do?' I said, 'I'm supposed to stop Hitler's army landing.' She said, 'What, YOU?' I said, 'No, not me, there's Bob Edwards, Charlie Evans, Billy Brightside – there's seven or eight of us, we're in a group, we're on guard in a little hut behind The Dog and Pullet.'

Wilton's stoical, aggrieved voice expressed in some way the sense of helplessness that ordinary people felt and their determination to do something, anything, to help the country. For many, he was the outstanding comedian of the war. Wilton took the nation into peace in typically lugubrious fashion, capturing the sudden emptiness which, paradoxically, so many people felt.

> The day peace broke out, I looked at the missus. I said, 'You don't look happy.' She said, 'Well, there's nothing to look forward to now.' I said, 'What do you mean?' She said, 'There was always the all-clear before.'

Over six years, a huge volume of series came and went. Some spluttered and died quickly, others caught and gave a glow that lasted for a season or two. Some, like *Workers' Playtime* and *Music While You Work*, continued into the peace. Few, like *Music Hall* and *ITMA*, were there at the beginning and the end, although *Monday Night at Eight* and *In Town Tonight* achieved this – indeed, the latter even made the transition to television in 1954. Both programmes added a middle-of-the-road solidity and a much-needed feeling that something, at least, was permanent. War-work and the *Luftwaffe* permitting, people accepted the invitation 'to take a chair, for *Monday Night at Eight* is on the air' (complete with Puzzle Corner, Inspector Hornleigh's detective quiz and the junkman-philosopher Syd Walker). On Saturdays they listened to the roar of London's traffic, overlaid by the Piccadilly flower-seller's cries and the swell of Eric Coates's *Knightsbridge March*, waiting for Freddie Grisewood's voice to shout 'Stop!' – when they would be introduced 'to some of the interesting people who are *In*

Town Tonight.' That opening was so evocative of home for servicemen overseas that many unashamedly wiped a tear from their eye when they heard it.

THE BRAINS TRUST IS BORN

In response to a request for something more informative on the Forces Programme, a few members of the Variety department went back to London at the end of 1940 to produce a half-hour show in which a panel of three experts would answer general knowledge questions sent in by members of the radio audience. The idea seemed as uninspired as the title, *Any Questions?*, and a run of only six shows was scheduled. No one guessed that, under a new name, this was to become the most influential talks programme in radio history.

Any Questions? went on-air, tucked away in the afternoon, on New Year's Day 1941, a Wednesday. In the first week it attracted fifteen letters: and then the explosion of interest was unprecedented. Soon – with its title changed to *The Brains Trust* – the show

The Brains Trust, under the chairmanship of Donald McCullough (back to camera) depended on the chemistry between Julian Huxley (top left), Commander A.B.Campbell (centre) and Cyril Joad (extreme right). Later, others joined the panel including Margery Fry (left) and the poet Robert Graves (on Joad's right).

was being listened to by one in three of the adult population and receiving a weekly postbag of more than 4000 letters.

Why *The Brains Trust* – quickly extended to forty-five minutes and repeated on the Home Service at Sunday tea-time – became the first serious programme to attract a mass audience had little to do with the information it imparted (How do flies walk on the ceiling? What causes a sneeze? Why do recumbent cattle rise forelegs first?) and everything to do with the contrast in the way in which the panellists answered the questions, and the chemistry between them. Producer Howard Thomas had cleverly brought together Julian Huxley, a biologist of world renown; the philosopher Cyril Joad; and a retired sailor, Paymaster Commander A.B. Campbell, an ordinary man who had not, he said, read much but who had travelled the world. The three could hardly have been more different: Huxley, the matter-of-fact man of science; Joad, who knew everything about everything and articulated perfectly formed thought in perfectly formed sentences; and the ebullient and irrepressible Campbell, already known on the BBC as a teller of tall tales. His 'When I was in Patagonia ...' became almost as famous as Joad's 'It all depends what you mean by ...'

The Brains Trust, wittily chaired by Donald McCullough, made eighty-four broad casts without a break, in an unprecedented run of eighteen months. When it returned, a pool of nine panellists had been formed. Many people resented the breaking up of the old team, but Howard Thomas felt that the unremitting exposure had worn their appeal a trifle thin and the load should be spread. The new team, including Dr (later, Sir) Malcolm Sargent, Kenneth Clark, Anna Neagle and Jenny Lee, made new reputations. Throughout the war, *The Brains Trust*, the forerunner of the chat show and the first programme to be broadcast entirely unscripted, remained an integral part of the nation's life.

As a matter of plain good sense, Thomas avoided questions about sex and religion, but did not shrink from controversial topics. There were few on-air lapses, although Joad upset one MP by quoting Confucius: 'What economy is it to go to bed in order to save candlelight if the result be twins?' Bracken, the Minister of Information, was asked in the House 'to take steps to prevent a repetition of such a disgusting incident'.

Another MP, the then Quentin Hogg, caused Thomas's departure from the BBC. Thomas had devised another talk show, *Everybody's Mike*, in which three male and three female MPs were to answer questions on parliamentary procedure. Hogg took part in the first recording, then complained that he had been misled about the nature of the programme. Under pressure, the BBC scrapped the series without broadcasting the first episode. Thomas, the future managing director of ABC and Thames Television, left. The BBC removed his name from the credits of *The Brains Trust*.

VARIETY IS HIT BY FLAK

There were all manner of criticisms of programmes in the course of the war. In the early days at Bristol, Leonard Henry was on the air almost as often as Sandy Macpherson. The heavy use made of the Variety Repertory Company, before

Noel Coward sings *Don't Let's be Beastly to the Germans* – a satire which some people misunderstood.

the Ministry of Information relaxed its vetting rule, meant that the same voices were being heard over and over again. When the Forces Programme unashamedly started up as an entertainments network aimed at men who would be listening in messes and canteens with the hub-bub of other men around them, there was an outcry that the BBC was 'pandering to the worst tastes' and transmitting 'filth' and 'tripe'. Later, when more than twenty dance-band programmes were on each week, there were complaints that there was too much of the stuff (research showed that most people did not think so).

A curious row blew up when Noel Coward sang *Don't Let's be Beastly to the Germans*, a witty put-down of those who, in 1943, were beginning to say that the Germans were not such bad chaps after all.

> Don't let's be beastly to the Germans
> For you can't deprive the gangster of his gun
> Though they've been a little naughty

To the Czechs and Poles and Dutch
I don't suppose those countries really minded very much.

Let's be free with them
And share the BBC with them
We mustn't prevent them basking in the sun
Let's soften their defeat again
And build their blasted fleet again
But don't let's be beastly to the Hun.

Coward first sang the song's many stanzas at a party marking the end of one of his West End seasons; Churchill was a guest and enjoyed it so much that he demanded several encores. Main Wilson describes it as 'one of the most brilliant, bitter pieces of satire' written by a man who was 'a patriot through and through'. But there was a furore in the Press: there were those who thought Coward was advocating some kind of conciliation. Eventually the BBC banned the song. 'But let's get it the right way round,' says Main Wilson. 'The BBC didn't ban it because they wanted to, it was in deference to public opinion – a few twits or twerps, call them what you will.'

Variety faced more criticisms from within the BBC than from without: the organization might have had the prescience to make entertainment a wartime banker, but living comfortably with the decision was something it never managed. There were 'drastic warnings' issued to staff on the need to eliminate 'vulgarity' and there were threats of suspension; no wonder Max Miller, undoubtedly the best but bluest comic of his time, did not get a wartime series, though at least he appeared more often than before the war. The minutes of one board of governors' meeting noted: '*Music Hall*: low standard deplored'. And two months later: 'Still declining, owing to competition of prevailing high stage fees and poor scripts.'

A variety censorship committee and a music censorship committee were put in place. Plays and songs were scanned for irreverence, lack of patriotism and lapses of taste. The producer of *Shipmates Ashore* was rebuked for allowing Phyllis Dixie, the striptease artist, to use the phrase 'tea and crumpet'. (Had crumpet been used in the plural, he was told, there would have been no objection.) Three George Formby ditties were deemed to be 'filthily suggestive' and Vera Lynn was rebuked for being too 'sentimental'. Sensing sin in the popular song *Why Don't We Do This More Often?*, the BBC amended the second line from 'just what we're doing tonight' to 'just what we're doing today'. An even more popular tune, *I'm Going to Get Lit Up When the Lights Go Up in London*, was banned for encouraging drunkenness.

Americanization of the airwaves also caused some soul-searching. There was no discernible unease when the somewhat Anglicized *Hi, Gang!* was joined during 1941

Bob Hope (second from left) appeared in *Yankee-doodle-doo*, an Anglo-American series written by Hal Block, an American scriptwriter signed up by the BBC in 1942 'to infuse new life and competition into our present set-up'.

by pre-recorded Bob Hope and Jack Benny pro-grammes from the US. But as American troops began arriving in Britain and an American influence be-came apparent in some of Variety's own output, the BBC worried it was casting itself 'as a Frankenstein'. And yet the BBC's attitude was ambivalent. Main Wilson remembers that the 'great unhappiness with the quality of entertainment, within the BBC if not the Ministry of Information or with the public' resulted in the assistant head of Variety being dispatched to the States 'to try and buy or pinch some ideas.... He came back pretty empty-handed.'

In the middle of the war, when the formidable ex-governor Lady Snowden was still calling for the elimination of vulgarity, the BBC asked Percy Edgar, the director of the Midland region, to make an assessment of Variety's work. He was 'appalled' at the low standard of many of the programmes and complained about 'persistent continuation of series which are obviously below-standard'. And he objected to 'undue attention' being paid to the size of audiences – one of the reasons Reith had resisted listener research until 1936 was his belief that getting answers to questions asked of the public could only tempt producers to make programmes geared to the lowest common denominator. Edgar seemed not to appreciate that the necessities of wartime broadcasting meant that the single standard of taste which had belonged to the BBC in its ordered, pre-war world no longer applied: other viewpoints had to be accommodated. He was a man so out of touch that he even suggested that artists used by the BBC should sign exclusive contracts – which overlooked the fact that BBC fees were minimal and someone like Max Miller was earning the wartime equivalent of a six-figure sum on the boards. It was a matter of great annoyance to the BBC that, in September 1939, when the theatres were briefly shut down and it would have been possible to get virtually anyone it wanted under contract, the Ministry of Information did not respond until it was too late.

No doubt some of the criticism of Variety's output was justified. The jokes in *Hi, Gang!* and *Happidrome* – not to mention other programmes – were elderly; *Old Mother Riley Takes to the Air* and *The Old Town Hall*, presided over by the brash Clay Keyes, were as low-brow as it was possible to be. And shows like *Factory Canteen* and *Works Wonders*, in which the workers themselves were the performers, were dire. Variety director, John Watt, was under no illusion about the general standard of comedy when he told his staff to 'try to be funny half the time and do more musical shows, though they invariably have only half the audience.' Yet he defended himself against Edgar by saying it was 'a complete myth that there are swarms of unknown talented artists rotting in the provinces.' How he would have loved to create another *ITMA*, which was both the jewel in his crown and his crown of thorns.

A GOOD PRODUCTION LINE

For six years, regardless, Variety stood on its production line and churned out the goods. During 1942 its forty or so producers (including the seven who concentrated solely on dance-bands) produced an average of 180 programmes a week – more than 9000 over the year. That figure dropped to around 120 shows a week by the end of the war, although that was still triple the pre-war output. Week in, week out, the producers got the stars to Bristol and then to Bangor (until the department's return to London in 1943) and to wherever else in the country they were needed. They knocked up adaptations of film musicals and cartoons, provided musical comedies, song-shows, revues, continuity shows, cabaret, stories with music, request shows and 'interest programmes'. They slogged around the country, providing relays from theatres and music-halls. They went to factories and dockyards in all weathers, sometimes rigging up in the open air. They trailed to concerts at barracks, aerodromes and naval bases and on the end of piers in the struggling seaside resorts. All of this was done in the face of bombing, black-out, cancelled trains, petrol rationing and, worst of all, the

Hi Gang! with the American husband-and-wife team of Ben Lyon and Bebe Daniels, aided by the comedian-violinist Vic Oliver, was such a success that it was moved from the studio to the Criterion Theatre which, although in central London, was underground.

loss of staff and performers to call-up in the Services.

The public's gratitude, whatever the passing grumbles, knew no bounds. Wartime entertainment coloured people's lives, enriched their conversation and made them laugh, despite everything. Good, bad or indifferent, the programmes made them instinctively aware, at the most basic level, that everyone was in the same boat. And they gave everyone a role against the enemy – even if, for most, it was only blowing raspberries.

In answer to a question about how he saw Variety's wartime role, John Watt said: 'In my mind's eye I see an embattled Mrs Mopp shaking her bucket and broom at Hitler. "I'll do yer," she shouts.'

As an epithet, it will do.

CHAPTER

4

KNITTING THE NATION TOGETHER

'It is a land of snobbery and privilege, ruled largely by the old and silly. But in any calculation about it one has got to take into account its emotional unity, the tendency of nearly all its inhabitants to feel alike and act together in moments of supreme crisis.'

The novelist and essayist George Orwell (who was working for the BBC as editor of broadcast talks to India) wrote those words about his country in 1941. The Battle of Britain had been won, the Blitz had been survived and Air-Marshal Goering's boast that the *Luftwaffe* would take two weeks to smash the Royal Air Force, leaving him free to bomb the British into submission at will, had turned to ashes in his mouth.

LIFE IN THE BLITZ

The air-raid sirens were first heard in earnest, over a wide area, on Wednesday 5 June 1940. Five days later the large-scale daylight raids began and on Saturday 7 September the prolonged onslaught on London began. An estimated 50 000 high-explosive bombs and incalculable numbers of incendiaries were dropped on the capital.

Britain soldiered on through the Blitz, an ant-hill of activity as evacuation, conscription and war-work moved millions of men and women around the country. In the summer of 1940, when German fighters sometimes strafed civilians, land girls donned their steel helmets and carried on digging out the crops; and tractor drivers ploughed the fields in pairs facing in opposite directions because their engines would drown out the sound of a diving plane. In London, where the barrage balloons wallowed in the skies like giant versions of Churchill's cigars, people picked their way over the rubble and struggled to work, took to the shelters during the air-raids which

'Their homes had been destroyed and everything around them was in flames, but they were out in the streets raging against the Germans...We're not going to give in...'

rose to seven or ten a day, and at night crowded into the biggest shelter of them all, the Underground system, in defiance of authority (although, with typical British phlegm, two-thirds of Londoners preferred to stay in their own beds, even though many moved downstairs).

As the number of new aircraft emerging from British factories began to exceed the number lost, the Germans were forced to shift from day attacks to night; and while they inflicted cruel damage, they were pounded out of the sky. The continuous offensive against London lasted until the all-clear on Sunday 11 May 1941, which signalled the end of the final and worst raid of the war. During this period, and for a while afterwards, before the *Luftwaffe* turned towards Moscow, most of the country's major ports and industrial cities absorbed even more concentrated attacks, although their ordeal usually lasted for only two or three nights at a time.

In this onslaught, Britain felt a surge of patriotism, a ferocious consciousness of itself as the last defender of freedom. 'I'm sorry for the cliché, but the true grit of the British came out in the Blitz,' says Frank Gillard. 'I was in city after city that had been hit disastrously and the guts and the spirit of the people never ceased to amaze me. Their homes had been destroyed and everything around

The Government forbade the use of the Underground as a shelter – but once the Blitz began, people bought a 1½d ticket and refused to come up. There were canteens, libraries and, as seen here at the Aldwych station in October 1940, entertainment.

them was in flames, but they were out in the streets raging against the Germans. "We'll get back at them for this. We're not going to give in."' It was the BBC's job to reflect this indomitable spirit and it did so. In October 1940, for instance, Robin Duff sampled life in a London shelter:

> It was a surface shelter that I went to … I've been round the streets most nights, on one job or another, but I've never seen anything to equal this for comfort and cheerfulness. All the people come from a nearby block of flats. There's a family atmosphere and the place looks fine. There are flags on the walls and pictures of film stars, and the children have hung paper streamers all around. Along one side there are chairs and a few tables; and when I went in, all the women were knitting very busily. There was a babble of talk, and most of the children were playing cards. Everybody was laughing and joking. And if there was any noise from outside they started singing. (*Sound of bombing.*) Their general motto seemed to be: take no notice. (*Sound of bombing.*)

Only once during the Blitz was the BBC badly compromised in reporting how Britain could take it. In February 1941, after three terrible nights of bombing on Swansea, the six o'clock news carried an interview with the head of the local *Evening Post* who talked in terms of such insensitivity about the cheerfulness of the city that Swansea was in a fury and the row reached the Ministry of Information. Charles Brady, a working man who lived through the raids, remembers the broadcast vividly: 'It was a bit of fancy prose stuck together without any relation to the facts, saying everyone was going around with their usual smiles. People said, "Damn it, it wasn't like that!" They weren't heroes. They'd lost their relatives, they'd lost their houses, they were grief-stricken, not the happy sort of nitwits they'd been made out to be.' But Brady adds: 'I don't blame the BBC: he wasn't a BBC man.'

THE BBC GETS INTO ITS STRIDE

The public had forgiven the BBC for the shambles of the early days of war. It liked the new hours of broadcasting. The old National and Regional Programmes had opened at a leisurely 10.15 a.m. The Forces Programme was on parade at 6.30 a.m., with the Home Service hitting the ground running half an hour later. The public liked the output, so much of which was different, even exciting, and yet so much of which was familiar enough to give a sense, at least, of normality. It liked the immediacy of wartime broadcasting. And it liked its own involvement in shaping what it heard.

The BBC spoke to the nation but it was also the conduit which allowed the nation to speak to itself. The news bulletins were reinforced by the voices of ordinary people – evacuated children, airmen, sailors, soldiers, munitions workers – talking, however

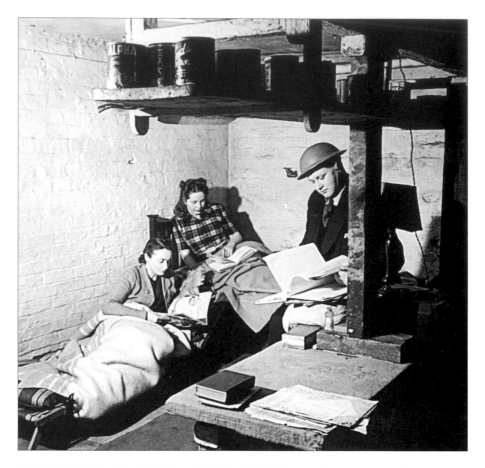

Communal living – an air-raid shelter at the the BBC in 1941.

haltingly, about their experiences. That, simply, had not happened before. From the beginning of the war to its end, officers from the Services gave the weekly *War Commentary*, which helped citizens and servicemen alike understand how the battle was shaping and how their contribution to its prosecution, however small, mattered. Across some 280 broadcasts, the series maintained a seven million listenership. And there were other voices, authoritative and trustworthy: the power of the spoken word did not rest only with Churchill and Priestley. Unknown, perhaps, to later generations, they included W.A. Sinclair, whose series, *The Voice of the Nazi*, was a brilliant analysis of the aims and methods of German propaganda, and Professor John Hilton, who before the war had won a reputation for advising the unemployed and who, now, addressed himself to the wives and families of serving men and their problems of evacuation, billeting and separation. His death robbed the nation of much good sense.

THE MODERN DOCUMENTARY ARRIVES

All sorts of voices, blended with the sounds of a nation at war, became the lifeblood of the documentaries which, more than any other area of wartime output, changed the face of broadcasting.

June 1940: head of Drama Val Gielgud (right) and writer Stephen Potter, discuss the placing of a programme with Harman Grisewood, who later moved to the European Service.

Before the war, the BBC documentary had been worthy and dull: a visit to an isolated lighthouse was typical of the kind of thing it considered exciting. Methods of inserting recorded material into live studio presentation had not been mastered and broadcasts were consequently jerky and largely formless. 'There was something a little humiliating in the fact that the best pre-war documentary feature was an American importation, *Job to be Done*,' admitted the *BBC Handbook* of 1940. All this changed as radio was catapulted into the final months of 1939. The documentary grew up with a bang. The universal changes and dislocation of national life made it vital to display every aspect of Britain in a fuller way than the news was able to do, and series like *Home Front*, *In Britain Now*, *Go To It* and *We Speak for Ourselves* provided vibrant sketches of how people were living, working and keeping going. A wealth of human-interest programmes showed how London and the country was coping: *Spitfire over Britain*, *Watchers of the Sky*, *Coastal Command*; and how

Britain was taking the fight to the enemy: *Bombers over Berlin, Swept Channels, Women Hitting Back.*

The dramatized documentary was born, a carefully shaped piece of writing which employed actors and music. Most memorable was the first of its kind, *The Shadow of the Swastika*, on the rise of Nazism, which was based on documented evidence and made all the more effective by a remarkable impersonation of Hitler by Marius Goring. In the main, however, this vivid treatment was reserved to portray the exploits of the fighting men, as in the immensely popular *Battle of Britain*, the weekly *Marching On* and the thrice-weekly *Into Battle*, which were all prototypes for countless individual programmes. Many were written at great speed and orchestrated only hours before broadcast. The dramatized technique reached its climax in *Victory in Africa*, which in May 1943 signalled the rout of the Germans at Cap Bon and was on the air within forty-eight hours of their surrender.

THE PROPAGANDA MACHINE STARTS TO ROLL

All of this was propaganda in the true sense that it disseminated a belief: that Britain would not be brought to its knees. The BBC spread that propaganda abroad. As part of its intensive efforts to bring America into the war, it broadcast in its North American service a series called *The Stones Cry Out,* which dealt with famous British buildings that had been demolished or badly damaged by bombing. Whether Americans, with their well-known respect for history, were suitably enraged is another matter, but Desmond Hawkins, one of the series' writers, has no doubt that 'it was blatant propaganda. I mean, we had no doubt that we were writing propaganda to get America to stir itself and come in. But it wasn't propaganda writing, if you understand me. I would have enjoyed writing a documentary about St Clement Danes whether it had been knocked down or was still standing.'

One of the BBC's small wartime triumphs was its dealings with the quite proper but frequently heavy-handed propaganda requirements of the Government. The BBC interpreted what was asked of it as imaginatively as it could and, by and large, managed to keep the ministries at arm's length. In the stalemate spring and winter of 1939-40 when good citizenship was all there was to talk about, there was a slightly absurd air about the 'home propaganda' envisaged by the Ministry of Information. Nonetheless, the BBC exhorted people to save and to salvage, to avoid careless talk and nip rumour in the bud, to watch their step in the black-out, to learn first-aid, to turn their wirelesses down in consideration of their neighbours, to stay put but evacuate their children, to dig for victory, to shop wisely, cook economically and keep pigs, chickens, rabbits and goats (but not, it was stipulated, rats).

There were other campaigns too during the course of the war. Wisely, BBC producers used comics in most of these endeavours. Syd Walker turned to good account a song of his, *Any Old Rags, Bottles, or Bones*. Will Fyffe gave a variety of tips. Will Hay and Claude Hulbert encouraged people not to leave their districts unless war-work took them elsewhere. Gert and Daisy and Charlie Chester talked about food.

DIGGING FOR VICTORY

Whether in the ground or in the pot, food was the subject of the most sustained campaigning: there were almost 2000 wartime broadcasts. These were of especial significance during late 1941-early 1942 when the already heavy losses being sustained by the Atlantic convoys rose to 50 per cent; 275 ships were sunk in March 1942 alone.

At the outbreak of war the Ministry of Agriculture, recognizing the part that the established series *In Your Garden* could play, wrote to the BBC to ensure that it would not be dropped. Nothing could have been further from the BBC's mind: the wrily humorous and casually dignified gardening journalist Cecil Middleton (who was never addressed as anything but Mr Middleton) received probably the largest fan mail of any pre-war radio speaker. If anything, his popularity increased during the war: three-and-half million listeners settled down to his fifteen-minute Sunday broadcasts, just after the lunchtime dishes had been cleared away. There were the practical reasons of wanting to know how best to raise vegetables in the back garden, but there was, perhaps, something in the notion that, as they fought for their land, people felt drawn to and comforted by a man who so clearly loved the soil.

Millions of men turned over their lawns and flowerbeds or more assiduously tended their allotments after Lord Woolton became Minister of Food in April 1940 and put backbone into the Dig for Victory campaign. Woolton was also responsible for the brilliant Kitchen Front campaign which won ordinary housewives to his side and helped them find ingenious ways of supplementing the ration, which had been introduced at the beginning of the year. The BBC quickly translated the campaign into *The*

The well-loved **Mr C.H.Middleton**, who delivered his 15-minute *In Your Garden* talks from a studio at Wood Norton, did no gardening himself – but was one of the great communicators.

Digging for Victory in *The Radio Allotment*, January 1942: broadcasters Wynford Vaughan Thomas, Stewart MacPherson, Raymond Glendenning and Michael Standing.

Kitchen Front series and *Backs to the Land*, a series for small-holders. In 1942 the BBC Outside Broadcast department adopted a piece of ground in Park Crescent, not far from Broadcasting House, and once a week listeners visiting *The Radio Allotment* were treated to a running commentary from the likes of Wynford Vaughan Thomas, Raymond Glendenning and Stewart MacPherson, who got the plot into shape in their spare time.

Country Magazine – the idea of Donald McCullough, chairman of *The Brains Trust* but in his professional life a PRO for the Ministry of Agriculture – began in May 1942, and it did much to acquaint farmers with the need to save imported feed, to set up pig clubs and to extend acreage of ploughed land. By 1945 the total amount of arable land in Britain had been raised from twelve million to nineteen million acres. Retired labourers came forward to work from sunrise to darkness, to plough by moonlight, to train the thousands of young women from shops and offices who volunteered for the new Land Army. *Country Magazine*, broadcast once a fortnight, helped to sustain that drive and it made people aware of what one section of the community was doing to help win the war, as many other radio series were designed to do.

Desmond Hawkins went to work on *Country Magazine* after *The Stones Cry Out*. It gave him an unexpected insight into censorship: 'The programme had to be scripted – and this is very hard for people nowadays to understand. There was no tape recorder. You couldn't go out to see a man on his farm and simply record him. You had to prepare a script. And you had to wait until the script came back with its two stamps from the two censors before you brought someone up to London and tried to make him work off the script so that he sounded more or less like himself.

I was doing an edition of *Country Magazine* which I thought couldn't possibly bother any censor at all. I'd been to see a dear old man who was talking about his early days fishing out of Lowestoft with the shrimp-boats just after the turn of the century – and the censor took out a whole lot and wrote against it: "References to navigation in the North Sea are not permitted".

Gert and Daisy (Elsie and Doris Waters) brought down-to-earth humour to helping the housewife in *The Kitchen Front*.

The Kitchen Front was by far the most successful of the programmes that in one way or another dealt with food. Like the Postscripts which followed the nine o' clock news on Sundays, it was a five-minute broadcast, following on from the eight o'clock bulletin every morning. In the first week alone it brought in 1000 letters, plus parcels of cakes and other gifts from women who had tried out the recipes. On some days Elsie and Doris Waters (until the war far better known than their brother Jack Warner) came to the microphone as Gert and Daisy, a couple of Cockney chars with husbands in the Forces. On other days it was the actress Mabel Constanduros as the cantankerous Grandma Buggins. Occasionally housewives were invited to come in and talk about their recipes.

The Kitchen Front was brief, friendly, humorous and laced, inevitably, with awful puns. (Grandma Buggins: 'Well, if you don't care about the nice recipes I bring you, I might as well go to Russia and fish for surgeons in the vodka.') And it undoubtedly appealed to the British sense of the ridiculous – fighting the war with Doctor Carrot and Potato Pete, who boosted the consumption of carrots, 'bright treasures dug from good British earth,' and potatoes, 'a rich store of all-round nourishment'. The programme did its best to help the beleaguered housewife, offering recipes for carrot flan, which had 'a deliciousness all its own', for banana cake made out of parsnips, for cakes made with dried elderberries and chopped prunes as substitutes for currants, for cakes made with nothing but flour, custard powder and dried egg. One recipe was called 'Pigs in Clover' – 'a novel way with baked potatoes and sausage' (sausages were unrationed, if you could find them and did not enquire too closely into their ingredients). Silly names rather appealed to *The Kitchen Front*'s frontman, Freddie Grisewood (who was affectionately known to listeners as Ricepud):

> Another letter gives a recipe called 'Fire-fighter's Pie'. That sounds to me a grand name. Almost as good as a wartime pudding I heard of called 'Skinflint's Joy'. Do you know, I think we could do with a few more names like these, if you would care to send them in.

Charlie Chester, who had become a Sergeant in the Royal Irish Fusiliers, appeared in a series of programmes that went out under the title of *Food Flash* to alert people to such things as the need to save milk bottles, the nutritional value of cod liver oil, the need to use only one spoonful of tea for each person 'and none for the pot'. 'To give you some idea of the shortage, if women saw a queue, they would join it, no matter what it was for,' he recalls. 'One joke that I remember was: My missus saw a queue and she joined it. After fifteen minutes she tapped the woman in front on the shoulder and said "What are we queuing for?" And the woman said "Tales of Hoffmann" and my missus said, "Well, you've got to eat anything these days."'

Chester wrote the sketches for *Food Flash*: 'I remember one where we were fishing in the desert. "Fish is cheap this week." You know, on occasions you got a glut. You didn't see many cows in the fields and there were no sheep. It amazes me even now when I see a field full of sheep.'

The British did not automatically follow the Government wherever it chose to lead. When the Board of Trade became alarmed that clothing coupons (introduced over the Whit weekend in 1941) were being used too quickly and launched a Make Do and Mend campaign, the public resented it. Whether people realized it or not, there was no real shortage: coupon rationing was a mechanism to divert factory workers into munitions. In any event, *Beating the Coupon* and *New Clothes for Old* were among the least successful of the BBC's wartime efforts.

All recipes for *The Kitchen Front* were tested in the Ministry of Food's kitchen at Portman Square. Scripts were also drafted at the Ministry, where Eileen Blair, George Orwell's first wife, was one of those responsible. Frequently there were tensions between the BBC and the Ministry, which often exercised an arbitrary control, for instance replacing a talk on swedes with one on green vegetables and cancelling another on the 'kitchen front' in the USA in favour of a directive about a hold-up in the distribution of ration books. In January 1943, when Lord Woolton wanted the phrase 'Eat potatoes instead of bread' broadcast every day for a month, Ministry writers managed to work it into the scripts for every day of the week except Wednesdays and Saturdays, and then insisted that the BBC's announcers should be instructed to use the phrase on those days. The BBC agreed but wrote, hoping 'there was nothing sacrosanct about this phrase since it would be a little bare to say: "This is *The Kitchen Front*. Eat potatoes instead of bread. Here is Mrs Buggins."'

In the middle of 1943, *The Kitchen Front* broadened its scope to include items about other household matters, something it had done occasionally in the past. In June 1942, for example, after the Minister of Fuel and Power had launched a national fuel economy campaign, the programme had plugged it regularly until *Fuel Flashes* were introduced after the six p.m. news. When told that in future *The Kitchen Front* would deal with food only on three mornings a week and would change its name to *The Household Front* on other days, the Ministry protested. But this time the BBC insisted and the Ministry reluctantly agreed, but with the proviso that *The Kitchen Front* should be the title used whenever the Radio Doctor was included in the broadcast.

THE RADIO DOCTOR AND THE NATION'S HEALTH

Wartime Britain, sustained on an adequate but meagre diet, was constantly concerned about its health; that was one reason why it listened to the Radio Doctor. But that alone did not explain the popularity of 'the doctor with the greatest number of patients in the world'. Why people listened to him – and could swell *The Kitchen Front*'s audience on such occasions from an average of six to fourteen million – was not only because his advice was sensible ('Don't give Father extra butter, Mother, that's your ration'), but because in his slow, fruity, compassionate voice he spoke in down-to-earth language like nobody else's.

The unidentified Radio Doctor was Dr Charles Hill, secretary of the British Medical Association. He had begun broadcasting by giving four talks on the Nutrition Report and later contributed to Freddie Grisewood's programme *The World Goes By*. Grisewood could hardly believe what Hill got away with on-air. In his autobiography,

Wartime Britain, living on a meagre diet, provided the Radio Doctor – Dr Charles Hill – with 'the greatest number of patients in the world'.

My Story of the BBC, he wrote that often he would protest, 'But Charles, you can't possibly say that,' only to be greeted with the reply, 'You just listen.' Hill was using the word 'belly' on-air at a time when a documentary about bomber crews was having to say that one of the crew was lying on his 'tummy'.

One of Hill's favourite themes was the need for regular bowel movements. He praised 'that humble black-coated worker, the prune' and described a pathologist as 'a man who sits on one stool and examines those of other people'. 'Another of Boxing Day's little troubles is constipation,' he told listeners in 1940. 'Too much food and too much armchair and the body's reply is "What I have I hold". Visit the throne at the same time each day, whether you feel like it or not.' 'And how's your stomach today?' he asked. 'Is it firm and steady or somewhat warm or a little wobbly and a trifle windy?' One wartime Christmas, when he was talking about the possible causes of a hangover, he remarked: 'It may even be due to too much drink, though if it was I'd like to know where you got it.'

Hill, who became Lord Hill of Luton and served as chairman of the Independent Television Association before taking over the same role at the BBC, once fell foul of the Ministry of Food. It was not because of his language but because his talk on spacing meals contained the statement that 'those who don't have breakfast won't work efficiently until lunchtime' – which was enough to have the talk rejected. The Ministry thought that men in canteens everywhere would be thumping the counter and demanding sustenance in the middle of the morning. But even the mild Mr Middleton managed to rub officialdom up the wrong way. It had been agreed that if one particular *In Your Garden* programme ran short, he would add a sentence or two about lettuces and dahlias. Instead, he talked about carnations, commenting that some people found them difficult to grow, because they like lots of lime. 'But cheer up,' he then added, 'the way things are going at the moment there will soon be plenty of mortar rubble about.'

In 'BBC at War', a pamflet it published in 1941 (6d, by post 8d), the BBC spoke of the need for good plays, good music and religion: 'A nation straining every nerve to win an arduous war needs food for its intellect and its soul as well as its body.' The language may seem a tad over-blown today, but the needs were real enough. And the

BBC met those needs – rather neatly, where body and soul were concerned, by introducing, in December 1939, *Lift Up Your Hearts* (the forerunner of *Thought for the Day*) and *Up in the Morning Early* (a programme of what was then referred to as physical jerks) back-to-back before the 8 a.m. news.

THE DRAMA DEPARTMENT'S WAR

Commentators tend to suggest that, during the war, the standard of radio drama declined in the face of the need to keep people cheerful, but that is not supported by the evidence. The head of Drama, Val Gielgud (the brother of Sir John), was determined that civilized culture should be preserved and, among the 400 or so plays which his department turned out during each of the war years, there was a healthy representation of Shakespeare, the classics and uncompromising new works. In 1941 the experiment of allotting almost the whole of an evening's listening to a single play, Shaw's *St Joan*, proved so surprisingly popular that it was followed by others including *Antony and Cleopatra*, *Julius Caesar*, and, in 1942, in celebration of the 450th anniversary of the discovery of America, Louis MacNeice's *Christopher Columbus*, with Laurence Olivier in the title role. There were also ambitious projects such as an eight-part adaptation of Tolstoy's *War and Peace*.

But drama was as much part of the BBC's war effort as the variety shows and in the main it strove to reach as many people as possible. The department revived programmes which gave extracts of plays running in the West End or on tour, with the original casts; ran a drama request week; supplied substantial dollops of Dickens, Trollope, Thackeray and Galsworthy – broadcasts of whose works guaranteed a heavy demand in the public libraries. In 1943 the two most popular drama series of the war began: *Saturday Night Theatre* (which the BBC itself described as 'determinedly middle-brow') and *Appointment with Fear*, an American-style thriller written by an American, John Dickson Carr, which came complete with shock-horror musical effects

March 1941: actresses Lucille Lisle (studying the rehearsal lists) and Lydia Sherwood (seated), in the Drama department Green Room in Manchester.

and the supernaturally deep voice of Valentine Dyall as the narrator, 'The Man in Black'. *Appointment with Fear* was so popular that it reached as many listeners as the most popular variety shows, with the exception of *ITMA*.

By 1944 the Drama department had doubled its pre-war audience. It owed much to the thirty or so actors of the resident repertory company who were signed up at the same time as the Variety Rep. They were just as hard-working, half of them looking after schools programmes and *Children's Hour* at Bristol, the others moving with the Drama department first to Evesham in Worcestershire and then to Manchester. The BBC found work for other actors when it could (there was a great deal of unemployment in the theatrical profession during the war) but still the stalwarts of the Rep. appeared in six or seven productions a week. Like those of the announcers, the voices of Gladys Young, Carleton Hobbs, Norman Shelley and others became so familiar that many people regarded them as family friends.

The first *Saturday Night Theatre* was adapted from a detective story by Dorothy L. Sayers. She was the writer who, in Christmas 1941, provoked one of the broadcasting controversies of the war with a remarkable religious series, *The Man Born to be King*, which went out in the Sunday *Children's Hour* and which, for the first time (by agreement with the Lord Chamberlain) included an actor playing Christ. The Lord's Day Observance Society denounced Broadcasting House as 'a temple of blasphemy', thereby ensuring the series of a massive listenership.

Valentine Dyall, the narrator of *Appointment with Fear*.

Children's Hour played its wartime role. It ran a *Blue Peter*-style salvage competition (the winners from Manchester collected nine tons of scrap) and produced its own brand of patriotic programmes such as *To Thee My Country, Men of Mettle* and *They Went to It* ('stories of civilian courage from the regions'). In October 1940, Princess Elizabeth made her first broadcast, appearing on the programme with Princess Margaret who joined her sister in bidding the listeners good night. The message was relayed to children of the Empire and included in the first of the weekly programmes for children who had been evacuated to the Dominions and the USA.

The BBC made heroic efforts to keep schools broadcasting on the air. Modern language broadcasts and the pre-war pamphlets that had accompanied all courses had to be abandoned, but by 1944, thirty-one weekly series, a daily news commentary and twice-weekly religious services were on offer. And the number of schools making use of the output rose from 10 000 to 12 000, despite the fact that many schools closed because of evacuation, bombing or because their premises were required for war purposes. This was a huge achievement which received little recognition, although one headmistress wrote to say that the broadcasts were 'like life-buoys in a queer, turbulent, scholastic sea'.

LET THERE BE MUSIC

Serious music gained a wider and more knowledgeable audience during the course of the war – though the offerings heard on the Forces Programme were rather sniffily described by Sir Adrian Boult (the BBC's director of Music until 1942 when he handed over to Sir Arthur Bliss in order to devote himself to conducting the BBC Symphony Orchestra) as 'the classics which have passed from "very popular" to the "hackneyed" class, without, of course, losing their intrinsic value …'

On the Home Service, however, there was a considerable increase in classical and contemporary output. Programmes were often shorter (taking the form of a single symphony) and there were fewer for the connoisseur, but two-hour periods were regularly devoted to symphony concerts and there were fortnightly lunchtime concerts. Those given by pianist Myra Hess at the National Gallery during the Blitz became a national institution. In late 1939, after years of obduracy, the D'Oyly Carte Opera Company signed an agreement which allowed the first complete Gilbert and Sullivan opera, *Trial by Jury*, to be transmitted. Subsequently, a full studio opera was broadcast each month as well as a short opera and a comic one. Britain also rediscovered its own national music as the BBC, as a matter of policy, devoted something like one-quarter of its output to British composers – Byrd, Purcell and Gibbons, as well as Elgar, Vaughan Williams and Walton – and to British folk music.

After a two-year absence from the air, the Promenade Concerts were re-instated in 1942, with Sir Henry Wood conducting his forty-eighth season. The Proms' traditional home, the Queen's Hall (where the 1939 season came to a precipitate end when the BBC Symphony Orchestra was ordered to evacuate to Bristol) had been destroyed by enemy action the previous year. For the first time the season was held in the much larger Albert Hall and, considering the circumstances, the BBC was concerned that the place might not be filled. They need not have worried – hundreds of people had to be turned away. The season coincided with the first anniversary of Russia's entry into the war and music-lovers were introduced to Khachaturyan and Shostakovich – whose *Leningrad Symphony* had been given its British première by the BBC Symphony Orchestra on the radio a week earlier. The conductor's score and the orchestral parts had been sent by diplomatic bag from Moscow on 900 microfilmed pages.

Early in the war the violinist Yehudi Menuhin twice visited Britain from his home

Twenty-eight-year-old Yehudi Menuhin rehearses with the BBC Symphony Orchestra under Sir Adrian Boult in October 1944.

in the USA, hitching a ride in a bomber so that he could play for the people 'when it was dark and there was nothing, no assurance, except their faith'. He came back in 1943 and 1944 to play for the Allied Forces; on the second visit, before his return to America, he gave the first British performance of Bartók's *Violin Concerto* with the BBC Symphony Orchestra. He had given concerts in Brussels, Antwerp and Paris, arrived having been up for days and, between rehearsals and performance, slept on a table at the back of the hall.

Why did he make so much effort? Lord Menuhin's answer is simple. 'I had known Britain since 1929 when I first gave my concerts. I had been given the key that unlocks British hearts. I offered immediately. The first trip would have taken place a year earlier, but they suddenly had to send aeroplane parts, which of course took precedence over violinists. For Menuhin:

The BBC was simply the reflection of everything that could be trusted, everything that was good, and people all over the world turned to the BBC. And in music Sir Adrian Boult carried the equivalent of the message that the rest of the BBC carried in words.... Great art is a form of inoculation against diseases which are unspeakable.

CHRISTMAS IN WARTIME

Another example of the BBC's message was the Christmas Day link-up, the climax of every broadcasting year during wartime as it had been in peace. King George V had made the first royal broadcast to the millions of listeners to the new Empire Service on Christmas Day 1932; at every Christmas throughout the thirties, Laurence Gilliam merged contributions from the Dominions into a loose whole that preceded the monarch's message. This tradition did not end with the war – indeed, probably more than anything else the BBC produced, it helped to knit the nation together, while throwing an invisible arm around the shoulders of the Empire.

The first wartime Christmas broadcast in 1939 went to a casualty-clearing station in France, to an RAF fighter station in Duxford, a farm in Somerset and a Cotswold hillside. And the King closed his message with some lines from a poem he had found in a book of *pensées*.

> I said to the man who stood at the Gate of the Year, 'Give me a light that I may tread safely into the unknown.' And he replied, 'Go out into the darkness, and put your hand into the Hand of God. That shall be to you better than light, and safer than a known way.'

Hitherto unknown, the poem brought its author, Minnie Louise Haskins, a middle-aged, retired university lecturer, fifteen minutes of fame, a reprint that sold 43 000 copies, an entry in *Who's Who* and, in due course, an obituary in *The Times*.

The round-the-Empire link-up charted the progress of the war. *Christmas Under Fire* in 1940 ranged from the ruins of Coventry Cathedral to the London Underground, where nearly 200 000 men, women and children sheltered from the Blitz. *To Absent Friends*, in 1941, came at the low point of the war, an appalling Christmas Day which saw the fall of the Hong Kong garrison, which was followed less than two months later by the surrender of Singapore, where 20 000 more lives were lost than at Dunkirk. In 1942, *The Fourth Christmas* reflected the build-up of nations against Germany; in 1943, *We Are Advancing* went into the newly liberated mainland of Europe, evidence that the tide was turning; and finally, in 1944, *The Journey Home* heard from Britain's liberated Allies in Europe and from British soldiers in Germany.

THE 'LITTLE BLITZ'

There was a note of exhaustion in that 1944 broadcast. To civilians as well as to soldiers, the journey home seemed long and slow. D-Day had not been followed by outright victory. Instead, in the summer of 1944, during the 'Little Blitz', the V1s had come droning across the Channel, only to be followed by the V2 rockets. In three summer months, some 3500 V1s and V2s landed, killing over 6000 people, seriously injuring 18 000 and raising civilian wartime casualties to 61 000 killed and 86 000 badly injured. Over one-and-a-half million houses were destroyed or badly damaged. Londoners took to the Underground once more and there was talk of abandoning the capital.

That year, the Proms should have been Sir Henry Wood's triumphal fiftieth season, but they were driven out of London by the danger of flying bombs. Only those concerts ear-marked for broadcasting were performed, at the Corn Exchange in Bedford. The rest were abandoned. Wood, who had wept amid the ruins of the Queen's Hall in 1941 and had continued to conduct for three seasons in failing health, attended a jubilee commemoration lunch on 5 June and said: 'I hope with all my heart that the BBC will carry on my concerts as a permanent annual institution for all time.' On 19 July, having conducted Beethoven's *Seventh Symphony*, he collapsed and was unable to attend the jubilee concert on 10 August. Nine days later, he was dead.

The flying bombs did what the Blitz had failed to do: they silenced Big Ben. From 16 June to 8 September 1944, while the most famous 'voice' of them all went unheard in London, a recording synchronized with the chimes boomed out on-air. Big Ben duly returned but, after tolling its way sturdily through the war, sounding the hour at 7 a.m. on the Home and Forces, at 11 a.m. on the Forces Programme only, and again on both at 9 p.m. (where it had been introduced by public request, in November 1940, ahead of the news bulletin), it stopped again on 10 December 1944 when an eighty-year-old suspension spring broke. Perhaps it, too, was suffering from exhaustion.

THE SEARCH FOR BATTERIES

Radios were certainly showing signs of fatigue. In 1942, one out of every five house-wives who tried to buy a high-tension battery was disappointed and by Christmas the figure was one in three. The number of mains receivers was over 80 per cent in urban areas, but only 60 per cent in rural areas, and by the summer of 1943 – when the German and Italian armies surrendered in North Africa – large numbers of people re-stricted their listening because of the shortage of dry batteries, the difficulty of getting wet batteries recharged and the near-impossibility of finding anyone able to carry out repairs. Valves were hard to come by although production rose from twelve million a year in 1940 to thirty-five million in 1944: a thousand-bomber raid – the first on Cologne in May 1942 – meant one-quarter of a million valves were in use in the sky. Radio licences rose to nearly eleven million by the war's end and might have gone higher, but there were no new sets for prospective licence-holders to buy. The danger from Germany's final bombing fling was over by September. On 17 September 1944, the national black-out gave way to the dim-out – officially called 'half-lighting':

windows other than skylights required curtains 'only sufficient to prevent objects inside the building being distinguishable from outside.' Two days later the broadcasting ban on weather details was also par-

Sir Henry Wood (centre) surveys the destruction of The Queen's Hall, home of the Promenade Concerts.

tially lifted: references could be given, but not to conditions more recent than the day before yesterday. The first climatic broadcast might have come straight from an Ealing comedy: 'Most people will have cause to remember … because in most parts of the country it just rained and rained…. So far this month we've had three times as much rain as we had last year' Britain had to wait just a little longer for its weather forecasts to be returned, as it had to wait for the total abolition of the black-out. But it had been given back its favourite topic of conversation; normal life must surely have been just around the corner.

5

THE FORCES' SWEETHEART – AND VERA LYNN TOO

The British Expeditionary Force (BEF) that went overseas in September 1939 got a different war than the one it had bargained for, just like the folks back home. The Army had expected to go straight into battle. Instead, it found itself kicking its heels in north-east France, which was soon in the grip of the same snows as Britain. Ill-prepared for the inactivity it met, it was without the radio sets that had been so much a part of barrack-room life at Tidworth, Aldershot and Colchester. But French sets were cheap and plentiful and the profits from canteen funds were quickly spent on them: everyone was desperate for news and voices from Blighty.

What the troops heard on the Home Service bored them out of their gaiters. With all haste they ransacked the airwaves, alighting on the English service put out by the French commercial station, Fécamp, which was bright, breezy and used top-class entertainers like Charlie Kunz, George Formby and Tessie O'Shea; they also found Haw-Haw. The Government and the military expressed worries about the men's morale, the question of the BBC broadcasting directly to the BEF was raised and at once became linked to the issue of a second network at home. It was an idea that the BBC had suggested at the time of implementing transmitter synchronization but which the Air Ministry had quashed.

THE BIRTH OF THE FORCES PROGRAMME

Reith's successor as director-general, Frederick Ogilvie, himself went to France to talk to the troops about what they wanted and there were consultations with the welfare officers of the three Services. Obviously something lively was required but the BBC concluded that Fécamp was 'too matey', which infuriated General Ironside, the Chief of

the Imperial General Staff, who let his views be known in no uncertain terms. It irritated the General still further that, when the Forces Programme did begin broadcasting on 7 January 1940, it was as an experimental service of six hours a day, carrying relays of the Home Service. If they wanted the news, the troops had to re-tune to the Home and probably not many bothered. Shortly afterwards the French High Command had Fécamp shut down and Ironside made strenuous efforts to have the order reversed. By mid-February, however, he was mollified by the full Forces Programme: plenty of light music and dance-bands, concert parties from Paris, record requests, sports commentaries and, before the end of the month, the first of the famous *John Hilton Talking* shows. The troops were said to be particularly appreciative of the *Bill and Bob* French lesson series because they wanted a working knowledge of the language to use in the local shops; more probably it was to chat up the local talent.

In March 1940 the War Office appointed a major in the Royal Engineers as its BBC

Live or on record, the dance-bands were heard on the BBC every day: Jack Payne, Geraldo, Joe Loss, Harry Roy, Victor Silvester, Billy Cotton, Mantovani, Jack Jackson and – most popular of all – Henry Hall (above).

liaison officer and sent him scurrying up and down the snow-bound roads and lanes of France, armed with a dossier of questions from the BBC's programme-making departments. Dutifully he ran the BEF to earth and collected his answers, which seemed to amount to a statement of the obvious. The lads wanted 'something to cheer us up', and 'to keep us in touch with home'. They wanted variety shows, musical comedies and crooners 'because they help us to learn the words'.

It hardly mattered. The Germans launched the offensive that culminated in Dunkirk and swept the BEF off the European board. The troops came back to Britain, creating an audience that for a time was not separable into Forces and civilians. The corporation took the opportunity to modify its output, including more spoken material – short talks, plays, features – and a little serious music, the amount of which was increased two years later, giving the network a better balance.

The Forces Programme was set up, first and foremost, for the fighting Services; its name made its purpose clear. The only other names that the BBC considered giving the network were the Services Programme (which would have given a nod to the Civil Defence) and the BEF Programme. Under the circumstances, it was just as well that the latter was not preferred to the Forces Programme. But one wonders why something that would have satisfied both the Services and the home audience was not found. The civilian population, after all, outnumbered Service personnel by ten to one; and as far as the civilian population was concerned, the Forces Programme was the alternative home network.

That there was a Forces Programme at all created widespread argument. Protests against low entertainment came from Parliament, the Press and the pulpit. Many of the clergy were distressed that the BBC board of governors had waived the pre-war policy which had frowned on Sunday entertainment. It was a revolutionary decision but a realistic one: the soldiers holed up in France would not have put up with the fare that had characterized Sunday listening on the National Programme. The decision was not before time, either. The Entertainment Act of 1932 had allowed cinemas and concert halls to open on Sundays and the majority of the country could not see how the music of Jack Payne and Henry Hall on the airwaves would have sullied the Sabbath. But Reith (*It's That Man Again*) had held the line against secularization, even though the BBC lost up to half its audience each Sunday to the Continental Radios Luxembourg, Normandie, Toulouse and Fécamp, as well as to Radio Athlone in Ireland.

The BBC's director of Religion, the Revd J.W. Welch, was among the protesters, although not in public. He had already been upset that the midnight news introduced on the Home Service had usurped the epilogue's rightful place at the end of daily broadcasting; later in the war he would complain when *Happidrome* was broadcast on the Forces Programme at the same time as a religious service on the Home. Now he expressed the view that the governors' decision was based on expediency and not on principle. 'I cannot see,' he wrote, 'why we should assume that because a few listeners had put on uniform and crossed the Channel they should be considered different persons religiously.'

His faith in the faith of British soldiery was somewhat misplaced. Even Army padres with the BEF told the BBC that the start of a religious programme was the sure signal for every set to be re-tuned or turned off. It was, of course, a different story once the fighting began and men who were suddenly faced with their own mortality and who worried about the safety of their families felt the need for some heavenly insurance: then the Sunday morning service put out on the Forces Programme became popular and Sunday evening communal hymn-singing attracted an audience as large as some variety shows.

Whatever opposition the Forces Programme experienced, the public at large loved it. Very soon 60 per cent of the population listened to it in preference to the Home Service, which the BBC, with its usual equivocation, found embarrassing. The 1941 pamphlet already quoted was defensive:

> If you don't happen to approve of the Forces Programme, remember that it was based on the expressed wishes of the soldiers, sailors and airmen for whom it was planned. Remember, too, the conditions in which it is usually heard. A man sitting quietly by his own fireside can concentrate on a Beethoven string quartet, or a Shaw play. No soldier, however intelligent, can listen in the same concentrated way in a crowded canteen with people calling for drinks, playing darts and keeping up a cross-fire of talk.

PUBLIC TASTE IS PUT ON THE LINE

If there was anyone in the BBC who thought that when the war was over broadcasting could return to dictating what people heard rather than what they wanted, harder heads were already analysing what was happening and concluding that the BBC would have to continue to pull in the crowds to stay in business. 'The new audience must be retained as a matter of policy,' an internal document of early 1942 noted. If it were not, the commercial stations, which would again 'spring up like mushrooms', would be waiting.

One of the fascinating things about the BBC during the war years was the way in which, despite the soundness of its instincts and of most of its judgements, it retained the capacity to shoot itself in the foot from time to time. The man with his finger on the trigger in February 1942 was B.E. Nicholls, the controller of programmes, who, evidently, either had not read the document or did not agree with it. On the basis of nothing but his own musical ignorance and prejudice, he decided, in effect, to change public taste.

A pre-war executive cast in the Reithian mould, Nicholls had not exactly caught the Dunkirk spirit of the country in 1940 when, while recognizing that 'recreational pro-grammes' were needed 'at a time when people were living under considerable stress and many of them are working long hours', he none the less decreed that the Home and Forces networks should never be devoted simultaneously to 'frivolity'. Two years later he was still making *ex cathedra* pronouncements from the moral heights, telling the Variety department that it should cut out 'dreary jazz sophistications' in favour of 'waltzes, marches and cheerful music of every kind'. As Nicholls was known to detest jazz (as did Reith and, so it happens, Hitler), no one was overly surprised. Unfortunately, Nicholls raised the ante by setting up a committee with the 'positive policy of the encouragement of better and more virile lyrics … the elimination of crooning, sentimental numbers, drivelling words, slush, innuendo and so on'. There was more of the same, including the barring of 'insincere and over-sentimental performances by women singers' – which dragged in Vera Lynn and started an almighty row in the papers.

VERA LYNN IS CAUGHT IN THE CROSSFIRE

In the wider context, Nicholls' directive angered music publishers and band leaders who pointed out that it would not only stand popular culture on its head, but that the BBC was now condemning what for years it had helped to promote. The issue dragged

on; in the end it came to nothing. It was all a side-show anyway: the controversy was focused on Vera Lynn and her series, *Sincerely Yours*, which had begun on the Forces Programme the previous November.

One MP called Vera Lynn's singing the 'caterwauling of an inebriated cockatoo' – but to British servicemen everywhere she could do no wrong.

Reaction was divided between the archetypal 'Disgusted, Tunbridge Wells' and the majority; between those who felt that Lynn would send the rank-and-file into battle in a debilitated state and those, including at least one senior commanding officer, who considered that the British soldier was more likely 'to be brought to fighting pitch after hearing sentimental songs than by martial music'. The BBC's board of governors sat on the fence: '*Sincerely Yours* deplored, popularity noted.'

A plumber's daughter from East Ham, Vera Lynn had been dubbed the Forces' Sweetheart after topping an on-air poll which the BBC had conducted among the BEF in France. After Gracie Fields' marriage to an Italian had turned public feeling against her and she had gone to America, Lynn's big, clear voice ('a gallery voice,' says Charlie Chester, 'she didn't need a microphone to reach the gallery'), perfect diction which belied her Cockney roots and a trademark catch in her throat, made her easily the most popular female vocalist in the country. In the early months of the war she appeared in *Ack-Ack, Beer-Beer*, the series for the men and women of the anti-aircraft and barrage balloon units which for the first time brought together Richard Murdoch and Kenneth Horne. But it was *Sincerely Yours* which rocketed her to fame and brought her 2000 requests a week.

The programme was presented in the form of a letter sent to the boys 'over there'. For it, she visited hospitals where servicemen's wives had just had babies, bringing them flowers and relaying personal messages from them – something which the BBC had never done before except in the pre-war *Children's Hour*. And she sang her way into the hearts of the men in uniform and their families at home with numbers like *It's a Lovely Day Tomorrow*, *Wish Me Luck*, *Room 504*, *Lovely Weekend* and many more. But all of these were eclipsed by *Yours* ('the love song', she called it), *The White Cliffs of Dover* ('the patriotic one') and *We'll Meet Again* ('the optimistic one'), the song of the war, which may have sounded like a greetings card but which expressed what so many ordinary people who were parted were too inhibited to say:

> We'll meet again,
> Don't know where, don't know when,
> But I know we'll meet again some sunny day.
> Keep smiling through,
> Just like you always do,
> Till the blue skies drive the dark clouds far away.

The song accompanied the British Forces in the Atlantic and the Pacific, in North Africa, the Middle and Far East and across Western Europe as the Germans were rolled back to Berlin. After the war it became known that many people in the occupied countries tuned in their clandestine sets to listen to Vera Lynn because of the sincerity in her

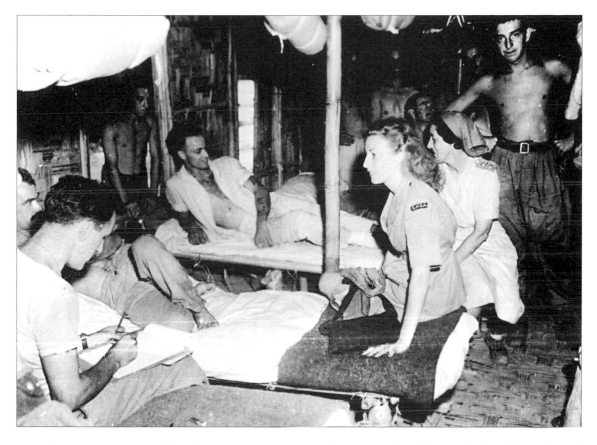

In 1944 Vera Lynn went with **ENSA** to entertain the troops in **Burma**, visiting the wounded in a casualty clearing station.

voice, just as they tuned to *ITMA* because the laughter was so infectious. It was irrelevant that most of them did not understand the words.

After listening to a concert Vera Lynn gave for the troops in 1941, a 'middle-aged listener' wrote to *Radio Times*: 'The words of her songs may have been so much sentimental twaddle. But she treated them with as much tenderness as though they were precious old folk songs, as though they meant something, something that she believed in and assumed that her audience believed in too. It may not have been great art. Who cares?'

Lynn paid her dues to the Forces. In 1944 she joined ENSA and undertook the difficult journey to Burma, where she entertained Slim's forgotten Fourteenth Army within singing distance of the Japanese forward lines. In Dimapur she fell in with BBC correspondent Richard Sharp who tried to take her to the front to have her sing against the background noise of battle. Some senior officer put a stop to that.

In her autobiography, *Vocal Refrain*, Lynn wrote: 'As I saw it, I was reminding the boys of what they were really fighting for, the precious permanent things, rather than the ideologies and theories. MPs, an ex-Minister and retired militarists fired off abuse at me and the programme, and the BBC, always ready to play the heavy father, set up an "Anti-Slush Committee" to try and protect the nation's moral fibre.'

Today she adds: 'I don't know how anybody could think that any of the songs could have lowered anyone's morale. They weren't war-mongering songs. They were gentle, sentimental, yes, to a certain extent, but they were all optimistic, every single one. You know, one of the things the boys always said when they came up was, "Well, we have, we have met again, haven't we?" I sang the songs then and I sing them now. They've survived in spite of it all.'

SOME FORCES' FAVOURITES

There was a fair amount of cross-over between the Forces Programme and the Home Service. Broadcasts of national importance such as Churchill's addresses and the news went out on both networks simultaneously; some programmes, especially variety shows, originated in one network and were repeated in the other. It was not always possible to satisfy civilians and Services at the same time, but the majority of the Forces Programme output, which was about or for the Services, suited everybody: for the most part, after all, the Services were made up of civilians in uniform. *Ack-Ack, Beer-Beer* was almost as popular as *Happidrome*, and from May 1940 the Variety department turned out 320 editions. *Shipmates Ashore*, devised for the Merchant Navy and broadcast from the Merchant Navy Club which the BBC set up in the West End; *Tom, Dick and Harry* the off-duty adventures of a soldier, sailor and airman; and *Irish Half-Hour*, designed to cater for the large number of men and women from Eire who were in the Armed Forces, were three other programmes which everybody enjoyed. Even when programmes like *Women at War* – for the ATS and the nursing profession – were more specifically targeted, people still enjoyed eavesdropping. Any programme like *Sincerely Yours* that linked servicemen and their families was assured of a big audience.

There were many such programmes but most of them were not heard on the Forces Programme: they went out on the BBC's overseas transmitters. *Calling Gibraltar*, with Joan Gilbert, was one. After the first transmission the BBC received a telegram which read: 'Fifty military police acting spokesmen all ranks Gibraltar report programme smash hit everyone wildly excited suggest extension immediately.' Another was *Your Cup of Tea*, beamed to the Army in North Africa, with the microphone suspended over the tea-table at which Freddie Grisewood presided. For *Over to You*, Jane Welsh toured the country with a recording van, collecting messages from the homes of RAF personnel who were training in Canada. Other programmes went out to men in India and Malta. Nearly every day wives, mothers and sweethearts came to the microphone to send little reassuring greetings, which were sparse, emotionally buttoned up, moving:

'Hello, Charlie. Hope you're all right. We're all fine here. Grandfather and Auntie May send their love. Baby's got a new tooth. Well, thumbs up, Charlie, and God bless you.' Other programmes kept Australians, New Zealanders, Canadians and South Africans serving over here in touch with their homes over there.

A development of *Over to You* was *Home Town*, for which the genial Cockney actor, Ronnie Shiner, went around Britain looking up soldiers' families and, in two or three minutes, painting such a vivid domestic picture that a man felt as if he had just closed his own front door behind him. Shiner also slipped in little bits of local news which made the programme as enjoyable to other men from the same district as to those he mentioned by name. Sometimes he would arrive when a woman had something on the stove that could not be left, so he would speak to her in the kitchen, much to her embarrassment as she would have preferred to use the best room. Sometimes it was washing day and Shiner talked to her as she pegged out the clothes in the backyard. To a man in the desert, the laundry flapping on the washing line was as good a symbol as any of what he was really fighting for.

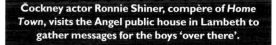

Cockney actor Ronnie Shiner, compère of *Home Town*, visits the Angel public house in Lambeth to gather messages for the boys 'over there'.

All of these programmes, which did so much to keep people alive in each other's memory, were spun out from an underground West End theatre, the Criterion, which became the wartime base of the BBC's Empire Entertainments Unit just before the Blitz. Here the staff worked, ate and slept in the dressing-rooms, cloakrooms and boxes, and broadcast from the stage. The royal box was the control room; the ante-room was fitted up with turntables; the theatre bar dispensed tea and biscuits. And through the stage door passed a stream of comedians, crooners and dance-bands to perform for an audience that was made up of members of the British and Imperial Forces on leave.

The unit knocked out fifty or sixty programmes a week, most of them the kind of stuff made by the evacuated Variety department. Many went out

Top: Much Binding in the Marsh – King George VI's favourite show after the end of *ITMA* – began as one segment of *Merry-Go-Round*. It was written by its stars, **Richard Murdoch** and **Kenneth Horne**.

Merry-Go-Round's army edition, *Stand Easy*, with its star, **Cheerful Charlie Chester**, second from right. **Arthur Haynes** (extreme right) made his name on television after the war.

on disc for rebroadcasting on Forces' stations, very few were heard in Britain. Exceptions among the request programmes were Roy Rich's *Record Time* and *Sandy's Half-Hour*, which brought Sandy Macpherson 5000 letters a week. Both these shows went out on the Forces Programme as well as overseas, as did the best of the entertainment shows, *Mediterranean Merry-Go-Round*, *Variety Bandbox*, broadcast from what had been the London Casino, and *Navy Mixture*, featuring ex-Flight Lieutenant Jimmy Edwards, DFC (shot down over Holland and a veteran of possibly more harrowing service at the Windmill Theatre, where the men in raincoats came to see naked if quite immobile women on stage). These were, in fact, the best variety shows of the second half of the war. In time, the three *Merry-Go-Round* programmes, each sponsored by one of the Services and written by their stars, split away from each other to become the leading series of the immediate post-war era. By then the Navy one, Eric Barker's *HMS Waterlogged*, possibly the most intelligent comedy of the war, had taken over the generic title; but the Army one, with Charlie Chester and Arthur Haynes, continued as *Stand Easy*; and the RAF one remained as *Much Binding in the Marsh*, the fictional Air Force station converted into a country club, with ex-Wing Commander Kenneth Horne as the Station-Commander-turned managing-director and ex-Squadron Leader Richard Murdoch as the Adjutant-turned-assistant.

BROADCASTING WORLD-WIDE

The complexity of broadcasting to the Services was something of which the public was unaware, although in the first year or two of the Forces Programme they would have realized that the BBC was trying to cater for minorities of listeners. While the BEF was in France, the network put out a half-hour programme, in their own language, for Indian troops serving with it. Later, when the Canadians became the first Dominion servicemen to arrive in Britain, there were newsletters and ice-hockey commentaries; later still, as Australians, New Zealanders, Rhodesians and South Africans arrived, there were other short specialist programmes. When the Americans poured into the country between 1942-3, the BBC provided them with short sports bulletins every night at 7 p.m. By then, the network was in danger of being overwhelmed.

Luckily, the US Army authorities wanted to broadcast to their own troops in Britain and, with the help of the BBC, they created the American Forces Network (AFN), which opened on Independence Day, 4 July 1943. It was made up of several low-power transmitters dotted around the country wherever there were concentrations of American troops and linked to London by landline. The programmes put out on AFN were mainly recordings of favourite American shows sent over from the States, but the most popular shows from the BBC Forces Programme were also carried.

Although Allied troops were no longer in Europe in 1940, there were hundreds of thousands of British and Dominion soldiers in the Middle East and Africa. As early as October 1940, *Sandy Calling* provided a slender bridge to them, transmitted in English on the World Service – the renamed Empire Service. By June 1942 new transmitters were relaying two hours of the Forces Programme to the Middle East every evening. But as the armies overseas grew, more of the World Service's output was devoted to servicemen and the network again changed its name, first to the Overseas Forces Programme and then to the General Overseas Service (GOS). It was heard by the British fleets in the Pacific and the Atlantic, in the commands of South East Asia, India, the Middle East, the Mediterranean and East and West Africa. At the time, it was the longest continuous daily broadcast in the world, on the air for twenty-two hours a day.

People in Britain knew nothing about the GOS until January 1944 when it was announced that, after four years on the air, the Forces Programme would close down at the end of broadcasting on 26 February and would be replaced the next day by the 6.30 a.m.-11 p.m. portion of the GOS, broadcast as the General Forces Programme. The GOS, in the shape of the General Forces Programme, came to Britain with many popular, original programmes, among them *Radio News Reel*, *Home Flash*, *Question Time*, *Forces Favourites*, and a daily five-minute review of the British Press, which was an entirely new feature to British listeners at home. And there were plenty of the familiar programmes including *The Brains Trust*, *Happidrome*, *Songs from the Shows*, *Music While You Work* and *These You Have Loved*. But although the network was largely the same, there was enough that was different to make the public feel lukewarm. By the time the General Forces Programme also bowed out in July 1945 to allow the introduction of the new Light Programme, one-third of the audience, which throughout the war had remained constant, had switched to the Home Service.

The introduction of the GOS in 1944 was a bold development, which helped to eliminate a great deal of duplication and make an enormous saving in running costs. But the reason for the change was more human: the BBC had taken heed of the men listening on the GOS (and they were now the majority) who asked constantly to share the same programmes at the same times as the people at home. That, the BBC strongly felt, was right. And it knew of something which was about to happen and which everyone would want to share with the fighting men everywhere: D-Day.

GETTING READY FOR D-DAY

The BBC's relationship with the US Army authorities was close from the moment America entered the war. The BBC not only gave assistance to the American Forces Network, it relayed broadcasts in nineteen different languages to Europe from the Voice of America network in New York and provided a news service to the American Broadcasting Station in Europe, which the US Office of War Information inaugurated at the critical psychological moment, a month before D-Day. And the BBC joined the Americans in creating a joint radio network – the Allied Expeditionary Force Programme (AEF) – to accompany the Allies in the invasion. Forces broadcasting had won its stripes and it went back into Europe, not for the ride, but as an intrinsic part of the military operation.

The AEF was the idea of the Allied Supreme Commander, General Eisenhower, who wanted to bind together his American, Canadian and British troops. It began broadcasting on D-Day Plus One – 7 June 1944 – staffed by members of the Services from the three countries, but with its direction and transmission in the BBC's hands. Broadcasting House was the AEF Programme's headquarters. Here, uniformed men and women of the three nations worked side by side and the Americans put their own white-helmeted guards in the foyer. They were promptly nicknamed Snowdrops.

BBC staff, recruited to the network, were not told why they were wanted and those who phoned Maurice Gorman, who had been appointed the director, could not be enlightened. An eighteen-year-old junior programme engineer, Reg Perrin, was working in Variety – by this time back in London and housed in the Aeolian Hall – when he received a message to report to Broadcasting House after work: 'It was all very secret. I was an effects boy and I wondered what on earth I was wanted for that could be so hush-hush. No one would tell me anything when I reached BH, except that I was to spend the night sleeping in the basement.' The next morning he was

In training for D-Day – war correspondent Stewart MacPherson.

woken early, taken to a studio and presented with an 'enormous mountain' of 78 r.p.m. records. From 6 a.m. his job was to play music for the invading forces and the reinforcements waiting their turn to cross the Channel.

It was the first of many regular morning programmes called *Rise and Shine*, hosted by Ronnie Waldman and the American Dick Dudley, who were unnamed at first. Two weeks after D-Day, when secrecy was no longer a factor, *Radio Times* identified them, and their assistant 'Shamus', said by the presenters to be a banshee who sometimes put a spanner in the works. (Longer recordings continued on the reverse of the disc; the trick, not always accomplished, was to judge when to switch from one turntable to a second.) Perrin was the first Shamus; others were to follow.

The AEF was a slick affair which put out the best entertainment that British, Canadian and American radio had to offer. In time, more shows were sent back from Brussels by the British Army radio unit and from Paris by Major Glenn Miller's Band. Special recording units toured the European theatre picking up material; among the

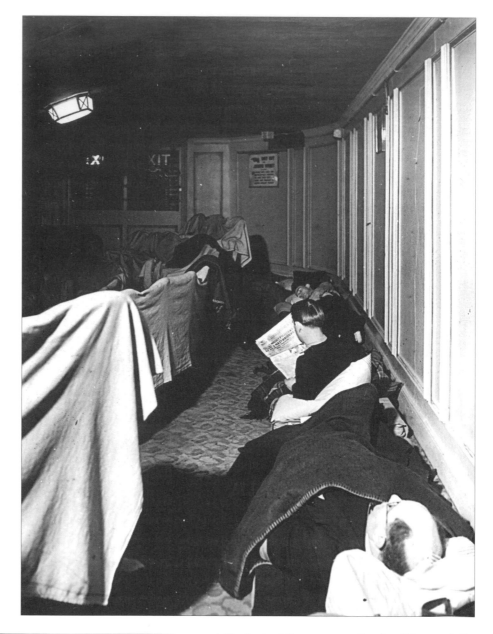

When the Blitz was bad and transport doubtful, performers, theatre and stage staff slept in the back row of the balcony.

specially devised features was *Combat Diary*, a daily news report from Service and civilian correspondents, which won an unparalleled reputation.

As the armies advanced from the Normandy beachhead they set up relay stations to broadcast local information but also to keep the AEF Programme transmitting. Finally, on the borders of the Reich, the Luxembourg station

Glenn Miller and his band played to packed houses in Britain. Over-age for call-up, Miller sacrificed a lucrative career to serve in the US army. He was lost in a small plane over the Channel when the war was virtually over.

was captured and pressed into service, with relays of BBC transmissions forming the backbone of the schedule. When the fighting was over and the armies had taken over their occupation zones, their radio units had the use of high-power local stations. The need for the inter-Allied network ceased. On 28 July 1945 the BBC closed down the AEF Programme – and launched the domestic Light Programme the following morning.

How many servicemen heard any of the AEF Programme in the early days of the invasion is something no one can know. Even *Radio Times* admitted: 'Many of you, probably, can listen only for a few minutes at a time, if you can listen at all.' But most of the men who hit the beaches knew the broadcasts were there with them and said that just knowing it boosted their confidence. There were more opportunities to listen later and the Americans and Canadians took them, as did many of the British. Others were inclined to tune to the General Forces Programme or the Home Service, if they could find them. They missed the voices of Lidell, Hibberd and co. But they did like the AEF Programme signature tune. After the war, many men who had sketchy memories of anything else they had heard remembered *Oranges and Lemons* blaring out of the signal trucks and the tanks as they advanced across Europe.

REACHING OUT ACROSS THE WORLD

It was very much harder for men in Burma to listen to the BBC, but they did manage on occasions to pick up the Empire Service broadcasts to the Pacific. Eugene Girot, a BBC recording engineer, remembers: 'Our vehicle had "BBC Mobile Recording Unit" painted on the side of it, and several times troops marching on the road stopped us. "Are you really from the BBC?" they used to ask. I'd say, "You can read – it says on the vehicle" and then they'd ask me if we'd recorded something or other. When I said "Yes", they'd tell me they'd heard it on the radio last night and I'd say, "Thank God for that – we haven't been wasting our time out here."'

Numerous films have shown the lengths to which prisoners-of-war went to find a way of listening to the BBC. David Porter, a Variety producer shot down by the Germans, described in the *BBC Handbook* how in Stalag Luft Three in Silesia, a short-hand writer with headphones would sit listening to the news on a set concealed beneath a lavatory pan. 'News was as vital as food,' he wrote. Tom Douglas, a BBC engineer who went into the Army and was taken prisoner by the Japanese at the fall of Singapore, also described how he made several receivers under the very noses of his guards. He got his first set going in the notorious Changi camp on Singapore Island, but had to leave it behind when he was sent, in June 1942, to work on the construction of the Bangkok-Moulmein railway:

I succeeded in collecting a few vital radio parts from people who had managed to hide them with their kit in case they might prove useful some day; and along with scraps of tin, wire and the ever-present bamboo I collected sufficient material to build five little receivers capable of sliding into a Service water-bottle. Power was the big problem, but we made contact with one of our native underground agents who obtained torch batteries. I distributed four sets to other camps and kept one, which I had with me all the time I was with the railway working battalions....

I remember one time when we were on a ten-day march we heard rumours that there had been a landing in Italy; everyone came asking me if I had heard anything 'Pukka BBC?'.... I waited till late at night.... But just as I was taking the news a Jap sentry took a sudden desire to sit down outside our tent and lean himself up against my part of the tent flap and my aerial wire as well. I was very scared but took the full bulletin without making a suspicious noise.

Towards the beginning of August 1945, the Japs decided to move us to a new open camp site in the centre of Siam. This meant the usual difficulty of transporting our set with its supplies and headphones, as by now the Japs were wise to water-bottles.... I found out that the camp commandant was taking along a lot of electrical material in his personal kit-box and I took the set to pieces and mixed them up with his stuff....

I think the only thing that gave us something to live for was the almost daily supply of news from the BBC in London. It was quite pitiful sometimes to see the look on a man's face when I had to tell him that there was 'No song from the bird today as the seed was done or it had taken ill.' The damp of the jungle played havoc with the delicate parts of the set …

August 1945: war correspondent Frank Gillard (holding the mike) and a BBC recording unit (engineer H.O.Sampson in the back of the truck) visit the 43rd (Wessex) Division in Germany.

Frank Gillard, who watched men in the North African desert tune their battered sets to the BBC which was being transmitted to them on crackly short-wave, has no doubts of the value of Forces' broadcasting. Up and down the front, in the lulls in fighting, while they were brewing up or taking their meals, men listened to the entertainment pro-grammes and the news and found both something to laugh at or hum along with, and something from which to draw reassurance. The very fact that broadcasting was still there meant that dear old Blighty, whatever battering it was taking, had not gone to hell in a handcart. In whichever of its guises BBC Forces broadcasting went out, it was more of a sweetheart than Vera Lynn. 'People back home could not conceptualize what broadcasting out there really meant,' Gillard observes.

Desmond Hawkins emphasizes the value of the news to which the troops listened:

> It was a big factor in the morale of the war and the huge difference between the First and the Second World War. During the First people at home weren't being bombed. And they were having a rosy picture of what was really happening on the Somme. It was obscene.
>
> But in the Second World War there weren't two different stories: it was the same news. A man in a slit trench in the Ardennes could listen to it and not burst out laughing because it was a load of codswallop. At the same time it was acceptable in a sitting-room at home with a couple of pensioners worrying what was happening to their grandchildren. The comradeship which the BBC news gave to soldiers and civilians was a great achievement.

Broadcasting for the Forces outlived the ending of the war. In September 1945, the Forces Educational Unit, set up quickly in the February, began to transmit twenty-minute programmes such as A Home in Civvy Street, Job in Hand and Clear Thinking. There were no headlines in the initiative, which lasted until 1952. But it was the BBC's contribution to the difficult task of easing demobilization and resettlement – something that was badly mishandled in Britain at the end of the first world conflict and in Germany sowed the seeds of the second.

CHAPTER

6

'MORE FAITH IN
THE BULLETINS THAN
THE BIBLE'

When a land-mine caused serious damage to Broadcasting House in December 1940, the European Service was obliged to move out to a disused ice-rink near the studios at Maida Vale, a nerve-racking place to be in during the Blitz because of its glass roof. Noel Newsome, the European Service news editor, was horrified that 'several hundreds of men and women engaged on the important task of radio propaganda to Europe [were] herded together at the height of the Blitz.... The hall had been partitioned into tiny offices and we were

The BBC's Maida Vale studios take a direct hit on 10 May 1941.

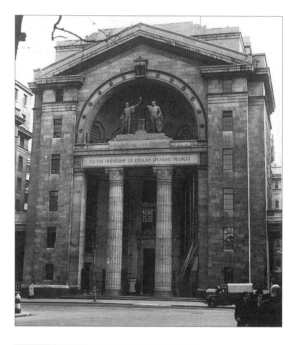

The most famous BBC building to the rest of the world: Bush House. Bombed out of Broadcasting House in December 1940, the European Service came here in March 1941. Over the years the rest of the foreign language sections have moved in.

packed into these like cattle in a market which might at any moment become a slaughterhouse.' In May 1941, two months after the Service moved to Bush House on the Aldwych island site at the top of the Strand, Maida Vale took a direct hit.

Bush House, a failed trade centre built by an American in the twenties, had imposing central halls and staircases of marble, but the accommodation in the south-east block, in which the rapidly increasing sections found themselves, was cramped and badly ventilated. In Parliament it was once referred to as 'the black hole of Tooting Bec' (its location obscured for security reasons, unlike its conditions). When he came to make a broadcast, Field Marshal Montgomery asked engineering operator Rowena Taylor, who was conducting him to a studio in the scruffy basement: 'People don't work down here all the time, do they?'

The staff settled in Bush House for the rest of the war. Most of them were dispossessed Europeans, passionate in their commitment, volatile, funny, cheerful, quarrelsome. The atmosphere was one of exhausting creative tension – and in it, as they carried on sending the BBC's message of truth and hope back to their occupied homelands, they forged the BBC's reputation as the most trustworthy international broadcaster in the world.

To Dennis Main Wilson, then a seventeen-year-old with good German who had landed a job as a recorded programme assistant straight from school, it was an exciting place to be: 'Bush House was seething. It was a marketplace, a football field: actors, writers, performers, philosophers, warriors – name it – all people who had fled the Germans.… I grew up among them very quickly.' It was an exciting place even for an old BBC hand like Harman Grisewood, Freddie Grisewood's cousin, who was the European Service's assistant controller: 'Bush House was a very special place, improvised, very crowded, where we felt part of the war in a very intimate way.'

THE BBC GOES INTERNATIONAL

Britain entered international broadcasting late, largely because the Government was unwilling to put its hand in its pocket. By 1933, when the Empire Service had just begun, the USSR was broadcasting in eight different languages and Britain was alone among the big nations in broadcasting only in its own.

Fascist Italy's invasion of Abyssinia (Ethiopia) brought a change in the Government's thinking. Following the invasion, Mussolini had opened a short-wave propagandist station in Bari, targeting the Middle East in Arabic to undermine British interests, particularly in Palestine. It was a brilliantly successful campaign, a mixture of entertainment and scurrilous allegations of British atrocities, which Britain felt it had to answer. The BBC Arabic service went on-air in January 1938. It was followed in March by Spanish and Portuguese broadcasts to Latin America, where Nazi Germany had also begun a propaganda onslaught.

In the autumn, with the Munich crisis, the BBC began broadcasting to Europe. The British fleet had mobilized in response to Hitler's claim to parts of Czechoslovakia and the news was not reported in Germany. On the evening of 27 September, when Chamberlain spoke to the people at home, the Government asked the BBC to broad-cast the text in German, Italian and French. No one realized how long it would take to make the translations and the German reader (dragged away from a cocktail party and never having broadcast in his life) ran out of air-time, leaving listeners   if there were any – with Chamberlain's unfortunate line about 'a quarrel in a far away country of which we know nothing'.

The BBC went into the war broadcasting in seven foreign languages and came out of it, as the world's largest international station, broadcasting in forty five. Russian was not among them; the BBC made out a case for it after the Soviet Union entered the war, but the Foreign Office said no. Broadcasting in Japanese was conducted, but it might just as well not have been: the corporation estimated it had fewer than one hundred listeners in Japan, although there was anecdotal evidence of some listening by the Japanese Army in the field. The Government wanted the BBC to launch a service as early as 1941, in the credulous belief that it might keep the Japanese out of the war. The BBC resisted until 1943, when Japan occupied most of Britain's colonial possessions in the Far East – and by which time it was illegal for the Japanese to own short-wave sets.

About half the languages put out by the BBC were beamed into Europe, the rest went around the world. While the bigger language sections such as the French and German, whose output rose to four or five hours a day, contained talks and other ma-terial, news made up 90 per cent of the output. 'News was the rock,' says the historian Lord Bullock. 'When people are listening to you with very considerable danger and difficulty, news is what they want.'

Down from Oxford University, Alan Bullock joined the twenty-four-hour central newsdesk in 1940. Here all bulletins were written by British staff with specialized knowledge of specific countries or regions, before they were translated within the sec-tions. Truth and consistency were the watchwords even during the considerable period

European talks editor Alan Bullock (left), with naval correspondent General S.R. Wason and European productions supervisor W. Gibson Parker.

when Britain re-armed and stood alone, when there seemed only defeats and retreats to report. 'Noel Newsome set the style and called the tune,' says Bullock. '"What we have to do in this period of the war when we're on the defensive, is to establish our credibility," he said. "If there's a disaster, we broadcast it before the Germans claim it, if we possibly can. And when the tide turns and the victories are ours, we'll be believed."'

Newsome had one of the most difficult jobs in the BBC. Every time a new language was added he somehow had to find the staff who could broadcast in it; and he had to ensure that the sections toed the official line which his daily directives laid down. He succeeded, says Bullock, 'because of the strength of his personality', and 'he combined a First in history with being a heavyweight boxing Blue.'

Language supervisors, who were also British nationals with linguistic skills, were attached to the sections to ensure that translations made from the original copy were accurate; finalized transcripts had to be approved by the central desk before transmission. As a further precaution, a language supervisor sat in the studio or the control cubicle during transmission with his finger on a switch which could take the announcer off-air 'if,' as Bullock says, 'he suddenly shouted hurrah for Hitler'. The switch was used from time to time to correct a mistake, but never for reasons of security.

Talks, which by their nature included comment and were prepared by the language sections, were trickier to control and sometimes caused conflict with the central desk, which had to ensure that the BBC spoke with one voice across all the output. According to Grisewood: 'There were occasions when some of the foreign staff tried to fight their war, not the war. This was something we could not allow – there were a few casualties.' Says Bullock: 'I think there was a degree of scorn for the British as being ignorant, knowing nothing about Europe. This was natural, because they regarded themselves as zealots, and on the whole we regarded them as that, while realizing that many of them in person were distinguished people. In the end, all the rows and arguments died away. They were insignificant by comparison with the fact that London went on broadcasting.'

The conflicts which were caused internally were as nothing compared with some of the problems the BBC experienced with the exiled European governments that were allowed by the British Government to produce their own programmes, but which the BBC was responsible for broadcasting. London had become the seat of government of Norway, Belgium, Holland, Poland, Czechoslovakia, Yugoslavia and Greece. It was also the headquarters of General de Gaulle and the Free French, a spiritual rallying point for those opposed to the quisling government at Vichy. The French, Dutch, Poles and Yugoslavs were given free transmitter time; the Norwegians seconded some of their own people to the BBC Norwegian section.

Although nominally independent, all the exiled governments had to submit scripts in advance, which led to frequent rows. 'We were very, very careful about what they were saying,' says Bullock. 'What we imposed was quite different from the normal censor-ship which said "You are not to say we've had a battle-ship sunk until we get the U-boat responsible." We exercised a political censorship on them.'

NOT ALL PLAIN SAILING

The BBC frequently found itself playing piggy in the middle. If its control was too rigid, it was censured by the Foreign Office; if its control was not rigid enough, there were repercussions which involved the authori-ties outside the FO. This was especially so where the Free (later changed to Fighting) French were concerned.

There were two major occasions when the British Government itself blocked French broadcasts and the BBC was caught up in the maelstrom. The first was in

The BBC went into the war broadcasting in seven foreign languages and came out of it broadcasting in forty-five, half of them to Europe.

July 1940, when Churchill ordered the sinking of the French fleet at the naval base of Mers el Kebir in Algeria, fearing it would fall into German hands. He had asked the French admirals either to scuttle it or put it under British command. They refused either option. In the action that followed, more than 1300 sailors were killed. It may have been necessary; it certainly became deeply ingrained in the French soul. The second crisis arose in November 1942 when, having landed in North Africa, the Americans decided not to deal with General Giraud, who had escaped from a German prison camp earlier in the year, but with Admiral Darlan, who happened to be in Algiers, 'in the name of the Marshal'. The Americans were expedient, because Giraud did not have the power to stop the French Forces stationed there and, loyal to the Vichy government, from putting up resistance which, for an unpleasant few days, they did. De Gaulle, however, who was keen to extend his power to France's colonial presence in North Africa, planned two broadcasts. The Foreign Office vetoed them. In fury, the Free French refused any co-operation with the BBC French section. The crisis was resolved by Darlan's assassination on Christmas Eve.

De Gaulle's relationship with the BBC started with one row and ended with another. A tank commander and one of the few military leaders to distinguish himself in the battle before the fall of France, de Gaulle came to Broadcasting House on 18 June 1940, the day after he had stepped off the boat from Bordeaux (and the day on which Pétain had announced his intention of suing for the end of hostilities) to make the broadcast that rallied the French and stamped him out as a potential leader of his country. The row occurred because, as he found out the next day, his broadcast was not recorded.

Leonard Miall, who was in charge of the European Service's news talks at the time (and who became controller of Overseas and Foreign Relations and later the BBC's research historian) had received a message from the Ministry of Information asking for arrangements to be made for a French general to speak to France on the ten o'clock evening news. The Ministry told Miall that the general's script had already been passed by the censor, which he found surprising, 'because the talk scripts were normally censored within the BBC'. But his attention was elsewhere: Churchill's 'finest hour' speech had gone out that day – and he was not to discover until later that 'passed by the censor' actually meant approved by the War Cabinet. 'There'd been a lot of French generals in the BBC the week before in hysterical mood, calling on Roosevelt to provide them with thousands of planes immediately or they were going to have to give in,' he says. 'There was no great excitement over another French general who was the Under-Secretary for National Defence in France. Most people in Britain hadn't the faintest idea who the Under-Secretary for National Defence in France was.'

De Gaulle broadcast again the following evening, and was taken to meet the BBC's director-general. While they waited, with Miall making small talk 'in my indifferent

French', the General suddenly asked if his broadcast the day before had been recorded. Miall had to tell him it had not: at the time the BBC had only six recording channels for all its services. Adds Miall: 'I

General Charles de Gaulle: his relationship with the BBC started with a row and ended with one.

was desperately trying to remember the French for "recording channel" and trying to explain. He was furious. He was a very frightening figure in his full military uniform and at his enormous height. He glowered down at me and tore strips off the BBC in general and me in particular for failing to appreciate the historical significance of this moment.'

Having been delicately advised that his first appeal to France had possibly had little impact, de Gaulle was persuaded to repeat the gist of it in a broadcast made on 24 June. 'This has gone down in history as the original General de Gaulle appeal,' says Miall. 'Only I and a few other people know that it was not so.'

The other row involving de Gaulle occurred on D-Day. The BBC broadcast a message on the European Service from Eisenhower, who was followed by such dignitaries as the King of Norway, the Grand Duchess of Luxembourg, the Queen of the Netherlands and the Prime Minister of Belgium. De Gaulle, angry that he had not been informed of the invasion plans until the previous evening, refused to take part. Says Robin Scott, who joined the French section from the Army: 'He said he would not follow anybody, least of all Eisenhower. For a time he huffed.' Told he could deliver anaddress if he chose, de Gaulle deigned to do so after the other broadcast had gone out, stalking in mid morning into Bush House where he pushed away a bouquet of flowers that the girl on reception tried to hand him. Scott, who was the assistant in charge of the studio session, recorded the speech in duplicate, just to make sure. It was transmitted in the early evening and five times more, the last at 1.30 a.m. 'De Gaulle radiated authority,' Scott adds. 'It was not always what you might call pleasant authority. He was a very difficult man. There was a lot of truth in the old joke about Winston Churchill saying "The heaviest cross I've ever had to bear was the Cross of Lorraine."'

As it happens, the Polish government caused the BBC far more difficulty than the Free French; frequently it tried to put out statements that might have damaged Britain's relationship with the Russians. The bitterness felt by the Poles was understandable. Britain and France had gone to war on behalf of their country, but had done nothing to help, even when Nazi Germany and the Soviet Union between them occupied the whole of it; they were not allowed to accuse the Russians of the massacre of Polish officers at Katyn; or broadcast their belief that the West did not have the will to assist the Warsaw Uprising (although after the war it became known that the West had tried, and was thwarted by Stalin). Even so, the BBC felt the Poles misused their position. When Bullock was editing talks, he remembers them coming in one day with a script that attacked 'our great atheist neighbour': 'I told them, you can't say that about the Russians. They said, oh, no, no, no, it's the Germans. But I knew damn well it was Russia, and so did they, and I crossed it out. That was the constant kind of problem. It was like stopping penalty goals.' The BBC felt pretty strongly about the Yugoslav government, too, which was not only 'quite incompetent, but rent by dissensions, Serbs, Croats and Slovenes all quarrelling among themselves.'

The nationals working for the BBC were not immune from such conflicts. One member of the French section became involved in a fracas with the French radio representative over Pétain's collaboration and challenged him to a duel. Dennis Main Wilson once went into a studio where the Serbs and the Slovenes fell out with the Croats over whose turn it was to broadcast: 'Communism versus Fascism and a punch-up which I had to sort out. It's sad how history repeats itself.' For the most part, however, people kept their emotions to themselves and got on with the business of broadcasting. There was a war to be won.

At the time that broadcasting in German, French and Italian started in the run-up to war, there had been the same old in-fighting about control which had accompanied the launch of Arabic the previous year. The Foreign Secretary, Lord Halifax, was of the view that 'the BBC could hardly be expected to possess sufficient knowledge of the facts to enable it always to be the judge of what should or should not be included in a bulletin.' And there had been the same outcome: broadcasting was left to the professionals.

The BBC's foreign language broadcasters were answerable to the Ministry of Information, as were the home services, but also to the Foreign Office's Political Intelligence Department and the Ministry of Economic Warfare. It was, as Harman Grisewood put it, 'exceedingly difficult to reconcile all these differing interests'. Leonard Miall tells a story which illustrates at the highest level the difficulty of getting any two sources to agree: 'There was a risk of Yugoslavia joining Hitler – the Prince Regent had made a pact with Hitler. Leo Amery, a Cabinet Minister with a remarkable command of languages, was to broadcast in Serbo-Croat and I'd sent his script to the Ministry of Information and got back the message that it was a bit flamboyant and ought to be toned down. I relayed this to Amery when he arrived at Bush House. He was a small man, very fiery, and he immediately got on the telephone to Churchill. And Churchill, who had the latest intelligence from Yugoslavia, immediately dictated a much stronger statement. Amery wrote it down with a little stubby pencil, kneeling at the side of my desk. The Yugoslav translator-announcer coached him on how to read this last bit as we went down in the lift, and he delivered it with tremendous aplomb. The next day there was a coup and Yugoslavia was firmly on the Allied side.'

SIMPLIFYING THE LINES OF COMMUNICATION

In early 1942, the Government pulled together the Political Intelligence Department (PID) and the Department of Enemy Propaganda (DEP) into a new Political Warfare Executive (PWE). This change in structure simplified the BBC's lines of communication as well as getting rid of some of the Government's own conflicts and clarifying Britain's propaganda aims. Until then, as Sir Bruce Lockhart, the director of the PWE, said, there was 'more political warfare on the home front than against the enemy'. It was also useful for the BBC to know what the DEP, which was in charge of subversive broadcasting to the Germans, was doing. But it kept its distance. The DEP ran a number of allegedly German stations, such as Soldatensender Calais, for the enemy forces, putting out fake news of the most unscrupulous kind. The BBC disapproved of this 'black' propaganda, as it was known. Bullock considered it 'sharp practice'. For Martin Esslin, a German section talks producer, it was 'almost pornographic'. He adds: 'We were as pure as Caesar's wife.'

The PWE did not have control of the European Service. It could consult and advise, but the BBC was able to respond to events, within the rules of censorship, without close supervision. At first the Executive was at Woburn Abbey and Miall remembers meetings at which 'we would thrash out a directive that was tolerable to both sides'. He adds: 'These directives were really rather ivory-towered: they were written by people working far away from the heat of the battle, and they didn't always make sense. And the news would change, anyway, and we couldn't carry out what they wanted us to do.'

When the Executive moved to the eighth floor of Bush House the contact was better but, says Bullock, the problem of time-scale remained: 'The news came in and within five or ten minutes, if you hadn't got it on the air in Italian or French or whatever it was, you were failing in your job. The PWE could draw up all sorts of directives but if the enemy, to your consternation, did something you weren't expecting, and did it in the middle of the night when everybody had gone home, then a decision had to be taken by the two or three men on duty. News is a very hard commodity to fit into a bureaucratic framework.'

He was on duty one night in December 1941, when the Germans had got to within 20 miles of Moscow and all the briefings indicated that Russia would not last six weeks, when a communiqué came in saying that one hundred Soviet divisions had gone into the field and thrown back the enemy. 'I still get gooseflesh when I think about it. The Germans had already taken nearly three million prisoners. Where had one hundred divsions come from, for heaven's sake? The answer was from the Far East. Instead of dribbling them into the battle,

The Red Army rounds up German prisoners on the Russian Front.

Zhukov had held back until he had a massive army. That was where the war turned, in one respect. But what was I to do? The PWE directive said we were not to encourage the belief that the Russians were going to make any difference to the war – and yet here was this sensational news. Well, I was young, I leapt about, I checked the sources. And I went with it.

'We never had time for inquests which was perhaps as well. They were always being held upstairs in the Political Warfare Executive and they would shake their heads over our sins. They always forgot about them if the news was good. If the news was bad then, of course, you were in for trouble.'

During May 1940, when the take-over of the BBC was a very real possibility, its external broadcasters were in much the same odour as their home colleagues. Touring the Middle East, Anthony Eden, the Secretary of State for War, sent back a telegram saying that wherever he went he heard complaints about the BBC's Arabic and English broadcasts. 'They are continually putting out rumours obviously emanating from enemy sources,' he complained. But once Ivone Kirkpatrick was appointed as the second of Churchill's internal BBC 'advisers', the foreign affairs counterpart of Patrick Ryan in home affairs, the pressure eased considerably.

Kirkpatrick, a Foreign Office mandarin who had held a senior post in the British Embassy in Berlin before the war and became the High Commissioner in Germany after it, was someone whom the Foreign Office thought would be their man. They were wrong. Kirkpatrick was 'extremely robust' where the FO was concerned; he also tended to treat the PWE with disdain. Grisewood remembered how the heads of the European language sections paraded in Kirkpatrick's office with the directives they had agreed with the Executive and how he would spread them out on his desk, say 'I'm going to biff out this and biff out that', and strike through item after item with his little gold pencil. 'It was one of the briefest meetings you can imagine and a great refreshment to me, coming from the old BBC where meetings were very long and everybody had a good yap.'

Kirkpatrick, a former soldier and linguist, ran Bush House as a kind of military command, but with the friendliness of a good commanding officer. He had the advantage of having Brendan Bracken's ear who had Churchill's – but he was such an attractive

Ivone Kirkpatrick. His role, along with that of Patrick Ryan, of preserving the BBC's independence has never been sufficiently recognized.

person that he seemed always to get his way without falling out with anybody. He was, in Grisewood's opinion, 'cleverer than anyone else'. Once, when Kirkpatrick was ill and had to leave his assistant in charge, he gave him two pieces of advice. One was to ensure that: 'When you see a Minister, make sure you know more than he does.' The other was what to do if an exalted figure from one of the exiled governments 'gave difficulties or became objectionable': 'Say with a heavy English accent, "*Je suis lié par mes instructions*" – and then leave the room.'

Bullock was grateful for Kirkpatrick's protection in late 1944 after he was responsible for putting out a digest of the Press coverage that had followed the suppression by the British Army of the Communist resistance movement in Greece, which looked likely to take over the country following the German pull-out. 'There was a great deal of criticism of Churchill, especially in America but also here,' Bullock says. '"There he goes again, with his right-wing sympathies. He's going to restore an unpopular monarchy." All I did was put together a series of newspaper extracts. They were very hostile, but no opinion was expressed by the BBC. We were just doing our job. But Churchill was in Greece and was told he was being undermined by the BBC from London. He sent back furious telegrams: "Take them all to the Tower and have them beheaded," roughly. Kirk – we always called Kirkpatrick that behind his back – sent for me and asked to see the script and the newspapers and we went through everything line by line. He said "Nothing else?" I said, "No". "All right," he said, "leave this to me." He didn't reproach me, he didn't reprimand me, he didn't say "You landed me with a nasty problem." He took it on his own back and I was never troubled. Now that was marvellous.'

AN OUTSTANDING BROADCASTING WAR

For all his geniality, Kirkpatrick was an authoritarian. But he let the men who ran the two most important language sections, the French and German, have their head: and Darcy Gillie, a romantic with a volcanic temperament, and Hugh Carlton Greene, an impassive sceptic, repaid him by conducting an outstanding broadcasting war. Both Gillie and Greene (the brother of novelist Graham and, in the sixties, the BBC's second-most famous director-general) had joined the European Service at the height of international newspaper careers, Greene's as the *Daily Telegraph*'s Berlin correspondent. Their sections were in as marked contrast as their personalities.

While both outputs stressed the inevitability of German defeat, the voices that predominantly carried the message to France were those of French nationals; Germany heard mostly British voices. The reasons were psychological. France, which had allowed German propaganda to contribute to its collapse, would have been hostile to any foreign broadcaster, but especially to Britain, which, by fighting on, represented a standing reproach. Germany required a different tactic. 'There had to be a very strong emphasis that Britain was conducting the broadcasts as it was conducting the war,' says Esslin. 'What the service was not to be seen as was a show run against Hitler by German refugees or political opponents. The news, which was objective and impartial, could be read by German voices. But almost all comment had to be British.' The exception was the author Thomas Mann who recorded a regular commentary from America. The main named speakers were Greene himself; Sefton Delmer, also previously a Berlin correspondent (of the *Daily Express*); Richard Crossman, a future Labour Government Cabinet Minister then working for the PID and assigned to guide the section; and Professor Lindley Fraser, Professor of Political Economy at Aberdeen University.

There were other differences between the sections. Where the French staff's job was to raise the spirits of France and talk of liberation, the German staff's job was to sap Germany's courage and confidence, though it did not leave listeners staring into a void, because it also looked to a post-war future in which the political and spiritual regeneration of the country would become possible.

Hugh Carlton Greene, who served as an RAF intelligence officer during the Battle of Britain, joined the BBC in October 1940. During the sixties he was to become the second-most famous director-general.

What the sections had in common was a singularity of vision. 'It was very difficult to interest them in anything not connected with France or Germany,' Bullock remembers. Half-way through the war he had ten talks prepared on the Beveridge Report which shaped the British Welfare State. These were broadcast by other language sections. 'The Germans said, "Phh, we've had all this since Bismarck's time" – you know, the British catching up as usual. Just to get them to put out one talk was a struggle.' That was another thing the sections shared: the power to buck the system. Bullock remembers the disputes that arose but is forgiving: 'Both had reasons for wanting nothing to do with the rest of the European Service, and both were superb – the French were one of the wittiest, most brilliant bunch of broadcasters there's ever been.'

THE FRENCH SECTION

Most of the French section arrived in the BBC after Dunkirk; they included actors, painters, writers and musicians. The first was Michel Saint-Denis, a celebrated theatre

February 1945: the war is not yet over, but France is liberated. Members of the Maquis, with a uniformed member of the Fighting French Army, tune into the news from London.

producer who had served as a French Army liaison officer with the BEF. Under the pseudonym Jacques Duchesne, he was the genius responsible for the section's most famous programme, *Les Français Parlent aux Français*, which went out at 9.30 every evening after the ten-minute news and the five minutes allotted to the Free French. Essentially, it was a half-hour of informal discussion, but themes were attacked from so many angles, with such speed and panache, blending news, commentaries, talks and slogans with jingles and music, that people in Bush House reckoned it was the most exciting thing they had ever heard. Robin Scott was one. He says: 'The French frequently were not scrupulous in following the official directives. If they had they would have sounded like official directives.... It meant that, on the BBC's behalf, they struck a note that the listeners understood instinctively. What they were being told was coming from intelligent people of independent mind.'

The section developed another very effective form of propaganda by taking well-known songs – *Frère Jacques*, *Auprès de ma blonde*, *La Cucaracha* – and rewriting the words, often twisting a piece of German propaganda. Every fortnight, a session was recorded at Maida Vale with a full orchestra, many with the comic actor Pierre Dac, who escaped to London in 1943 after a year in prison. The German section also made telling use of parodying popular music. The cabaret star Luci Mannheim sang a ver-

sion of *Lili Marlene* in which the girl waiting in the lamp-light was told that her soldier was missing in Russia and that the lamp-post could be used to hang Hitler.

THE GERMAN SECTION

Satire was used more extensively in the German output than the French. There was a weekly letter home from Lance-Corporal Hirnschal, who found himself kicked from one end of Europe to the other as everything went wrong, and Frau Wernicke, a Berlin Mrs Mopp, talked about the difficulties of rationing and air-raids, letting fly at the authorities. And there was *Kurt and Willi*, such successful characterizations that they had their own series. Kurt was the kindly schoolmaster who believed everything he heard; Willi his cynical friend at the Propaganda Ministry who made up some of the things Kurt believed. 'They'd meet for a drink every night,' says Main Wilson, 'and Kurt would say, "Did you hear the Fuhrer last night? Wasn't that good – we sank the entire British merchant fleet in the Atlantic." And Willi would say, "Yeah. I thought we did that last month." Great stuff. I was seventeen years old, waiting to go into the Army, and I'd discovered comedy. And to think I'd been worried about not going to university!'

The French put out an early-morning programme for workers, but the Germans went further, aiming at different strata of society – intellectuals, workers, women, youth; they had special slots for the Forces which included details of prisoners-of-war. From 1943 some of the hundreds of thousands of German prisoners spoke on a daily programme, revealing the distortions they had been told by their commanders and exposing incidents of maltreatment. The section used prisoners in a Sunday programme, *Anthology of German Literature*, utilizing the humanistic poems of Goethe, Schiller and Heine 'to do a bit of cultural propaganda'.

The bulletins in German were as starkly truthful as any put out by the BBC. Even in the despairing early years of the war, the subliminal message was that, whatever happened, Britain believed it was ultimately going to win. Once the victories began to come, the policy increasingly forced the Nazis to admit what they would have preferred to conceal, or to make such exaggerated claims that the German people and its Armed Services, like everyone else in Europe, came to see them for the lies they were.

On Crossman's advice, the section also pinned Hitler down on his promises. On the last day of 1940, the year of Dunkirk, he issued a proclamation that 1941 would be the year of final victory. From then on the broadcasters started every news with the words: 'This is London with the news on the first/second/third day of the year in which Hitler has promised you final victory.' On 31 December, the bulletin began: 'This is the last day of the year in which Hitler has promised you final victory.' The same stratagem was employed with the Battle of Stalingrad. Effective use was made of Hitler's

In *Mein Kampf*, Hitler wrote 'in wartime, words are acts'. Unlike Churchill and the American President F.D.Roosevelt (famous for his 'fireside' style of broadcasting), Hitler preferred to address his audience not from a studio but from party rallies.

speeches, with recorded extracts used to show that what he said had been contradicted by events. Esslin made one programme in the form of a conversation in which an Englishman asked questions and received contradictory answers from two Hitlers, with extracts again being taken from recordings. 'I think we had considerable success in undermining the idea of Hitler as the God-ordained Führer,' Esslin says. 'Of course, in many ways, he was a very ridiculous person.'

The German section twice rejected Hitler's offers of peace even before the Government did so. The first was after Poland had been overrun in the autumn of 1939. That made headlines: 'BBC rejects Hitler peace offer'. There might have been repercussions but there were not, nor were there the following year, when the same thing happened after the fall of France. This time Sefton Delmer, who was making his first broadcast and knew Hitler well, delivered the reply in earthy language: 'Let me tell you what we here in Britain think of this appeal of yours to what you are pleased to call our reason and common sense. Herr Führer and Reichskanzler, we hurl it right back at you, right in your evil-smelling teeth.' The effect was dramatic. The reply was printed round the world. And Germany was dumbfounded that the answer had come back within three hours of Hitler's speech. Says Leonard Miall: 'Looking back, the interesting thing is that not for a moment did it occur to any of us involved that we should do anything other than reject the offer. Churchill had said we would never surrender and that was that.' The Government's formal rejection came three days later.

THE ITALIAN SECTION

Broadcasting to Italy, the second member of the Axis, employed the same mix of news, talks, satire. In *Sotto Voce*, Leo and Paulo, Romans with no strong political leanings, discussed current events with Rossi, a firm Fascist, driving home Italy's uncomfortable position as Hitler's 'tattered lackey'. The voices used were mostly Italian, but the most popular was that of an Englishman, Colonel Stevens, a former British military attaché in Rome, who became known as 'Colonello Buonasera'. The Italian section's job altered radically in mid-1943 after the government that had replaced Mussolini surrendered to the Allies. The goal became, according to the *BBC Handbook* of 1944: 'The rebirth of a fighting spirit in a country which has changed from being an enemy to a co-belligerent.' The BBC sent messages to the partisans who had taken up arms and gave instructions to factory workers in the industrial north on the best way to obstruct the Germans.

KEEPING HOPE ALIVE

The relationship between the BBC and the emergence of national resistance movements across occupied Europe is easy to exaggerate and impossible to unravel. There is no doubt, however, that the BBC played a part, though its main role was in keeping hope alive in the breasts of the ordinary millions whose greatest act of resistance was listening to the BBC. 'Our role was to encourage people not to collaborate with the Germans' says Robin Scott. 'For example, the Germans set up a system of so-called "labour exchange" – if a Frenchman agreed to go to work in Germany or on a German project, then a French prisoner would be released. A lot of people fell for that and we ran a long campaign, "*Ne vas pas en Allemagne.*"'

There were many such campaigns in the various sections, the Danish Den Kold Skulder, for example, ensuring that the occupying Germans were given the cold shoulder whenever possible. The Danes also got people to knit and wear red, white and blue bobble hats which, when a head was inclined, displayed a copy of the RAF roundel. The Czechs were particularly successful with a boycott of the Nazi-controlled newspapers: sales fell to practically nothing while the citizens were seen on the trams and in the coffee houses ostentatiously reading their country's classics. 'But there was a great hesitation about giving any kind of false lead to people to start firing guns or declaring themselves and openly attacking German installations until the time was right,' Scott emphasizes. To everyone in Bush House, the possibility that they might be encouraging listeners to acts which would have repercussions was 'a thing of continuing anxiety'. As Dennis Main Wilson observes: 'We weren't the one who'd be put up against a wall if anything went wrong.'

V FOR VICTORY

There were some qualms about the V for Victory campaign, the best known of all the BBC's propaganda activities, which developed a life of its own. It began in minor key, when Victor de Laveleye, the Belgian programme organizer (who became his country's peacetime Minister of Education) introduced it in his own service in January 1941, suggesting to his compatriots that the letter, standing as it did for the French *victoire* and the Flemish *vrijheid*, was an appropriate rallying emblem. News quickly arrived from Belgium that placards and posters of the pro-German Flemish separatist organization VNV were being changed into VVV. The V campaign was taken up by the French, Dutch and Norwegian sections and the message reached a crescendo as a cascade of Vs appeared, chalked on walls, roads, pavements, telegraph poles.

By May the whole of the European Service was involved. Soon after, someone realized that the Morse for V, three dots and a dash, was replicated by the opening of Beethoven's *Fifth Symphony*. It immediately became the European Service's call sign and interval signal, beaten out on a muffled timpani. The imaginative French section gave it words, '*Chantez le V, sifflez le V*' and they, too, spread. Across occupied Europe, people hummed the *Fifth*, whistled it, tapped it with teaspoons on teacups in the presence of their occupiers. In the English service to Europe, 'Colonel Britton' (actually, assistant news editor Douglas Richie), dealt 'with points of correspondents'.

Furious, the Germans tried to neutralize the campaign by appropriating the opening bars of the *Fifth* as part of their radio call signs. They exploited the V in news papers, erected a V-sign on the Eiffel Tower, renamed one of Prague's main through-fares Victoria Street. Meanwhile, England was struck by V-madness. There were V-badges, brooches, ear-rings. In Leicester a giant V was displayed on the city's clock tower. In the Press, 'Colonel Britton' became 'the Scarlet Pimpernel of the radio'. Brendan Bracken told Parliament that the campaign was a 'sort of *Lift Up Your Hearts*'. Churchill adopted the sign, making it as much his trademark as his cigars and romper suits.

If you can't beat them...In August 1941 the Germans had V for Victory painted in the streets of Prague to try to convince the population that they had originated the sign.

Churchill gives the V-sign.

As acts of sabotage increased across Europe, the campaign was in danger of turning ugly, but in June Russia joined the party, followed by the Americans in December, and the V campaign lost its impact – but never its emotional significance. It had been the first pan-European gesture, helping people defy the physical presence of the Germans who paraded in their streets, filled their restaurants and were billeted in their homes. For millions the V campaign was the simple assurance which said: we are not alone.

GOING UNDERGROUND

In 1942, the BBC began to broadcast in Morse code in the early hours of the morning, to help the clandestine newspapers which were beginning to appear in most of the occupied countries. Half an hour of news was tapped out in English, French and German. Morse was replaced in 1944 by speech transmissions. A Norwegian told listeners in England and America:

At this very hour, the secret journalists are at their underground work. The day's work has finished on the farms and in the factories and offices. Now the more important part of the day has come. In a cellar, somewhere in my snow-covered country, a girl is crouching in front of a muffled loudspeaker, taking shorthand notes of the BBC news. In his lodging, a student is typing the stencils for tomorrow's *Radio Post*. In a boathouse a young factory worker turns the handle of the duplicator. In a deserted office, three young clerks are pinning the sheets together, folding the finished papers, and putting them into envelopes. Or they may be walking the streets and roads in the black-out, dropping envelopes into pillar-boxes or delivering small bundles of paper at houses as they go along. Hundreds and hundreds of people are at work just now, producing and distributing the illegal papers in my country, and before midday tomorrow their duplicated paper, bringing the latest war news, will have covered the greater part of Norway.

The same kind of thing was happening all over Europe, even, by the end of the war, in Germany itself.

As D-Day approached, the BBC contributed directly to the war effort by broadcasting coded messages in its normal programme output. These messages derived from Colonel Buckmaster's French section in the Special Operations Executive (SOE), and were sent to resistance groups and British agents in the field; some were to mislead the Germans into thinking that the landing would be in the Cherbourg peninsula. They were described as 'personal messages' to give the impression that they had no connection with the war, which fooled nobody. Their meaning was unknown to the broadcasters and sometimes the sheer number of them (each one repeated twice), was resented, particularly by the French who received the bulk of them. On the eve of D-Day, when the troopships had already left British ports, at least 200 were transmitted.

The most important message was the one announcing D-Day, which the French section broadcast in two halves. Peter Carr Foster – an Englishman whose family had lived in France for two generations and who was a French section announcer – was on duty the first day: 'It was a quotation from a poem by Verlaine, "*Les sanglots longs des violons de l'automne*", which means "The lengthy sobs of autumn's violins". A few days later, when D-Day was actually upon us, the second half went "*Bercent mon cœur d'une langueur monotone*" – "Cradle my heart in a languorous monotony". I hope Verlaine will forgive that.'

MOBILIZING FOR D-DAY

In the run-up to D-Day, Eisenhower's first instruction to the people of Europe was broadcast on the BBC by a member of his staff (Eisenhower was simultaneously talking on the Home and Overseas General Forces networks). France, Belgium, Holland, Norway and Denmark were asked to observe the movements of enemy troops and supplies and advised what to do when the fighting started. On D-Day, 6 June 1944, a warning was given to all those living within 22 miles of the coast that an air attack was imminent. More instructions were broadcast: to Poles forced to serve in the German Army, to fishermen in specified areas, to dock workers in Cherbourg who were asked to protect installations.

Unlike the Alps and Pyrénées, the Normandy countryside was not suitable for guerrilla operations. The crucial work of the Resistance here during the waiting period was in intelligence and weapon drops. D-Day was the call to arms, the chance, at last, to restore French self-esteem. Roads were mined, bridges and railway lines blown up; the destruction was so great that one SS division was delayed from reaching the front line for a fortnight. The Resistance's contribution to the liberation of France, Eisenhower said, was the equivalent of fifteen divisions. One wonders how many divisions the contribution of the BBC was worth. It carried on broadcasting (a message put out on 8-9 June instructed teams from the SOE to rendezvous with and arm 30 000 members of the Resistance), issuing warnings about air attacks to French civilians living behind the retreating Germans, advising the Belgian and Dutch resistance movements to protect factories and industrial complexes and to harry the enemy wherever possible. As the Allies pushed on to Germany, broadcasts were made to civilians and foreign workers in the Ruhr and Rhineland, telling them to evacuate the battle areas. As mopping up continued and Allied military rule was imposed, broadcasts explained what people should do.

THE BBC MONITORING UNIT

The BBC announced the D-Day landings before the Allies had done so themselves – the news had been picked up from German radio by BBC monitors. In the course of the war, the BBC assembled first-class sources of intelligence, but none was sharper than its own monitoring unit which fed 'hot flashes' (as they were known) into the teleprinters that were linked to all the BBC's news departments, to the Government ministries, the Services (which were particularly interested in lists of prisoners-of-war) and to Number Ten. In late 1944,

March 1941, a BBC Monitering department gains valuable intelligence.

the unit was the first to learn, from his own broadcast, that Hitler had survived the bomb attempt on his life; in May 1945, it was the first Western source of Hitler's death, announced in Germany to the strains of Bruckner. By then the monitors were listening to one-and-a-quarter million words a day in thirty-two languages, which were reduced daily to a 50 000-word printed digest.

The Foreign Office had started listening to the Arabic output of Italy and Germany during the thirties, but as war loomed it asked the BBC to set up a monitoring operation, which it did at Evesham, on the edge of the Cotswolds in Worcestershire. In 1943, the station moved 70 miles closer to London, to Caversham Park, a nineteenth-century, no-longer-stately home that had been a boys' school in the inter-war years and was about to be used as a hospital.

Here the staff, which rose to nearly 1000, most of them foreign nationals, had adequate accommodation: at Wood Norton, where they were based in huts, there was never enough room for anyone to occupy a listening position throughout the day and an elaborate rota of comings and goings had to be strictly fol-

From 1939 to 1943, BBC Monitoring worked in these wooden huts at Evesham, Worcestershire. When the huts were demolished many years later, a cigarette packet found in the walls had written on it: 'Whoever finds this will know who won the war'...

lowed. Vovo Rubenstein, a Russian monitor, remembers 'quite a few' elderly academics who found difficulty in tuning their sets. Old wax-cylinder recorders were used and, although better equipment gradually replaced them, they did not go out of use entirely. 'Prehistoric, absolutely,' says Rubenstein. 'The cylinders were very brittle and broke easily. Particular recordings were kept for a week or two, or perhaps forever, but generally the cylinders were shaved and re-used, time and again. Sometimes they were shaved very badly and you might get the sounds of the preceding recording mingling with yours. You can imagine the confusion, particularly if both were in the same language.' When a major speech was coming out of Europe, half a dozen monitors would handle it as a team, each taking down two or three minutes' worth and completing the translation almost as the speech finished. Rubenstein remembers the tension at the station. 'If someone had a "hot flash" they ran, not walked, ran, to the information bureau which was wired up to all our outlets.'

For Rubenstein, the most momentous day of the war came at the beginning of July 1941. The German invasion of Russia had taken place early in the morning of 22 June, Soviet radio had not reacted, and for eleven days the situation remained unclear. Then one night, when he was on duty, there came an announcement that an important statement would be broadcast. Was Stalin going to conclude a pact with the Germans? Would he draw back behind the Urals and leave Europe to its fate?

'When you are nervous and excited you are not at your best as far as hearing is concerned,' Rubenstein says. 'What made matters worse for me was that Stalin was broadcasting from what sounded like an air-raid shelter somewhere underground – the acoustics were terrible. Add to that his Georgian accent and the fact that he was pouring water into his glass near the microphone – I could hardly make out what he was saying. I struggled alone, trying to understand the tenor of the speech and gradually it became clear. He was calling on all Soviet citizens to resist to the last.… Now we had a big strong ally, which made it quite certain there would be no invasion of this country, at least for some time to come. And there was a fair chance of victory in the end, which before had been extremely doubtful.'

HOPE IN A SEA OF HOPELESSNESS

Few people in Europe listened to the BBC at the beginning of the war. Why should they have done? It was hard enough surviving under the Nazi yoke without risking your life to hear broadcasts from a country that would soon go the way of the rest of the Continent. But after Britain sent the *Luftwaffe* packing and there was hope, the BBC became a life-raft to which the occupied nations could cling. A girl who escaped from Czechoslovakia in March 1941 wrote to the BBC: "People who were almost too poor to buy bread have now a radio. They need it. A man told me, "The stomach is hungry but the soul still more so. London is the only thing to feed the soul.'"

In Denmark the Nazi paper *Faedrelandet* concluded: 'Many people have more faith in bulletins from London than in the words of the Bible ...' The Vichy and Italian authorities imposed punitive fines on anyone caught listening and sets were confiscated in all the countries under Nazi domination. In France and Poland there were imprisonments, deportations and some executions. In the end, the Germans gave up: the task was beyond them from the beginning. A letter, typical of the time, smuggled from a French village in May 1942, read: 'Out of 150 households there are 110 wireless sets. Out of the 110 owners of these sets, 105 at least listen to the BBC regularly.'

When they were forced to divert troops into Italy after the Italian government capitulated, the Germans issued threats about listening, but they never imposed the death penalty. Had they done so they would have had to shoot almost the entire nation. By early 1944, they would have had to shoot most of the *Wehrmacht*, too.

The restoration of the postal service at the end of the war brought an avalanche of letters of gratitude into Bush House from all over Europe: 4000 in the first month from France alone. Thousands more came from Germany, most of them saying that the writer remembered this or that broadcast in this year or that, and asking for confirmation: many Germans had reason for wanting to show that they had been anti-Nazi and there was no better proof than listening to the BBC. In fact, the BBC audience in Germany was huge; after the German section revealed that a high-ranking submariner, presumed dead in Germany, was, in fact, a prisoner of the Allies, no one turned up for his memorial service – everyone had heard the broadcast. After the war, people like Hugh Greene and Lindley Fraser found they were more famous in the eyes of Europeans than anybody else in the country. 'For years afterwards, it was almost embarrassing to go to Europe because there was so much fuss made about the BBC,' Lord Bullock comments.

To him, the BBC meant Bush House, not the home services; he never went near Broadcasting House once the European Service moved out. 'We thought of ourselves as an élite service,' he admits. 'I listened to my radio at home and I thought the home news pretty sleepy. They seemed to lead with the same story in the evening that they'd led with at lunchtime. You'd have been fired at Bush House if you'd led with the same story in two separate transmissions.'

Robin Scott, unlike Bullock, stayed to make his career in the BBC: 'It's curious how independent of the mother house we were. I felt that they weren't anything like as clever at the broadcasting game as the people in Bush House, who were not only winning the war but shaping the future of broadcasting.' Even Harman Grisewood felt no split loyalties, for all his years of pre-war service: 'We did not feel part of the BBC. I certainly knew that the powers that be at Broadcasting House were a bit suspicious and I think envious of the European Service as it developed.'

CHAPTER
7

MIND MY BIKE!

Templemeads Station, Bristol, one morning in April 1941: BBC Variety was on the move again, this time by special train; 432 comics, singers, musicians, producers, actors, writers, wives, children and others, plus seventeen dogs, an unknown number of cats and a parrot. The guard's van was piled high with equipment, the instruments of the Variety Orchestra, tea-chests full of band-parts, luggage, prams and bicycles.

The first move, on the declaration of war in September 1939, had been out of London to Bristol, where Variety, with the Music, Religious and Children's departments, had gone in the mistaken belief that they would be safe from the bombing. Drama had gone to Wood Norton Hall in Evesham, Worcestershire, a few days earlier, when the announcer Stuart Hibberd had noted in his diary: 'The entrance hall of Broadcasting House looked like King's Cross on Christmas Eve.'

In *ITMA 1939-48*, the producer Francis Worsley wrote: 'The BBC is a good organizer, but moving hundreds of people and their families to different parts of the country gave the accommodation and catering officers headaches.' That was an understatement in the first few days at Bristol. The evacuees were not expected to arrive when they did, nor were so many of them anticipated. There were insufficient beds, bedding and billets and the canteen, used to serving meals for sixty, could not cope with an influx that rose, eventually, to nine hundred.

BRISTOL IS BATTERED

In the early summer of 1940, the *Luftwaffe* presented a more formidable problem when Bristol became one of its first consistent targets. Rehearsals and transmissions went on in rocking buildings. Over and over it seemed impossible that a particular programme would go out that night, but it did. Frequently the lighting was knocked out and broadcasts were made by the light of hurricane lamps. The alerts became so frequent, interfering with scriptwriting and production, that the staff finally disregarded orders to go to the shelters and remained where they were unless the planes and

the bombs were getting near. In due course a band of voluntary spotters was formed and took turns sitting on the roofs. One by one the makeshift studios were damaged and programmes could no longer be broadcast live in the evenings, but had to be pre-recorded during the day.

On one occasion, a *Music Hall* show was recorded in Bristol Central Hall which had

On 15 October, 1940, a delayed-action bomb smashed through the telephone switchboard room on the seventh floor of Broadcasting House. BH was bomb-damaged for the second time in December 1940 but again stayed on-air.

been so badly damaged the previous night that it had no roof or windows. Two thousand factory workers came in their lunch-hour and sat in the pouring rain singing songs until the engineers repaired the landlines to London. During a heavy raid one Sunday evening, the planned religious service had to be broadcast from a small emergency studio in which the Revd Welch delivered the talk from under a table, with Stuart Hibberd giving readings from the Bible beside him and Paul Beard playing the violin on his knees.

In January 1941 part of Music's headquarters in a house in Pembroke Road was destroyed by a fire which was not caused by enemy action but by a fire-watcher who had recently been released from a mental institution. The music library was lost and with it most of the control scores which contained the timings of the works.

The BBC struggled on until, on 17 March, the regional centre in Whiteladies Road was badly maimed, with two of the three major studios destroyed, and it became impossible to stay. 'Religion leaving Bristol' a local paper announced ambiguously. So was Music, and both departments went to Bedford, where religious services were broadcast from the parish church and the Bunyan Chapel, and concerts were staged in the Corn Exchange; from September 1941 it became possible to broadcast all home network music programmes live.

And Variety boarded its train and travelled up through the valleys to the small university town of Bangor in north Wales. A small party went to Weston-Super-Mare to see if it might make a better base and produced some programmes from there. But the resort was bombed and the party rejoined the department in Bangor – where in October two sea-mines, intended for the Mersey, were dropped by parachute and did a lot of damage, killed a BBC driver and took *ITMA* off the air.

THE BBC IS BOMBED

The Blitz on London had lasted for eighteen days in September 1940 before the BBC received its first blow: St George's Hall, abandoned by Variety almost a year before, was gutted by incendiary bombs and the theatre organ was destroyed. On 15 October, the day on which its exterior camouflage painting was completed, Broadcasting House took a direct hit from a 500-pound delayed-action bomb which entered a window on the seventh floor at 8.15 p.m. and crashed through to the music library on the third. Its impact caused so much damage that, at first, staff did not realize it had not exploded. Shortly after 9 p.m., someone with more courage than sense decided not to wait for the disposal squad and tried to shift the bomb to the outer corridor to save the building's central structure from further possible destruction.

The bomb exploded while Bruce Belfrage was reading the nine o'clock news in a basement studio. Listeners heard a distant crump, there was a slight pause, a clearly

The bomb which landed on the seventh floor of Broadcasting House finally came to rest in the music library.

audible 'It's all right', and Belfrage, who was covered in fallen plaster and soot, carried on as if nothing had happened, although he was shaking from a severe attack of claustrophobia, something that had affected him when he was younger but which he thought he had mastered. His only fluff came at the end, when he announced that the *Postscript* which followed was by Lloyd Lord

The bomb which hit Broadcasting House in October 1940 exploded about 45 minutes later – while Bruce Belfrage was reading the nine o'clock news.

instead of Lord Lloyd. He was back on-air with the midnight bulletin.

Seven staff (four men and three women), died in the blast. Half a square mile of the area surrounding Broadcasting House was devastated. The top bedrooms of the Langham Hotel across the road had plunged into the street and part of a London bus was perched on a nearby roof. Inside Broadcasting House, studios had been ravaged (it took three years to restore them), the switchboard was a tangle of splinters and broken wire, thousands of precious gramophone records had been destroyed and the news library was wrecked. At 6 a.m. the following day, the news librarian, trying to save some of his files from the heap of rubbish in Portland Place, was almost arrested for looting.

Even more serious damage was done in the late evening of Sunday 8 December 1940 when a landmine exploded in the centre of Portland Place, killing a policeman and taking out the side of Broadcasting House. Blast fire raged inside the building for seven hours while water from smashed pipes and firemen's hoses cascaded down the stairwell and turned the entrance hall into a lake. Desks floated in the newsroom, which had been moved into the basement at the start of the Blitz. Outside the main entrance, an armoured car waited to drive announcers to the Maida Vale studios if broadcasting became impossible. There were no BBC fatalities but there were serious injuries, and the infirmary was overwhelmed with casualties, most of them from the neighbourhood.

In the kitchens, the catering staff were first choked with soot and then flooded. There was no electricity and nothing to cook on but two picnic-sized primus stoves. Yet by early morning 500 breakfasts were being served amid the wreckage. Many people remained on duty for several days without a break, sleeping in wrecked offices or in nearby Egton House. Once again the news library was destroyed, as was the repaired switchboard. In the October 1940 bombing, eight of the normal seventy telephone exchange lines had been kept going; this time all the lines were down and programme-makers queued at public kiosks to make whatever calls were necessary to keep their programmes on the air.

On 10 May 1941, when the Queen's Hall next door to the gutted St George's was totally demolished, a high-explosive bomb struck the Maida Vale studios, killing the back-up announcer of the European Service German section. Since the raids of the previous year, the BBC had set up belt-and-braces cover for all its home and foreign-language services, with a team of announcers spending the hours of darkness at Maida Vale, ready to take over if Broadcasting House or Bush House were put out of commission. During the same night, Bedford College, one of the scores of buildings around central London which the Overseas Service occupied, was severely damaged by fire.

Bush House remained unscathed until the 'Little Blitz' of 1944, when a flying bomb came down in the Aldwych, killing a number of people outside the building, in front of the Post Office, and seriously injuring several BBC staff inside. Peter Carr Foster, returning to the French section, found a female colleague named Madeleine Hume apparently drenched in blood and thought that she was another victim until he realized that she was covered in red ink. A spate of V1s fell along the Thames, disturbing the river rats, and it became commonplace in the mornings to find them sitting on the studio turntables preening their whiskers.

When Broadcasting House opened in 1932, its slightly eccentric shape (which maximized an irregular piece of land) was likened to an ocean liner; during the Blitz, pitted and scarred, its pristine stone rendered a sombre grey, it had all the appearance of a battleship damaged in action. In 1939, when anti-gas doors were fitted, sandbags were piled at the entrance and, because the building was 'an obvious target for fifth columnists and subversives', a squad of police guarded it night and day. Once the bombing began, soldiers replaced the police, a wire and steel anti-blast pillbox went up in front of the handsome doors, and the sandbags were augmented by concrete blocks 6 feet square that ran right around the perimeter. (After the war it took nearly a year to remove them with hammers and chisels because the noise of the pneumatic drills with which the builders started the job penetrated the studios.) A concrete bunker nick-named 'The Stronghold' was constructed in the hole at the north end, where the big extension to the building, begun in the months before the war, had been abandoned at foundation level. This bunker contained a broadcasting station in miniature comprising studios, control room, recording rooms and transmitters, and would have come into use if Broadcasting House had been obliterated.

Inside Broadcasting House, a group of Local Defence Volunteers (LDV) patrolled the studios and corridors, wearing armbands and carrying truncheons. Godfrey Talbot was one of them and he did his stint of guard duty outside the anti-gas door leading to the sub-basement, armed with a double-barrelled shotgun, with two cartridges in his pocket and an instruction not to insert them without permission. In May 1940, the LDV became the Home Guard – Churchill finding the new, less cumbersome, name in the course of giving a broadcast talk. Units were formed across the BBC, marched and drilled by the corporation's own commissionaires who were all ex-Service types. In Bristol, an enthusiastic actor demonstrated how to shoot a rifle,

Because Broadcasting House was 'an obvious target for fifth columnists and subversives', it was guarded day and night. No one without a pass was admitted.

which he did not know was loaded, and put a bullet through the ceiling into the room above, in which Derek McCulloch (*Children's Hour*'s Uncle Mac) was working. Not long after, in Broadcasting House, where the newsroom was preparing the nine o'clock news, two brown-paper parcels came thumping down on to the desks from the gallery and a voice said: 'You're all dead. Them's bombs and we're Jerry fifth-columnists who've got yer!' Talbot recalls: 'There were four grinning men in khaki above us. They were from some other Home Guard unit engaged in a defence exercise; object, to penetrate and capture Broadcasting House. And they'd achieved it without a pass in sight.'

There were few such moments of light relief once the bombing began. Broadcasting House developed a siege mentality. Churchill took to ringing the duty office late at night or early in the morning to comment on what was being broadcast. Producers, announcers and artists lived and slept there, often because the air-raids made it too dangerous to leave. The Queen of the Netherlands was forced to stay one night (and trod on Alan Bullock, who was lying in the corridor, on her way to the loo). The newsroom in the bowels of the building had its own bunks. 'Safe but sordid,' Talbot comments. The concert hall was used as a dormitory, with tickets issued on a first-come basis. Here a curtain of blankets divided the sexes from each other. Many of the staff wondered whether the puritanical Reith would have countenanced such an arrangement, but they were mostly too dog-tired to care. No one had anything in mind other than sleep, although that, as Freddie Grisewood wrote in his autobiography, was not easily achieved:

> To begin with, the place was like Piccadilly Circus, with a constant traffic of people coming from or going to their various jobs and the recumbent sleepers were more often than not heavily trodden on by some careless newcomer trying to find his rightful place by the inadequate beam of a blacked-out torch. Nor was the atmosphere conducive to sleep. Never in the whole of my experience have I heard such a varied assortment of noises issuing from the human frame. Snores, grunts, whistles, moans and occasionally deep sobs were mingled with sad sighs, and even snatches of song …

THE BBC BILLETEES

Outside London, many of the BBC's evacuees were having to put up with sleeping arrangements that were no less unpleasant. The Government had made billeting compulsory where necessary; one guinea (one pound ten pence) a week for bed and breakfast, inside sanitation and bathroom not guaranteed. 'Do not confuse billets with lodgings,' a BBC memorandum warned. 'The lodger is desirous and desired. You are a billetee; you probably don't want to live in a billet. Remember that it is even more probable that the billetor doesn't want you.' BBC billetees nicknamed themselves 'guinea pigs' and tried to establish good relations without always succeeding.

'Breakfast was nine to nine-fifteen,' the actor Maurice Denham recalls from his days at Bristol. 'If I wasn't down then I didn't get breakfast. I was entitled to a

The Government made billeting compulsory but, as billetees everywhere – including the staff of the BBC, some of whom are seen here outside the billeting office at Wood Norton – were to find, they were not always welcome…

bath a week on a Friday at six. If I was late, I didn't get that either.'

Francis Worsley wrote: 'It is hard if you are working on night-shift in such a nerve-racking job as monitoring, for example, to be frowned on for staying in bed part of the day. It is hard to have no privacy, except in an unwarmed bedroom, to have to bicycle 2 miles to get a bath and wash your clothes or, as happened, to be thrown out of your billet for being rung up on urgent business at the immoral hour of ten at night.'

The chapel-going, Welsh-speaking inhabitants of Bangor were not welcoming when Variety arrived in their midst and started fitting up more church halls, though this time it had a cinema at its disposal as well as the Grand Theatre, Llandudno. It was not just the business of billeting: there were such outrages as women wearing trousers and smoking in public and long-haired males walking affectionately hand-in-hand. (It is said that a telegram was sent to London, 'For God's sake send more stags Bangor', but that smacks of BBC folklore.) Gradually the Welsh warmed to Variety's free-spending habits and generous support for local charities, and they grew used to the more extravagant behaviour of the artists who came and went. 'The tobacconist's had a notice, "No cigarettes", which was on the counter all the time. But he always kept some under the counter for the BBC,' says Charlie Chester.

ON YOUR BIKE!

Variety was spread out to a radius of about 25 miles around Bangor and buses were needed to take staff to their billets in places like Benllech and Penmaenmawr. Those who lived in or near the town acquired bikes if they did not already have them: even people who owned cars used bikes because they frequently had no petrol coupons. The whole of Bangor came to a standstill when a producer named Ernest Longstaffe appeared. His machine was painted red, white and blue and had a basket on either end – and he rode it wearing a plus-four suit.

For the BBC's Drama evacuees in Evesham the bicycle was, if anything, a bigger part of daily life: even Val Gielgud took to riding one ('after fifteen years!' he groaned) and Bruce Belfrage, the department booking manager who had not yet become a newsreader. 'This form of transport,' he wrote, 'was unfamiliar to some and several casualties resulted.' Maurice Denham remembers some of the casualties caused by the steep hills of Bristol when Variety was billeted there. 'It was hard to get about to some of the places we broadcast from and a lot of people used bikes – very dodgy in the black-out. I preferred to walk.'

The flamboyant Variety producer Ernest Longstaffe, 'customized' his bicycle while in Bangor, patriotically painting it red, white and blue.

When Variety's staff left Bangor, the mayor presented them with a plaque: 'To commemorate the sojourn of the BBC's Variety department in the City of Bangor from May, 1940 to August, 1943.' If the language lacked the inspired Welsh way with words, it also belied what was in people's hearts. There was no such token of friendship from the small West Midlands town of Evesham, when Drama packed its bags, which it did in November 1940, less than three months after its arrival. Bombs had nothing to do with it. The department simply could not wait to get out of the place.

Drama output had already increased by at least 50 per cent, while time for rehearsal had been reduced by 75 per cent. Producers who for years had been trained in the technique of the multiple studio and the drama control panel, had to adapt themselves overnight to the American single-studio system. And the makeshift studios which they now had to use had none of London's sophistication. The main drama studio in Broadcasting House had been equipped with 'a large tank for water noises; a wind machine; a railway noises group; various types of floor materials for floor effects; a compressed-air group including hooters and fog horns; a small piano; a barrel organ; special doors for opening, shutting and slamming, etc.; suspended sheets for thunder; and drums of various sizes.' Some of these things had been salvaged, but the change in Drama's circumstances, Gielgud felt, was 'shattering' and production standards had to be deliberately lowered.

He detested Wood Norton Hall, which the BBC had bought in April 1939 against the eventuality of war and where a dog, rescued from Battersea Dogs' Home, patrolled the grounds. Once the home of an exiled Duc d'Orléans, with fleurs-de-lis on everything from its weather-vane to its bath-plugs, it was, Gielgud wrote, 'the appropriate setting for nightmare'. He was 'deafened by typewriters operated upon parquet floors' and described his producers as being 'wild-eyed, trying to cope with the peculiar acoustic qualities of metamorphosed stables and billiard-rooms.' And, to Gielgud's horror, he was not allowed to smoke in Wood Norton Hall.

His complaints did not end there: 'My billet is vile. Its owners seem to regard one rather as if one was … likely to steal the silver and ravish the daughter as opposed to hoping for bed and breakfast. I fancy, too, that one's inevitably irregular hours of going and coming have raised doubts in their minds about one's morals.'

One wonders whether he laughed at the Wood Norton standing order, as everyone else did, which stipulated that 'in the event of an air-raid, staff are instructed to go to the wood and lie down, preferably in pairs.' Perhaps he just wanted to put whoever was responsible for landing him in Evesham, famous for nothing but its Brussels sprouts, in the bear-pit in the garden. By November 1940 he had persuaded his superiors that the state of affairs was intolerable and, quintessential metropolitan man that he was, he escaped to the comparative sophistication of Manchester.

The growing numbers of monitors stayed on, working in their huts which were

located some distance from the hall at a spot where the reception of incoming radio signals was clearest. Most of them were already resident in the UK when they were recruited, men and women not only with linguistic ability but many of high intelligence who distinguished themselves after the war in many walks

Immediately before the outbreak of war, many big companies bought country mansions to accommodate their evacuated staff. The BBC purchased Wood Norton Hall – and a Battersea Dogs' Home stray to patrol the grounds.

of life. The local population, however, regarded them all with the deepest suspicion and the German-speakers among them were regularly reported to the police as enemy infiltrators. 'It would need a very great writer like George Eliot to describe the social and sexual revolution that was caused,' says Martin Esslin, an Austrian who left Monitoring for the German section at Bush House and ultimately became the head of Radio Drama. 'Almost every possible nationality was here. Arabs, Russian counts, French gigolos.... Some of these foreigners were great seducers. The impact on Evesham was absolutely hilarious but tragic, too, in some ways.'

Monitoring did leave Evesham, in 1943, coming 70 miles east to Caversham Park near Reading to what had been the country house of a nineteenth-century iron-master. The move upset the staff who could not see the logic of it and were worried about the lack of accommodation in the area. The three senior members of the service resigned in protest and joined the Forces. What the BBC could not tell them was that the Government, which from mid-1941 suspected that Germany was in possession of the atomic bomb, now feared that it might be used on London as a last throw of the dice. Had the BBC been forced to flee the capital, it would have needed Wood Norton to house its broadcasting departments.

That did not happen. Had it done so, the Clifton Rocks tunnel would have come into its own.

THE CLIFTON ROCKS TUNNEL

A view down the stairs of the Clifton Rocks tunnel, an abandoned funicular railway cut through solid sandstone, to which the BBC would have retreated if the Germans had invaded and the capital been overrun.

One of the secrets of the war, the tunnel was constructed in 1940 when it seemed possible that London might be paralysed by all-out conventional air-attack. If that had happened, the control and direction of the BBC would have passed to Bristol where an underground fortress had been prepared beneath 50 feet of solid sandstone.

The BBC had planned to construct this final stronghold in a disused tunnel on the old Bristol to Avonmouth railway. The full BBC Symphony Orchestra, consisting of nearly one hundred instrumentalists, tested the tunnel by playing in it, but before conversion work could begin, Bristol was heavily bombed and hundreds of people began using the tunnel as a shelter. The corporation's civil engineers turned to an abandoned funicular railway that had been driven through the rock of the Clifton Gorge near the suspension bridge.

With a steep gradient of one in two, the shaft presented huge difficulties, but in three months the framework of four large chambers had taken shape, one above the other. These were now fitted out. The topmost one, about half-way up the shaft, housed the radio transmitters which would maintain contact with other BBC centres even if all communication lines failed. The aerials were erected on top of the gorge – and were duly replaced when a bomb blew them up. The chamber below was the studio, with an upright piano (to save space), gramophone turntables, and enough general equipment to make it suitable for music, features and small-scale drama. The recording room below that had enough recorded programmes stored in its lockers to maintain a radio service for weeks. Below that was the control room, into which was squeezed apparatus which it had never before been thought possible to assemble in an area twice the size. Eighty pairs of telephone lines terminated here, linking the shelter with the outside world and the BBC's transmitters throughout the United Kingdom. The lines were so routed that if bomb damage severed some, there was a good chance that others would remain intact.

At the touch of a button in the control room, big diesel motors could generate an independent power supply. There was a canteen with enough food to last three months, tanks of water, a ventilation plant, gas-doors. When the sirens sounded in Bristol, the essential programme staff raced from the regional centre to the tunnel, where the control room was manned by technical staff round the clock.

The tunnel was never brought into full operation. But until the war ended the facilities played a routine role in the BBC's network, passing broadcasts from London to the transmitters in the West of England on their way to listeners at home and overseas.

MAKING 'DAISY CHAINS'

Engineers were the unsung heroes of the BBC's war. Had they not devised a way of disguising the signals from the transmitters, the Ministry of Air would have seen to it that the BBC was side-lined for the duration. That, indeed, was what the Ministry demanded as war loomed and before 'synchronization' saved the day.

This ingenious method of 'daisy-chaining' transmitters in a group ensured that, even if an aircraft knew the location of an individual transmitter, it was unable to hitch a ride on the signal because of the collective tangle of interference. A reliable fix was only possible within about 25 miles of the transmitter, after which point it was taken out of commission on the instructions of Fighter Command – and listeners continued to receive the broadcast from a more distant member of the group, albeit a little less clearly. Only once was it necessary to shut down one of the two four-transmitter groups – an achievement in sharp contrast with German radio, which did not implement synchronization and which frequently went off the air under ;the impact of Allied bombing attacks.

The engineers also developed low-power 'in-fill' transmitters, known as H's, which did not have to close down when their big brothers did but which were able to stay in operation until an enemy aircraft was within a few miles. Even during raids the H's kept going a large part of the time, correcting the slight deterioration in sound that occurred when a primary transmitter had to switch to another in its group. The first ten H's were in operation by November 1940, close to the biggest areas of population;

eventually there were sixty of them, all using one wavelength: special equipment had been developed which ensured that they did not interfere with one another.

To ensure that Britain's voice reached the occupied countries of Europe, the engineers increased the number of transmitters at existing sites and built new, more powerful short-wave stations in Cumberland, Shropshire and Dorset. These had the great advantage that they gave no navigational aid to the enemy and so did not have to be shut down. The BBC began the war with 24 transmitters and ended it with 121. The engineers also found ways of getting round the often heavy jamming that the Germans threw up to block the European Service. They developed a system of relaying German radio stations through a BBC transmitter, thereby confusing incoming aircraft which sought to use it as a direction-finder. The engineers also helped the RAF by using transmitters to guide bombers over Germany. They tapped into German telephone and non-public broadcasting circuits and passed information to the intelligence services. And they patched up the studios damaged by bombing; fitted up 150 more in the course of the war; cannibalized equipment when parts were unobtainable to keep the BBC on the air; accompanied the programme-makers wherever they went to send back live programmes; and took their equipment to record the correspondents in the danger zones.

Says Lord Bullock: 'We never met them, we never saw them, but you realized as you sat there broadcasting from your little cell that you might just as well be talking to a hole in the wall unless there were people doing technological wonders somewhere else.' The publisher Lord Weidenfeld, who was a monitor at Wood Norton before becoming a news commentator in the Overseas Service, adds: 'The engineers came down from the hill in the evening, smoking their pipes and knowing they were the kings of the universe.'

ROYAL RECORDINGS

It may not have been exactly a technological wonder, but one engineer aided the war effort by taking the stammer out of the King's Christmas broadcast.

Usually the broadcast was recorded at Windsor, where the BBC had equipment fitted permanently in a passage. (An engineer named Alan Scottdack used to go every Friday to check the batteries which were used instead of Windsor's unreliable mains electricity.) In December 1941, however, the King spoke from Sandringham and performed so badly that Churchill, having heard the broadcast, contacted the BBC and asked for it to be 'doctored' before going out in the Empire link-up. David Martin was given the job.

'It's well known that the King had a speech impediment, but the media didn't talk about it as they would today,' he says. 'He must have been more nervous than he usually was, because the broadcast was awful. Churchill wanted a confident face presented to the world. As it was, he thought people might think England was on its uppers.'

Martin had two recordings to work from: the recording of the live broadcast and one made earlier in the day which would have been patched in had the line from Sandringham been bombed. Each recording was on four 12-inch acetate discs, with only the outer 2 inches or so of each one having been used because that was where the best sound-quality was. Martin set them up on a bank of eight turntables, then identified the stutters and pauses, putting yellow marks with a grease pencil where one word finished and the next word began; there were sometimes three or four grooves between them. When the link-up began, he hopped the pick-up from groove to groove. 'I did that for Africa, then for India, the two North Americas, east and west, the Pacific. There was no tape and no fancy editing devices in those days, it was all done by hand – "just like that", as Tommy Cooper used to say. The Pacific broadcast finished at 6.20 the following morning. I was knackered.'

WOMEN TO THE FORE

Of all the changes that war brought, none was greater than in the employment of women. In 1939 any woman who did not need to work was frowned on for doing so. In 1940, when women had taken over many traditional male roles, that view was merely quaint; by then even the white-collar occupations – which included the BBC – had abandoned the practice of asking women who got married to hand in their resignations. The BBC issued a memo to this effect, but added to it, as if afraid of losing its authority, that, whatever their marital status, all women continued to be obliged to wear stockings. That directive lasted only as long as stockings remained available.

In 1939, the BBC employed just over 4000 people (800 in Broadcasting House); by the end of the war, the figure had risen to a peak of 11 600, with 5800 of them women – and women were an intrinsic part of broadcasting as they had never been before the war. Married women at one BBC hostel even had a nursery where they could leave their children while working their shift. At the sharp end, there were now women with their own record request shows, including Jean Metcalfe, Barbara MacFadyden, Marjorie Anderson, Lilian Duff and Joy Shelton. And the first commère, Doris Arnold, whose show *These You Have Loved* was a particular favourite with the Forces, became a Variety producer, the first in the BBC's history to make the grade. No woman made it into newsreading, but a handful – Joy Worth, and the three Joans, Burman, Gilbert and Griffiths – became continuity announcers. There were women in the Engineering division, too, and not just in secretarial capacities.

'Until 1941 there were enough men to go round,' says Rowena Taylor, one of the

Doris Arnold, the first woman to become a BBC Variety producer.

800 females (along with twice that many males) who passed through the training school which the BBC opened in the May of that year. 'Then things got tight, the transmitter network was expanding all the time and operating round the clock and they had no choice but to recruit women. But they didn't want us, we were the last resort. There was chauvinism, there's no point in saying otherwise.'

Before she joined the European Service in Bush House, she was posted to Newcastle, which was an H station. There she had to learn Morse before she could be promoted: twenty words a minute, taking and receiving through a haze of 'mush'. If Britain had been invaded, this was how London would have tried to keep in touch with the rest of the country; the 'in-fills' would also have been used by the twelve government-appointed regional commissioners, who were named in April 1939, to give instructions to their populations. Every day messages were transmitted from the Broadcasting House control room and sent up one side of the country and down the other through every H station. When a message arrived back in London it was supposed to tally with the original transmission. If it did not the error was traced back through the system.

All maintenance was done at night because the equipment was in use during the day. A night-shift consisted of four people – 'an engineer who was too old to go to war, a youth who was waiting call-up or a chap with some disability, and two women. If one of the women was taken ill, the other one was sent home – she wasn't allowed to work with two men on her own'. Taylor laughs. 'We did exactly the same work as the junior maintenance engineers, we did the heavy work on the transmitters and we worked in the studios and the recording rooms. But we weren't allowed to work with two men unless we were chaperoned. Mind, we weren't allowed to be called engineers, either, not the women. We were "operators".'

RESERVED OCCUPATIONS

The National Services (Armed Forces) Act, which Parliament passed without debate within hours of the declaration of war, made all fit men aged between eighteen and forty-one liable for military call-up. A further Act in 1941, which extended the call-up to women, increased the male age-limit to fifty-one, although in practice few over the original upper limit were conscripted and none over forty-five. At first, under the Schedule of Reserved Occupations, men in a wide range of trades and professions from steel-workers to teachers were exempted; gradually one occupation after another was removed from the list, deferment was decided on an individual basis and the age of reservation was raised. BBC staff were not exempted, but compulsory service was not done by anyone over thirty-five.

There were some people, perhaps with husbands or sons at war, who resented those in reserved occupations, as John Longden, an engineer in Outside Broadcasts, has reason to remember. Early in 1941, when he was nineteen and waiting to go into the RAF, he was aware that 'there was a rumour that the BBC was full of Hooray Henrys ... that once you got in it was a soft job and you wouldn't be called-up', but he paid little attention. He was too busy working on two or three jobs a day at the height of the Blitz, lugging his equipment around the country, usually by train because the vans had no petrol. 'Anyway, one day I was derigging the equipment after this *Workers' Playtime* and a woman came up to me and pushed a cigarette packet into my hand which I took. People often gave you things like that, people loved the BBC. When I opened it, there were three white feathers inside. That really shook me up.'

Most people believe that the BBC made a significant contribution to victory by carrying on with the job of broadcasting. Nearly one-third of the BBC's pre-war staff went into the Forces or other war-related work. Twenty-three were taken prisoner of war; eighty-two were killed on active service or as a result of enemy action. Those who worked for the organization did not shrink from doing their bit for their country in the more conventional manner when called upon to do so.

Bricked up, sandbagged and sentried, the foyer of Broadcasting House still manages to retain some of its art-deco splendour. Bicycles were just as important a means of transport in London as in the provinces.

8

REPORTING GETS IN
THE GROOVE

As soon as war was declared in September 1939, a saloon car fitted up with recording equipment was loaded on to a cross-Channel steamer at Dover. It passed through French Customs without delay and was driven to Paris, where it was hidden in a deep garage. Early in October, when the BBC was allowed to follow the British Expeditionary Force (BEF), Richard Dimbleby arrived and took possession of the car. Broadcasting had moved to the front line.

Dimbleby had established himself as the BBC's

In Town Tonight's Cecil Meehan watches engineer Kenneth Hughes edit an acetate disc on a bank of machines typical of the period.

best-known reporting voice. Early in 1939 he was the first man to go on a royal tour (of Canada) and he caused something of a stir at the end of the Spanish Civil War when he covered the retreat of the broken Republican Army at the Franco-Spanish border.

He went to France expecting, as everyone did, that the war would explode into the immediate violence that had characterized the 1914-18 conflict. Instead, little happened and, in the uneasy calm, the military authorities, unused to radio's presence, wanted to censor material almost out of existence. Dimbleby had his share of problems with the BBC, too, which was moving cautiously and not yet consistently into direct news reporting: it carried the sounds of a German air-raid on the Firth of Forth, but was unwilling to allow a recording of Maginot Line guns.

Dimbleby reported the King's inspection of the troops and their positions, and the decoration of the British Generals Gort and Ironside by the French Commander-in-Chief Gamelin, amid much Gallic kissing. The weather worsened. Dimbleby moved about the front; once, in the Jura Mountains, he recorded a march-past of the band of the Chasseurs Alpins at 6 a.m. in a blinding snowstorm. From time to time the mobile unit went to Rheims where fellow reporter Charles Gardner was with the Advanced Air Striking Force. In temperatures as low as -40° Fahrenheit, frost patterns formed on the blank discs and the engineer took them to bed so that he would be able to record on them in the morning.

THE DEVELOPMENT OF OUTSIDE BROADCASTING

The BBC was slow to develop on-the-spot reporting. The newspapers fought the development of the infant medium's news service and the BBC was embarrassingly cautious in taking them on; during the twenties its coverage went little beyond limited news bulletins. Technology, as so often happens, changed the rules of the game. In 1931 came the Blattnerphone, a device which recorded magnetically on to a large reel of steel tape at 3 feet a second. Although prone to snapping with a nasty twang, steel-tape transformed broadcasting for programme-makers, who were relieved of the pressure of having to produce every programme live. The effect on news was minimal, but at least some possibilities were opened up. In 1935, while it experimented with several Continental recording systems, the BBC moved to disc-recording on machines rather like gramophone players which cut grooves on acetate-covered aluminium discs that were instantly ready for playing, without the elaborate intermediate process involved in making gramophone records.

The following year the BBC converted a laundry van, fitting it with a small studio and twin turntables that could be used in tandem to make a continuous recording. Weighing 6 tons fully laden, it was subject to a 20 m.p.h. speed limit and was difficult to manoeuvre in narrow streets. Dimbleby and Charles Gardner, the News department's

BBC chauffeur Marshall Raper sleeps beside an old-fashioned steel-tape Blattnerphone which was pressed back into service during the war to free newer machines for the vital business of news coverage.

roving reporters (at first called 'mobile topicality assistants' so as not to upset the newspapers, and later 'BBC observers'), begged for something speedier and more tractable. In 1939, months before the outbreak of war, several saloon cars were converted. There was room in them only for a single turntable, which limited a recording to four minutes. But the equipment could work off a 12-volt accumulator and its output could be fed back from any telephone line or, less reliably, short-wave transmitter. While it was bulky, it was compact enough to be man-handled where the vehicle could not go. When Dimbleby went to the Maginot Line, the equipment was set up on a truck on the miniature railway system that ran through the underground forts.

In the spring of 1940, there seemed more likelihood of action in the Middle East than in France and Dimbleby sailed for Cairo. Bernard Stubbs, who had transferred to News from Outside Broadcasts to cover the Royal Navy, went out to GHQ, where he was joined by Edward Ward. Dimbleby was hardly over the horizon when the Germans launched their offensive. The BBC recording car accompanied the British Army as it fought its way to Brussels and beyond, then back to Lille, Arras, Amiens. Stubbs and Ward got some recordings out through Boulogne and talked live from

Paris, before making their escape, Stubbs directly from the French capital, Ward through Bordeaux. Stubbs was home in time to describe the return of the bloodied and exhausted troops at Dover:

BBC correspondent Robin Duff (with recording engineers A.R.Phillips and L.F.Lewis) back at 'bomb alley' during a raid on Dover in August 1940.

> It was astounding to walk along carriage after carriage of soldiers and to find in each one silence, for most of the men were fast asleep where they sat. In the dining cars they sat, most of them, with their heads on the tables or on pillows improvised out of their equipment. Train after train passed out of the station, all full of sleeping men. All the way along the line the people of England stood at the level crossings and in the background to wave. And so the men of the BEF came home.

Shortly afterwards Stubbs enlisted in the Navy. He lost his life when HMS *Hood* was sunk in May 1941.

A second recording car had gone to support Gardner at Rheims, in France. He had it camouflaged and then took it to within 85 feet of the enemy front line. On another occasion, a Heinkel dropped a 500-pound bomb so close to him that the equipment which he was using from the vehicle was thrown up into the air, destroying his recording. But he did capture on disc the first sounds of falling bombs which listeners ever heard. And then he, too, high-tailed it out of France.

Back with his recording car in July 1940, Gardner recorded the most sensational eye-witness account of the war to be made before El Alamein more than two years later. The Battle of Britain had begun and Gardner went to Dover to see what he could find. The mobile unit had just taken up position when a convoy steaming slowly up the Channel was attacked by German dive-bombers supported by fighters, and an RAF squadron went up to meet them. The coastal batteries had already opened up. Gardner, leaning on the rail looking out to sea, described it all:

> We've just hit a Messerschmitt! Oh! that was beautiful… He's come down, he's coming down like a rocket now. Absolute nose-dive. I'm trying to move round so I can watch him a bit more… looking for the parachute – no, the pilot's not getting out of that one… There's another. I don't know whether he's down or whether he's trying to get out of the anti-aircraft guns which are giving him a very hard time… Oh! darn, they've turned away, I can't see, I can't see… One, two, three, oh! whoops! there's a dog-fight going on up there, five, six machines wheeling and turning… Yes! they're being chased home, and how they're being chased home! Three Spitfires chasing three Messerschmitts now. Oh boy! Look at them going! That is really grand! And there's a Spitfire just behind the first two. He'll get them! Oh yes! Oh boy! I've never seen anything as good as this!

Already at heart a member of the RAF, in which he shortly became a pilot, Gardner was so worked up that his account was virtually a sports commentary, delivered above the sounds of the bombs being dropped on the convoy, the engines, the anti-aircraft guns, the excited voices of the gunners. Passed by the censors, part of it was broadcast in the nine o'clock news and it created a controversy. Some people felt it trivialized life-or-death combat. Others objected to the tally-ho language (though in truth it was the language that the RAF itself used) and yet others disliked what they thought was gloating: 'You've got him. Pump it into him. Pop-pop-pop – Oh boy, oh boy, he's going down!' One retired major-general wrote to *The Times* saying the broadcast was an insult to a civilized society. Most of the newspapers thought it quite brilliant and Gaumont British Movietone secured the film rights. Frank Gillard found 'Gardner's "gotcha" approach' both exciting and acceptable and points out: 'There was no agreed technique for reporting this kind of conflict.'

In the USA, the commentary was heard on *Radio News Reel* and the Americans asked for a recording. But a programme entitled *London After Dark* caused a sensation when it was heard in the States. A round-up of various points in the capital had been arranged, including shelters and railway stations. The sirens sounded just as the broadcast was timed to begin and as Michael Standing reported from under the glass roof of Waterloo Station, and Wynford Vaughan Thomas chatted on the steps of a

church, the bombs, the guns and all the sounds of a
bad raid were captured. Shrapnel even tinkled on
Vaughan Thomas's mike. The Houses of Parliament
were damaged, witnessed by Robin Duff.

The BBC had increased the number of its reporters in London and other cities once the Blitz enveloped the country. The regions were equipped with
recording cars or vans as well as with secret lists of
transmitters and telephone lines; if the Germans had
succeeded in landing and occupying parts of the
country, the BBC's intention would have been to go
on broadcasting from wherever it could. The mobile
units went to dockyards, hospitals, munition factories and the bombed-out streets. One car went back
to the cliffs of Dover, to record the long-range guns
firing shells into the port from across the Channel,
and was machine-gunned by a Messerschmitt.
Removed from the vehicles, the recording gear was
taken out in destroyers and minesweepers, down in
submarines, up in planes. The microphone went to
the people: to the farmers who apprehended Rudolf
Hess in Scotland; to the Clyde bankman who boiled
the baby's milk on a spent incendiary; to the woman
in the south of England who answered her door in the
middle of the night and found a German airman who
thought he was in Holland.

L.F. Lewis sees to the controls of the recording
car equipment.

By 1941, ninety news-talks a month were being broadcast, many of them
eye-witness accounts from the correspondents in the far-flung theatres of war.
Without mobile recording, none of this type of reportage would have been possible.
And yet the BBC seemed to regard material recorded in the field as being in some
way inferior, not only to live broadcasts but to recordings made in the studio. What
it described as 'this travelling equipment' was, the *BBC Handbook* of 1942 stated, 'at
moments of emergency … an invaluable assistant. But, of course, the majority of
news-talks are either spoken directly to the listener through the microphone, or they
are recorded at one of the stations of the BBC. (If they are recorded, the listener is
always so informed.)'

One can assume that by 1943 the attitude had changed. The number of
disc recordings had risen to 5000 a week – and that went up to 7000 during
D-Day week in 1944.

OUR MAN IN ...

By the end of the war, a handful of correspondents had become as famous as the news-readers at home. Edward Ward might have been one of them – except that for three years he was a prisoner-of-war having been, in his words, 'put in the bag' in the Western Desert.

Ward, the Viscount of Bangor's diffident and debonair heir, was an announcer in September 1939. When it was his turn to spend the long night-shift in Broadcasting House, standing by in case the invasion came, he sat drawing exotic Chinese characters. He already felt that announcing was a dead-end job and when he was asked to go to Bristol he talked his way into being made a correspondent. At the end of November, Russia attacked Finland where it wanted a small but strategically important area of the Karelian isthmus and the Hango peninsula as a naval port. The established names were tied up elsewhere and Ward got his big chance, becoming the first radio reporter to send back live dispatches from a front line, through a local Finnish station.

The Finns had no hope of holding out, but before they conceded after four months, they inflicted great losses on the enemy in the wastes of the eastern boundary. Ward sent this report from Suomussalmi, where two Russian divisions lay dead in the snow:

> Never, I should think, has there been such a scene of frozen horror since the retreat of Napoleon's grand army from Moscow, and even that cannot anywhere have been so concentrated. Some of the best war material had been taken away, but the bodies were there – the ground was far too hard for them to be buried – they were there in their thousands, frozen as hard as stone in the ghastly attitudes in which they had fallen. There was a terrifying unreality about these bodies. Somehow they didn't look human. The terrific cold had made them look like rather badly executed waxworks. They were a curious brown colour and when, once, I stumbled and hit a dead man's hand, his finger snapped off as if it had been plaster. The bodies were everywhere: on the sides of the road, in the makeshift shelters and dug-outs where they had tried to escape the relentless fury of the Finnish ski patrols.

When Dimbleby transferred to North Africa, Ward went to France, treating himself to lunch at Maxim's in a deserted Paris before beating his retreat. The next guests, that evening, were the German General Staff.

Ward now hot-footed after Dimbleby and spent an eventful eleven months in the Western Desert, which Bob Crawford remembers all too well. Crawford, who was in the Seventh Armoured Division fitting radios in tanks, was assigned to Ward as his engineer. 'He had to be top boy, he had to be there and the first with the news, and he pressed on regardless,' Crawford says.

There were times we went out on the desert with a vehicle that shouldn't have been off the tarmac. There was one occasion when he wanted to get to this particular unit and we followed the telephone wires which should have led to them, except we met a signals unit vehicle coming in the other direction, rolling the wires in. Now the sensible thing to do would have been to go back to the starting point, but Ward reckoned that we were fairly close so on we went. We went 10 miles, 15 miles, another 15: and now we were in trouble because we were at a barbed wire fence and the posts with the death's head on them; we were either in a minefield or the other side of a minefield. It got dark so we bedded down. The next morning, looking over this little hill, we could see a sandbag enclosure with anti-aircraft guns. But we hadn't a clue if we were in front of our own troops or what. So we put our hands up and walked forward. Luckily they were British and we got breakfast. Another thing about Eddie, he had no understanding that there were technical limitations. We were running two 12-volt car batteries and, of course, they had to be charged up regularly. We always had to find a signals station or RAOC depot for that. He absolutely fumed about the delay.

May 1941: Richard Dimbleby records the Battle of Keren while under shell fire.

Five times during the Desert War, Tobruk changed hands. On 18 November 1941, knowing that a push to win it back for the second time was about to be launched, Ward and Crawford drove through a gap in the Italian-laid wire and struck out with the long-range desert group. Crawford went reluctantly: 'When I was with Seventh Armoured Div. I accepted, as a soldier, that I might be killed. I was less keen to risk my life for the news. Eddie, now, he'd have died for the BBC.'

Days later, the enemy came in behind them, cutting them off. Like the troops, the BBC men dug in. Crawford, with deadpan humour, asked the shovelling Ward whether this was the scoop he was after. Under bombardment, they kept recording, cutting their last disc on Sunday, 23 November. They handed it in to the armoured command vehicle, the divisional HQ. Crawford knew they were only going through the motions. Shortly after, the vehicle was shot up. Then someone shouted: 'The tanks are coming – we're OK.' Says Crawford: 'He was right, the tanks were coming. But I'm afraid they had big black crosses on their sides. It was the Twenty-first Panzers.'

The British surrendered. The Germans took their watches and other valuables, including Ward's camera. Ward, who spoke fluent German, said something which caused a stir and Crawford asked what he had said. Ward replied: 'I asked him for a receipt.'

REPORTING ON THE DESERT WAR

Dimbleby's war in the desert had become as unsatisfactory as it had been in France. At first, his dispatches were well received. He risked his life, lying on an exposed plateau with shells falling all around him, to record the guns at Tobruk; he used his microphone under the very noses of German and Italian snipers. And he scored a number of triumphs outside Egypt, notably in the Abyssinian campaign in which he covered the return to Addis Ababa of Haile Selassie, who had been removed from power by the Axis. He also went to watch the Italians being kicked out of Albania by the Greek Army and the humiliating retreat from Greece of the British, who lost all their equipment. But his later reports from the Desert War were criticized for over-optimism and he was accused of allowing himself to be manipulated by the High Command. He was recalled to London.

The full-scale invasion of Germany from the West began with the crossing of the Rhine on the night of 23–24 March 1945. Richard Dimbleby (with engineer Bob Wade, left) flew in one of the 'tugs' that towed in the gliders of the 6th British and the 17th US Airborne Divisions.

In January 1943, Dimbleby became the first correspondent to fly on a bombing raid to Berlin. He was in the air for eight-and-a-half hours and shot at for six-and-a-half of them. The Air Ministry was so slow in clearing his report for broadcast that the Germans had already bombed London in reprisal for the raid by the time his report was on-air. In the September, Wynford Vaughan Thomas went on another raid, noting how his voice slurred when he moved about under oxygen and memorably recording the conversation of the Lancaster crew as they came in over Stetten to attack the German capital. When the bombs were released, his recording engineer, Reginald Pidsley said, 'it was like going up in a lift' and the cutting head dug into the disc.

For both Godfrey Talbot who replaced him in North Africa, and Frank Gillard who followed Talbot, Dimbleby was largely the victim of circumstance. With Ward's capture he was alone in trying to cover the war and he felt he had to base himself at GHQ in Cairo. 'Every war reporter has to make a decision as to whether he is going to report on things that he has seen with his own eyes, or whether he will report on information which he has gleaned from Army headquarters,' says Gillard. 'There's an argument in favour of both. Poor Richard again and again was caught out on-air with information which was either inaccurate, because he'd been wrongly briefed, or else was already hopelessly out of date. And his prestige and his standing with the troops was greatly diminished.'

Gillard agrees that Dimbleby was 'a little too fond' of hob-nobbing with the generals. 'But it pays to hob-nob with the generals to some extent. The great thing is you must hob-nob with the lower ranks too. You need to be able to talk to the troops, to tell them what's happening on their right flank, their left flank, what the tittle-tattle is. I learnt from Richard's mistakes and I did that. He was a pioneer; pioneers make mistakes.'

'Richard was as brave as a lion,' says Talbot. 'He didn't get up to the front as he'd have liked to have done because we needed a man in Cairo. The trouble was the nature of the Desert War, advance, retreat, the situation swinging from moment to moment. The beautifully Sam-Browne-belted chaps at GHQ, the "gabardine swines" as they were called, wouldn't have given him so much duff information if they'd been in the desert with the battle-soaked warriors.'

Talbot, who had got out of the Broadcasting House newsroom to look after news-talks and covered wartime Britain with the mobile units, reached Cairo on 2 August 1942. He was wearing soldier's khaki, his shoulder flashes said 'British War Correspondent' and his green cap-badge was inscribed with a golden C. It had taken him six weeks to get there, on a merchant ship via West Africa and by a series of hops in a sea-plane across the Congo and Uganda. If he were taken prisoner-of-war, he was told, he would have the privileges of a major.

MONTY'S WAR

Talbot stayed in Cairo only until Army workshops had converted a 30-hundredweight truck into a recording studio and living quarters. Then, in a staff car driven by an RASC private assigned to him, with another behind the wheel of the truck, he and his engineer, 'Skipper' Arnell, went into the desert, accompanied by a liaison officer from Middle East public relations.

There was little fighting to be recorded. Having licked the Italians in Libya and swept far beyond Benghazi (over which Ward had made a recording in a plane), the Eighth Army had been pushed back by the Germans to within 70 miles of Alexandria and was now making a last-ditch stand behind the mine-strewn sands of the Alamein Line, which was 35 miles wide. By the time this Empire force of Britons, Aussies, New Zealanders, South Africans, Indians and others had dug itself in, it was badly

Monty at Alamein. The first general to be able, via radio, to speak to all his men, Montgomery believed in the BBC as part of his army's 'crusading spirit'.

dispirited. It had no faith in the commanders it hardly knew and it harboured a growing conviction that Rommel was invincible. But Talbot found a new mood taking hold, thanks to a new general who had arrived in Egypt at about the same time as himself. Bernard Law Montgomery, who believed that morale was the greatest single factor in battle, had 'come out like a fire rocket'.

'He used to say that in the First World War he had never seen the top brass and he was determined that in his Army his troops would know him,' says Talbot. 'If they had confidence in their Supreme Commander they would fight and win, whatever the circumstances. But in order to have that confidence, they had to know him. So he got around more than any other general had ever done before, stopping to talk to the men, spreading out a map to show the state of the battle, throwing cigarettes from his jeep. And when the Australians gave him a bushwhacker's hat, he wore it; when he was given a black beret by the Tank Corps, he wore that. His cockiness, his uncompromising enthusiasm of purpose, was infectious.'

Later, perhaps, Montgomery became too enthusiastic about broadcasting as a means to an end – and was told so by Frank Gillard who took over from Talbot in the last months of the desert campaign. But through the power of the BBC he became the

156

first general in history who was able to speak to all his troops. Says Gillard: 'Generals used to say that in war you only tell the public when it's beginning and, when it's over, who's won – that's all they need to know. Monty never took that view and increasingly he saw broadcasting as the fourth arm of warfare, after the Services. His Army was his first concern, but he used to say to me "I'm also talking to the wives and fathers and mothers and sisters back home, and they'll trust me too. And that will be reflected in the letters they write to their men out here."'

Talbot was lucky in having Montgomery, a general who not only believed in publicity but who lived permanently among his troops. He was also lucky in that the combatants in the coming decisive battle were squaring up from static positions. He was able to go up and down the line on the wide, stony plain, seeking out infantry command posts and forward batteries; men lived in holes like the desert rats after which they were named. They were, he remembers, the same colour as their surroundings, their faces the same khaki as their shirts and shorts. Often he would recce in the staff car before bringing up the recording truck, which was affectionately known as 'Belinda'. She was large and fat and friendly-looking, but she was too conspicuous for the really advanced positions and once the Battle of El Alamein started – and in the months that followed – the BBC were on occasions told to 'Get that bloody thing back!'

If he typed a story before recording it, Talbot could make any amendments demanded by the field

Godfrey Talbot (centre) with his recording truck in the background. 'Belinda's' sides pulled out to provide extra accommodation.

censor. If he had recorded directly on to disc and something was regarded as being dangerous to security, the censor defaced the recording which was thereby lost, unless it could be done again, which was frequently impossible. Self-censorship was critical. Even when a disc was passed, Talbot's difficulties were not over – a dispatch rider or, with a bit of luck, a plane, had to be found to take it back to the Egyptian State Broadcasting studios in Cairo to be beamed to London.

On one occasion Talbot found himself in trouble with the peppery, sharp-nosed little General who listened to the BBC's Overseas Service in his caravan. It was night and Talbot was asleep under Belinda when he was shaken awake: the Army Commander wanted to see him.

'I got up and dragged something on. We were quite near, only a short walk from Monty's caravan. And there was Monty, sitting on the edge of his bed, saying "Talbot, sit down, sit down. The BBC is saying my men, my soldiers, are having a lull. Nothing about what they're doing on night patrol, nothing about our preparations, nothing about the Desert Air Force combating the bombers. Are they using your stuff, Talbot?" I said, 'Well, some of my stuff. And some of it's simply the communiqués issued by your headquarters and your intelligence officers, going through Cairo to London." "Well," he said, "it won't do. Tell London it won't do. Tell them that the Army Commander has heard them and they're not giving a true picture." I said, "I'll try and put the picture right, sir." And indeed I did.'

Talbot will never forget the sight of Churchill when the Prime Minister came to visit Montgomery, whom he had taken away from the defence of the south-east of England to put him in charge in North Africa. 'Churchill was wearing one of those siren suits, those romper suits, that he used to wear during the Blitz. He must have been rather hot in Egypt. On his head he had a sola topi which he must have worn in the Sudan when he was a young soldier, long ago. He had moccasins on his feet with "WSC" embroidered on each foot. He was carrying a sunshade. And yet, you know, he looked formidable, not a laughable figure at all.'

Talbot tried to interview Churchill, producing a microphone from behind his back, but he was met with a curt 'Let us dispense with this device'; Churchill would never be interviewed, not even after the war. But he did record a message, which was released for broadcast when he was back in England. After making it he remarked that the desert was 'miles and miles of arid austerity. How Stafford Cripps would like this!'

Montgomery's first desert victory was in August 1942 at the Battle of Alam-el-Haifa, where he threw back Rommel's attempt to crash through with his armour. The Battle of El Alamein began at 9.40 p.m. on 23 October 1942, Monty telling the gathering of war correspondents that he was now ready to 'hit the enemy for six'. Listeners to both the Home Service and the Forces Programme heard Talbot's recording of the General's clipped briefing to his commanding officers:

In a visit to North Africa in June 1943, Churchill takes off his hat to men of the RAF and the Army, after addressing them in the ancient amphitheatre of Carthage.

Here we will stand and fight. There will be no further withdrawal. I have ordered that all plans and instructions dealing with further withdrawal are to be burnt, and at once. We will stand and fight here. If we can't stay here alive, then let us stay here dead.

I want to impress on everyone that the bad times are over, they are finished. Our mandate from the Prime Minister is to destroy the Axis forces in North Africa. I have seen it, written on half a sheet of notepaper. It can be done, and it will be done, beyond any possibility of doubt.

What I have done is to get over to you the atmosphere in which we will now work and fight. You must see to it that this new atmosphere permeates right down through the Eighth Army, right down to the most junior private soldier. The great point to remember is that we are going to finish with this chap Rommel once and for all.

Now, my forecast of this battle is that there will be three definite stages. First, the break-in to the enemy's positions. Then the dog-fight. And then the break-out....

I believe that the dog-fight battle will become a hard killing match and will last for ten or twelve days. The enemy will crack. Then will come the break-out, and that will lead to the end of Rommel in Africa. Make no mistake about that.

The battle gave Talbot some of the most historic recordings of the war. On the first night, he captured the sound of 1000 guns along a 6-mile front laying down an opening barrage of such ferocity that the desert heaved and many of the discs Arnell tried to cut were spoilt because the pick-up arm bounced and dug into the soft acetate. Twelve days later, in line with Montgomery's prediction, the tanks bored a hole through the German defences. Talbot's report spoke of a fog of sand thrown up by the moving armour. In fact, to capture the sound of the squadrons rumbling forward, he was standing out in the fog, unable to see anything, judging where the vehicles were by their creaks and squeaks. Several times he had to jump for his life and his microphone cable, connected to Belinda by several hundred feet of cable, was cut in two.

On 4 November, the BBC news began with a communiqué from Cairo: the Axis forces were in full retreat. On 10 November Churchill made a broadcast which began:

Rommel is in retreat from El Alamein, but British troops approach these abandoned vehicles keeping an eye out for snipers.

I have never promised anything but blood, tears, toil and sweat. Now, however, we have a new experience: we have victory.... A bright gleam has caught the helmets of our soldiers.... This is not the end. It is not even the beginning of the end. But it is perhaps the end of the beginning.

Rommel continued his flight west, pursued by the Eighth Army and Belinda. Tobruk fell on 14 November and the sound of the Tobruk church bell was heard in Britain – where the church bells rang out in celebration of El Alamein. Denis Johnston, the Irish playwright who had been in television before the war and who had come out to help Talbot, made the broadcasts, when he was not stalking about the desert in a German officer's greatcoat. Just before Christmas, Talbot recorded some soldiers singing Christmas carols to a clarinet accompaniment and ended his report: 'There may be a few extra things coming from NAAFI, but for the most part it will be a Christmas of bully beef, biscuits and sand. But they'll be thinking of home and I hope that all of you will be thinking of them.'

Talbot returned for a spell in Cairo after that and then went elsewhere in the Middle East. Gillard took over from him and went on with Monty. By the time of the German surrender in Tripoli in May 1943, Cairo was 1500 miles away and getting his recordings back was 'one hell of a job' for Gillard. Even so, material was generally on the air in England within twenty-four hours. In the last three months of the Tunisian fighting the problem eased. The Eighth Army linked up with General Anderson's First, which came in from the west, accompanied by the BBC's Robert Dunnett and Howard Marshall; after that, the discs went through Algiers.

REPORTING IN ITALY

Gillard accompanied the Eighth Army through the bloody thirty-eight-day campaign in Sicily, then went back to Tripoli to go with the Fifth Army to Italy. For four days the Army's open assault landing craft were bombed, but spirits were lifted, just before Salerno was reached, by the radio news of the Italian surrender. Then, when the Fifth believed its arrival was unopposed, it ran into the murderous fire of the Germans who had occupied the artillery positions.

While the British and American armies were pinned down on a narrow strip of beach, Gillard asked the American Army Commander, Mark Clark, for his view of the situation. 'The only time I feel depressed about the situation is when I listen to your goddamn BBC,' replied Clark. 'Your BBC insists in reporting the German communiqué that they're going to push us off this beach. You think of the effect of that on my soldiers who are listening and wondering if it's true.'

Gillard, who had arrived only with a typewriter (there was no room in the crammed boats for his recording gear) told the huge and intimidating General that he had no means of refuting the Germans. Clark immediately gave him time on his own radio to transmit 200 words direct to the War Office. The transmission not only went to the BBC but was released by the Ministry of Information to the Press. Gillard was given the same access daily – and Clark found him a radio set, which was probably torn out of a tank, so that he could monitor what the BBC was saying.

In December 1943, what the BBC was saying from Italy involved Gillard in a curious conflict with General Alexander, the Commander-in-Chief of the Army Group.

The incident started with a message delivered by motorcycle dispatch, telling Gillard to report for dinner at the General's headquarters at Bari. Going there meant a 200-mile drive in an open jeep across the bleak Apennines, which was no joke in the middle of a freezing winter; but Gillard went, wondering what was wrong. After a congenial dinner in the mess, he was invited into Alexander's office – and asked how it was that the BBC was reporting what was happening on Clark's and Montgomery's fronts before the information was received at headquarters. Gillard replied that all his dispatches were censored and passed through the proper channels and he could only suggest that there was something wrong with the Army's communications. Alexander took Gillard's breath away by saying: 'No, no, that can't be the answer. You're beating the gun. And you can only do that if you've got a secret transmitter.'

Gillard insisted on an inquiry, Alexander informed Brendan Bracken, the Minister of Information, and William Haley – who had just joined the BBC as editor-in-chief and was recovering from pernicious anaemia – was sent out to investigate. In the meantime, Gillard had put together enough of his reports, stamped by the censor and the communication people, to prove that they had been transmitted legitimately. In half an hour Haley demolished the case. Alexander shook Gillard's hand. 'But it was a very unusual experience for a war correspondent,' he observes.

Talbot got to the Italian war early in 1944. He should have been covering the fighting in Burma but, having been called back to London the previous October, he went down with an infection that kept him off-duty for two months; it was small comfort that a fellow Yorkshireman, Richard Sharp, got the assignment. At one time or another, seven or eight correspondents contributed to the BBC's Italian coverage as the Allies made painful progress up the peninsula against the twenty-eight divisions thrown in by Kesselring; Italy was no longer the soft underbelly that Churchill had referred to. For six months Cassino stopped the advance to Rome, the Germans holding the heights in and around the Benedictine monastery on the hill 2000 feet above the town. To his dying day, Gillard will be able to close his eyes and picture the scene: 'This enormous, almost bottomless chasm in the mountain range, with the little town down on the northern slope and the great towering ridges and peaks of the Apennine mountains rearing themselves up to an immense height – and on the top of one of those peaks, the golden abbey of Monte Cassino.... In military terms it was almost impregnable. No vehicles or tanks could get up there. The infantry had to scale the heights. And my main memory is of the dreadful carnage as one division after another of crack troops was hurled at this almost impossible barrier.'

General Alexander once again invited Gillard to his headquarters, now based at Caserta, and then, over a friendly lunch produced a document. It was from the Pope, addressed to the commanders-in-chief on both sides: 'I write to notify you that the abbey of Monte Cassino is Vatican property and therefore is neutral ground. I trust you will respect it accordingly.'

'What do I make of this?' Alexander asked. 'All my men, hundreds of thousands of them down there, believe that every movement they make is being observed by the enemy located in that abbey – it's an observation post to control their attacks on our positions. Shall I destroy it or shan't I?' Gillard's advice was that the abbey should be allowed to stand. Alexander ordered it to be bombed. 'And', Gillard says, 'it remained just as much an obstacle after its destruction as ever it was before.'

The abbey was taken on 18 May 1944. It was left to Talbot to make one of the most poignant broadcasts of the entire war. Having filed an earlier and fairly brief, dispatch, he reached the abbey with his recording gear after an exhausting two-hour climb. Two newspaper reporters had been blown to pieces by trip-wire mines as the party of war correspondents edged through the rubble which had once been Cassino town.

A phase in the bloody battle of Monte Cassino. Allied artillery concentrates its fire on a small stronghold of Germans at mid-slope. The town is already destroyed. Still the Allied Command is reluctant to sacrifice the abbey...

… as for today's taking of the great Abbey of Monte Cassino on Monastery Hill, this was an enormously hard-won triumph for Polish troops against an enemy from whom they had suffered much. In the mountain height to which the Poles broke to get round the back of the ruined monastery fortress, fighting had been severe in the extreme. Men fought till they dropped, dropped exhausted or dropped killed or wounded.... The Poles were counter-attacked time after time when they gained a height and there was no way up to the hill positions except by mule and finally on foot. Always the supply, ammunition and water parties had to go up through heavy German fire. In many positions you could by day remain alive only in a hole in the ground. To show yourself and move in daylight in these awful positions was death....

As we wound our way higher, the number of rotting mule corpses increased. There were bodies of soldiers lying around, too, bodies hurriedly covered with blankets weighted down with stones. Enemy fire day and night had made it impossible to get to

The Allies march into Rome, 5 June 1944. Godfrey Talbot speaks to the rapturous crowd.

these corpses and bury them. There on the mountainside, the stench of dead men and animals was strong and sickening. Near the forward positions we passed infantry resting for a few moments under a bank. Their clothes were black with sweat. They were examining their feet – the rocky trails are cruel to them.... The high wall of the abbey's west front was still standing. Only that: the rest was just a pile of stone. That was all that remained of this famous religious house and seat of learning in this the last act of its 1400 years of history....

... a Polish soldier, with whom I'd been climbing for the last 3 miles, showed me why he had been carrying four wooden posts, each about 10 feet long, made to slot into one long staff, for he and others were now scrambling with great difficulty up a mound to the highest point of the rubble, and there, on top of the ruined abbey ... in a moment the red and white Polish flag fluttered out against the sky. And then the Union Jack was put up beside it. The Germans on neighbouring hills would be able to see those flags, I thought. At any rate, when we were leaving the abbey soon afterwards, mortar bombs began to drop near....

You could see what a fortress the place was, commanding on all sides. But only these few small rooms were remaining. No great halls, no libraries, no seminary, no courts, no cloisters, everything flat rubble. We found candles, we lit them, and we went down a ruined passage to where three wounded German parachute troops lay.... The room was a shambles and stank almost unbearably. All over the floor there were remains of food, smashed boxes, ripped up ecclesiastical robes, altar candlesticks, rifles, blankets, charred wood, mattresses, billy-cans and bullets, and bits of German uniform. The next room was in a similar state. It had shafts of sunlight coming through a narrow latticed window through a haze of dust and on to religious gilded mosaics and figures about the walls. We could see Latin inscriptions on the walls extolling saintly virtues and extolling peace. And then, worst shambles of all, there was a small chapel and on the altar there was a German soldier's bed and a pin-up, a German bathing beauty, was pasted up on the chapel wall. Also on that altar were a hand grenade, two small mortar bombs, a knife and fork and an electric iron....

I went out in the fresher air ... and there before me, far below, was the whole countryside — Route 6, the road to Rome, and the smoke-filled, embattled valleys ...

Eighteen days later, on 5 June, the Allies marched into Rome from which the Germans had withdrawn. Talbot reported the rapture of the city, the troops almost having to fight their way through the delirious crowds.

I myself have been literally pulled out of my jeep three times in the last hour, pulled out and had both my hands nearly shaken out of their sockets by handshakes, and kissed and hugged almost to suffocation point. My battledress is torn with the violence of this welcome and my jeep is half-full of roses ...

The broadcast from the first capital city of Europe to be freed swept almost all other news out of the BBC's bulletins. There was plenty of fighting, and reporting, left in Italy: Florence, Bologna, Milan – where Talbot reported finding Mussolini's corpse hanging by the heels in a petrol station. But twenty-four hours later Britain, and the rest of Europe, had forgotten Italy. The beginning of the liberation of Western Europe had arrived.

CHAPTER
9

'THIS IS THE DAY
AND THIS IS THE HOUR'

During the course of the war, newspapers were restricted to one correspondent each in any theatre of war and that did not change with D-Day. But when the Allies launched their assault on Hitler's 'Atlantic Wall', seventeen BBC correspondents sailed with the Navies, flew with the bombers, jumped with the paras, landed with the gliders and hit the beaches with the US and British Armies. How the Press complained and continued to complain, in Normandy and beyond: about the BBC's mob-handedness, about the speed with which its dispatches went back; there were even mutterings that the BBC was given the best news opportunities. How things had changed since 1939 when, in thrall to the Press barons, the corporation's news service had been token, dull and second-hand. 'In the desert and in Italy we were two or three reporters trying to be everywhere, never sure,' says Frank Gillard. 'In Normandy we were an army.'

THE WAR REPORTING UNIT BEGINS WORK

The idea of a radio commando unit took shape in the January of 1943 when Germany's surrender at Stalingrad, following its humiliation in North Africa a few months before, raised the prospect of the Second Front. The BBC began to woo the Services so that it would be able to put into action what it wanted to do and in March 1943 was presented with the opportunity to prove its point. The Military fought a mock battle, code-named Spartan, across the Thames and up beyond Oxford in order to test new methods and equipment. Two teams of BBC correspondents and engineers were allowed to accompany the opposing sides. Dispatches were recorded in the midst of the sham fighting and then sent back to Broadcasting House where they were handled, censored and edited as if for transmission against a real-time schedule.

The War Office was impressed by what it heard. But, it emphasized, if it were to allow the BBC to go to war in numbers, its correspondents had to fit into the Service landscape. That view had already been expressed by Richard Dimbleby in an internal report on Operation Spartan, in which he spoke of the need for 'a sense of military discipline and bearing'. It had angered him that the young engineer who accompanied him during the exercise not only wore his cap on the back of his head and smoked incessantly, but also called everybody from private to senior officer 'old boy'. Dimbleby wrote: 'This is a delicate point ... but recording engineers must be trained to behave like the officers whose status they assume by putting on the uniform.'

Men like Godfrey Talbot and Frank Gillard learnt the military's ways in the field. Those who now joined what was called the War Reporting Unit were on a steeper if less dangerous learning curve. In the following months a physical training instructor tuned them up for life in the front line. They were instructed in gunnery, signals, reconnaissance, aeroplane and tank recognition and map-reading. They went on assault courses and battle courses, crossed rivers on ropes, ducked under live ammunition, lived rough. Some were attached to regular Army units, finding themselves competing physically with men fifteen years their junior; Stewart MacPherson, for example, a Canadian who had joined the BBC Outside Broadcast department in 1941, trained with the Grenadier Guards. 'The compelling objective was to become a member of the Unit,' he wrote. Others were filtered among the Navy and the Air Force, picking up their jargon, getting to understand their mind set. All of them were inducted in the pitfalls of censorship and watched an intelligence officer demonstrate, with a specially made recording, how seemingly innocuous remarks could be of significant military value. And they were taught enough of the engineers' trade so that, in an emergency, they could work the recording equipment.

In the autumn of 1943, when the Supreme Headquarters of the Allied Expeditionary Forces (SHAEF) was set up and Eisenhower was appointed as Supreme Commander, there was briefly a suggestion that the BBC's plans would come to nothing. SHAEF was at first inclined to regard the BBC as merely one claimant for the limited places in the Press pool. But the BBC was quick to make clear that it was not the equivalent of an American network: it was the voice of Britain in the English-speaking world and it spoke not only to the Allied troops in every theatre of war but to the countries which the invasion was to liberate. Ike agreed that the arrangement with the BBC should stand. Perhaps there had never really been any doubt that it would. Montgomery, the man who in Africa had called the BBC a part of his Army's 'crusading spirit', had been appointed Eisenhower's Commander-in-Chief of Land Forces. 'Eisenhower endorsed the BBC's position, but Monty's influence had a lot to do with it,' Gillard says.

'D-DAY HAS COME'

The landings might have happened in 1942; supplies had been accumulated and in March that year the BBC broadcast a Navy plea for holiday snaps of the French coast to help map coastal areas; 30 000 letters arrived the following day. After the disaster of Dieppe, however, Churchill was cautious, resisting calls for the Second Front from Roosevelt and Stalin. He moved only when he was sure. 'This is the day and this is the hour,' reported one of the BBC's correspondents, Colin Wills as, about 6.30 a.m. on Tuesday 6 June 1944, he moved on a rough sea towards Gold Beach with the infantry of the Second British Army.

For days the south of England had known that the big push was about to happen. Two million men, 10 000 trucks, 3000 guns and 1500 tanks moved towards the invasion ports. On 4 June the news carried a dispatch from Gillard which began: 'England has become one vast ordnance dump and field park.' He remembers:

June, 1944: D-Day on the Normandy beaches.

'I drove 100 miles across southern England and it was incredible. Wherever you looked, literally, anywhere there was any kind of cover – in the hedgerows, in people's private gardens – there were military vehicles, trucks, ambulances, tanks, armoured cars, carriers, jeeps, bulldozers, ducks [DUKWs, amphibious landing-craft]. And, of course, there were endless columns of soldiers.

'In one place there was a bit of clear ground and there were a couple of dozen Tommies in their uniforms and their heavy boots having a knock-up game of cricket, and I couldn't help thinking of Drake and Plymouth Hoe. I hoped that the outcome of our adventure was going to be as successful as his.'

Millions knew that Operation Overlord had been launched many hours before the BBC told them. Through the night of 5 June, they had been kept awake by the roar of more than 10 000 planes taking off from the airfields, carrying with them the three British and American Airborne divisions or the 6000 tons of bombs that blasted the German coastal defences between Cherbourg and Le Havre. At 5.20 a.m. Stuart Hibberd, who had spent the night in Broadcasting House in case he was needed to read the momentous news, was awoken by the heavy drone of the endless stream of aircraft making for the coast, some with gliders swooping behind them. At 8 a.m. Freddy Allen read the bulletin, which included an item, picked up by Monitoring from German radio, that paratroops had landed in France. And then, at 9.32 a.m., John Snagge, speaking from Eisenhower's Supreme Command beneath the Senate House of London University, broke into the Home and Overseas General Forces networks with this announcement:

D-Day has come. Early this morning the Allies began the assault on the north-western face of Hitler's European fortress. The first official news came just after half-past nine when Supreme Headquarters of the Allied Expeditionary Force, usually called SHAEF from its initials, issued communiqué number one. It said: Under the command of General Eisenhower, Allied naval forces supported by strong air forces began landing Allied armies this morning on the northern coasts of France.

The first wave of BBC correspondents was already at war. MacPherson and Kent Stevenson had covered the air strikes that preceded the landings. Dimbleby had recorded the take-off of the first paratroops – among them was his colleague, Guy Byam, who jumped with them – and then had flown in a Mosquito over the Normandy beaches. The BBC's Australian, Chester Wilmot, had landed with the gliders. Others now in France were those who had come in from the sea: Wills; another BBC Canadian, Stanley Maxted, from a minesweeper; Richard North, from a landing craft; Howard Marshall – who had to half-swim ashore after his barge struck an anti-invasion mine; and Robert Dunnett, who had gone in with the First US Army. In the

The scene in mid-July, as reinforcements and supplies are landed to pursue the retreating Germans. The Press was resentful that the BBC accompanied Eisenhower's armies in such numbers.

Channel, where the greatest armada ever assembled stretched as far as the eye could see – 5300 ships, including 4000 assault and ship-to-shore craft, six battleships, twenty-two cruisers, ninety-three destroyers – Robin Duff was with the US Navy, Michael Standing and Alfred Fletcher with the Royal Navy and David Bernard with the Merchant Navy.

The first eye-witness report was heard on the one o'clock news. It came, not from a staff man, but from Air Commodore W. Helmore who had made a dawn run in a Mitchell bomber as an observer, a BBC recorder at his feet. 'I don't think I can talk to you while we're doing this job, I'm not a blinking hero,' he shouted against a colossal static storm. That evening, after concluding the nine o'clock news, Joseph McLeod announced:

War Report! Night by night at this time, this programme will bring you news from correspondents and fighting men. It will contain live broadcasts and recordings made in the field, special broadcasts from forward areas, and dispatches and expert comment – to give you the latest and fullest picture of the war on all fronts.

The programme carried the first account from the Normandy landings. An exhausted Howard Marshall, whose returning craft had capsized, throwing him into the sea for the second time, got back to the main transmission point, on a hill at Fareham near Portsmouth, to tell listeners: 'I'm sitting in my soaked-through clothes with no notes at all; all my notes are sodden – they're at the bottom of the sea …'

Elaborate arrangements had been made to cope with the return of correspondents who were not staying in France, and with the recordings made by those who were, which Service couriers ferried back by ship or plane. In some cases the BBC's permanent facilities in the coastal towns from Plymouth to Ramsgate were used; but the bulk of the traffic came through Fareham, where a small brick building standing in a field had been taken over and two wireless masts erected. Cars stood by at the ports to bring in the correspondents (American and Canadian as well as British – they were sending their stuff home via London), but there was a lot of improvisation. One correspondent hitch-hiked from Hamble, having persuaded a Wren to run him to the mainland from the Isle of Wight, where a ship's picket-boat had dropped him.

Whether a dispatch went up the line to London live or recorded, it was simultaneously re-recorded on disc and on wax cylinder for copy-typing. Next, the script was checked against the recording and then duplicated for circulation and censorship. When cuts were indicated, further re-recording was necessary.

WAR REPORT GOES INTO ACTION

On D Day, the War Reporting Unit, which thought it could handle all the material itself, was overwhelmed; the Roneo machine flooded and the secretaries were in tears. Robert Reid, a correspondent who had yet to join the Western Front, got the duplicating office to help run off the stencils. Mary Lewis, the supervisor, was still there operating the machine after midnight. 'Robert said, "What you need is a good stiff whisky,"' she recalls. 'I asked him where on earth we would get such a thing at one o'clock in the morning. He disappeared and was soon back with a hip flask. The second wave of correspondents was sleeping in BH before going out next morning and he'd sneaked in and taken the flask from one of their kitbags. We managed to get all the work finished by about 3.30 a.m. in a slightly alcoholic stupor but apparently in the right order. History doesn't relate the reaction of the correspondent who found his baggage sadly depleted!'

The BBC had carried nothing like *War Report* before. Until now, it had injected brief war dispatches into the news after the formal bulletins or given them more air-time as impromptu news-talks. None had exceeded fifteen minutes and most were less. Now the war had been given its own daily half-hour programme and that was revolutionary. So was the manner of its production. *War Report* was in the hands of a team drawn from the News and Documentary departments, who merged their techniques to splice the best of all the material they received into a fast-moving commentary that was unique. Once communications were established and the Western Front fanned out, the team was able to co-ordinate what the correspondents did, and that had never happened before, either. Before *War Report*, Broadcasting House received whatever the men in the field could get. Now the central unit, in possession of the bigger picture, was able to give briefings, could ask for specific items of coverage and get correspondents to 'version' some of their pieces for *Combat Diary*, the equivalent programme that went out on the Allied Expeditionary Forces network for those who were doing the fighting.

Up to fifteen million people in Britain listened to *War Report*: the size of audience that the nine o'clock news had commanded in the bad old days of the war. Countless millions more heard its dispatches in *Radio News Reel*, broadcast in the Overseas Service to the English-speaking world. In the United States, 725 out of 914 radio stations carried *War Report* on D-Day; by the close of the war in Europe an estimated fifteen million Americans were listening to one or more editions every week. They listened, of course, because they were concerned for their own servicemen; but they listened, too, because *War Report* shattered the American conception of reporting. Traditionally, the American news commentator went to the scene, then returned to the studio to deliver his piece. After *War Report*'s rushing blend of sound and voices torn from the events unravelling around them, studio commentaries delivered in stasis suddenly seemed contrived and lifeless.

But none of what the BBC achieved in *War Report* would have been possible without without 'The Midget'.

'THE MIDGET' HAS A MIGHTY EFFECT

It was obvious from Dimbleby's early months with the BEF that correspondents needed a truly portable recorder, and the Desert War rammed home the message. Dimbleby's recording car offered at least limited portability; Belinda, whose recording gear weighed about 450 pounds, offered none. Yet it took the BBC Research department until early 1944 to come up with something that fitted the bill.

Officially, it was called the Riverside Portable: spring-wound, with two recording positions (one to cut out background noise, the other to open up the field of sound so that the pandemonium of battle could be heard); a clip-on mike; twelve double-sided 10-inch discs slotted inside the lid, giving seventy-two minutes' worth of recording. By

The mighty Midget: it was not, as war correspondent Frank Gillard says, very reliable. But the portable recording machine brought the sounds of war into people's homes in a way that had been impossible before.

today's standards, the Midget hardly justified the diminutive. It weighed 42 pounds and must have been a bitch to hump in and out of trenches. Not only that, it was unreliable, too, working on only two out of three occasions. It had no playback facility, either, so there was no way of knowing if it had recorded. And it was fragile: when they could, the correspondents used the detachable dry battery to save wear on the wind-up handle, but breakdowns were frequent. And yet it was on a dozen or so of these machines – the first tested by Wynford Vaughan Thomas on the beach-head at Anzio three months before D-Day – that much of the final struggle for Europe was captured for all time.

Gillard's Midget was put out of action almost as soon as the ramp of his landing-craft was lowered: he tripped in the chest-high water. He had wrapped the machine in his gas cape and sealed the seams; but the first message the BBC received from him read, 'Recorder unworking'.

REPORTING FROM THE SCENE OF ACTION

The BBC had learnt a valuable lesson in the last months of the fighting in North Africa when its dispatches went out through Algiers. There, the Americans had controlled the transmitter facilities and the BBC was short-changed in using them. That was not going to happen in Europe. A week before D-Day, a quarter-kilowatt mobile transmitter, call-sign Mike Charlie Oboe, was mounted in a 3-ton truck with a power generator, amplifiers and other equipment for direct broadcasting from the beach-head. Two 5-kilowatt mobiles were crated to follow.

On the night of 17 June 1944, Mike Charlie Oboe (MCO) was landed at Arromanches in the tail-end of a heavy gale that worked itself up into the worst Channel storm for forty years and wrecked one of the two concrete Mulberry harbours which the Allies had towed in sections to Normandy. Within hours, MCO was assembled in a tent on the beach, its aerials were up and the first dispatches sent by it were already in London.

MCO arrived in the nick of time: the storm had so badly disrupted communications that the Army transmitter which the BBC had been allowed to use was now restricted to operational material only. Next day, MCO was moved to the turret of a fourteenth-century castle at Creully near Bayeux, where the shutters were kept closed to keep out the noise of the guns and the aircraft. For two weeks, the military authorities had allowed material to pass uncensored from the battle zone to England, during which period Broadcasting House was the only source of spoken news dispatches to the world. Normal censorship was now re-established. But whereas the newspapermen were going through the field censors as Talbot and his colleagues had had to do in

North Africa, here the BBC was given its own small censorship unit. It was a privilege that afforded the correspondents the chance of discussing sensitive matters freely and speedily. It was also yet another indication of the BBC's standing.

For a while the studio at Creully, with its vaulted roof, narrow slit windows and worn stone floor, was the most important communications centre in the world. An endless procession of reporters of every nationality passed through it; from here the BBC's correspondents spoke not only for the Home Service and the General Forces Programme, but broadcast at odd hours to Africa, the Pacific, the Near and Middle East; and from here Pierre Lefèvre from the BBC French section addressed his fellow-countrymen – by way of London. Montgomery, who set up headquarters in a château visible across the fields, gave the BBC a signed photograph, which hangs on the stone wall of the preserved studio to this day.

By the time the Allies had broken out of the bridge-head and prised the Germans out of Caen and St Lô, the first of the BBC's recording trucks had landed; soon the first of the more powerful transmitters, Mike Charlie Nan (MCN), was installed near Bayeux; but the speed of the hue and cry across the Seine into the Low Countries left it high and dry. In an attempt to catch

Chester Wilmot and his engineer H.F.L.Sarney among the wreckage of German radio equipment near the River Elbe in April 1945.

up with the armies, its 3-ton trucks, which towed 7-ton trailers, broke down: late September had arrived before MCN was eventually on the air near Brussels. It was left to little Mike Charlie Oboe to pursue the pursuers, hugging the Channel coast road all the way so that its weak signal might reach England. After Arnhem, when the front stabilized, *War Report* used MCN, which accompanied the British and Mike Charlie Peter, which was with the Americans. Hundreds of live broadcasts were relayed from these transmitters, besides the thousands of recorded dispatches which were often received in such good quality that they could be broadcast as they were, without waiting for the original discs to arrive by air.

There were times when the correspondents arrived ahead of the transmitters and had to improvise. On 19 September, listeners to the Belgian six o'clock news suddenly heard an English voice, Frank Gillard's, telling them – and BBC Monitoring – about the 30-mile push across Holland which had taken the British Second Army to within 7 miles of Germany itself. When Chester Wilmot reached Brussels five days later with his account of the desperate fighting for the bridge at Nijmegen, Mike Charlie Nan was out of service and nobody was listening for it. Somewhere, Wilmot found a suitcase radio that had been dropped by the RAF for the use of the Underground during the occupation and broadcast on that. The wavelength was outside the BBC's reception, but Wilmot asked anyone who was listening in Britain to ring the BBC – which many did; an Army receiving-station passed on the dispatch. By then Howard Marshall and Robin Duff had nearly finished serving a thirty-day suspension for not waiting for SHAEF approval of their copy before broadcasting the news of Paris's liberation from a city radio station. The original suspension was sixty days but this was halved when the BBC appealed on the grounds that, if the correspondents could get into Paris, so could the censors.

RUFFLED FEATHERS

There had been still earlier rows. Bogged down at Caen, under sharp criticism from Eisenhower and in danger of being sacked by Churchill, Montgomery objected to details of his offensive being broadcast in the nine o'clock news. He told Marshall that valuable information had been given to the Germans and for a while put an embargo on all news from the front. A week later he was angered when a speech he delivered to the Sixth Airborne Division was transmitted. He had not wanted it released although Wilmot, who made the recording, was not to know that. Wilmot was sent home but, almost at once, allowed to return, with Monty apologizing for the 'misunderstanding'. A more serious difficulty arose when General Omar Bradley, Commander of the US Twelfth Army Group, told a Press conference 'that the BBC had cost the lives of American soldiers by making a premature announcement closing the Falaise gap'.

Later the chief Press censor at SHAEF wrote, clearing Robert Dunnett and admitting that 'the error was one of censorship here and the BBC is entirely without fault'.

Monty caused an unintentional rift with the Americans, and dragged in the BBC, when he held a Press conference after the Battle of the Bulge had been fought and won. He had ceased to command all the ground forces on 1 September (when he was promoted to Field Marshal), but for the action against the Sixth Panzer's counter-offensive in the Ardennes during December-January, Eisenhower returned two of the six American armies to his control. Montgomery regarded the battle, in which he and his armies had driven in from the north, while General Patton in command of the other US troops had pushed up from the south, as a great example of Allied co-operation. Unfortunately, Montgomery, who was no orator, got into a tangle at his Press conference and gave the impression that he had had to take over personally to bail out the Americans because of their incompetence. Bradley received so many complaints that he took the matter to Eisenhower. By the time Churchill and Brendan Bracken had become involved, it appeared that the BBC – which had picked up the story from a news agency tape, not from one of its own correspondents – was in some way to blame for what Montgomery had said. The upshot was that the BBC was requested to give more attention to the Americans (who now had three million soldiers on the front, almost three-quarters of the total) and Gillard was detached to work with Twelfth Army Group.

TROUBLE-SHOOTING

Montgomery was unhappy at losing Gillard with whom he had a close personal relationship which had developed since their days in North Africa. The Field Marshal regarded the BBC man as his broadcasting expert – a reputation which Gillard had enhanced, a few days after the Normandy beach-head was established, by rescuing a tricky situation. Montgomery had issued one of his famous Orders of the Day but, as he also wanted it heard on the radio, he had sent for Gillard. Because his own recorder was useless, Gillard borrowed another to take to Montgomery's caravan. This broke down, Monty was aghast, and Gillard was sitting there feeling small when he suddenly spotted a red telephone on the desk, which he had not seen before: Montgomery had just been connected to the War Office.

"'Could I speak to the War Office?' He looked at me as if I was rather crazy, but he said, "Well, I suppose you could, if you like." I asked his operator to put me through and when a voice said "War Office" I said, "You've got a line to the BBC, please put me through on it." The next voice was the BBC's. I said, "This is Frank Gillard in Normandy and I'm with General Montgomery and I want a recording channel right away." Through to the recording channels. The next voice said, "Recording." I said again who I was and that I wanted a channel immediately. Sorry, I was told, every channel was occupied. I said, "One of them has got to be disconnected and switched over to me, this is vitally important." Would I take responsibility for it? asked the wretched engineer. Right then. And thirty seconds later a voice in my ear said "Go". I made a little opening announcement, handed the telephone to Monty, with the printed copy of his Order of the Day, and he read it. Then I made a little closing statement and told him, "I'll swear to you that within thirty minutes you'll hear that coming back over the air." And we did. Nowadays, telephones are used in broadcasting all the time, but nobody had used one for broadcasting before, it had never been done. Everything just clicked. Monty thought it was a marvellous trick.'

Shortly afterwards, Gillard went down with malaria, picked up in Africa. Through a feverish haze he saw one of Monty's ADCs standing by his camp bed, who told him 'the boss' was sorry to hear he was unwell, then added: 'But when you're better he wants you to get him a puppy.' Montgomery was mad about animals, as Gillard knew, but how was he supposed to do this? 'He thought you might just mention it in your next broadcast,' the ADC said.

Gillard was unable to meet the request: 'Even if my editors had allowed it, which they wouldn't, he'd have got 10 000 sent over, he'd have kept one and I'd have had to do something with the rest.' But as soon as he was well, he scoured the beach-head until, in the devastated little village of Douvres, almost under the German guns, he found a Frenchman whose fox terrier had had three pups. Buying one cost Gillard the equivalent of twenty-five pounds; a lot of money. Monty was delighted and promptly named the dog Hitler. It lived until the last day of the war when it was run over by a tank.

Initially, Gillard was as unhappy to join the Americans as Monty was at losing him, but in the three months that remained of the war in Europe, he covered the fall of Cologne, the capture of the bridges at Remagen and the Rhine, the encirclement of the Ruhr and then the link-up with the Russians at the town of Torgau on the River Elbe, where the soldiers of both sides crossed to meet each other in rowing boats paddled with reversed rifles. 'All these stories dropped into my lap, which wouldn't have happened if I'd not been at Bradley's headquarters,' he says.

Torgau, on 25 April 1945, was one of the stories of the war, the meeting of East and West, and Gillard wanted to be the first to broadcast it to the world. But three American reporters were there, too, and they disagreed with Gillard that, just because the transmitter, Mike Charlie Peter, was BBC property, he automatically had the right to go first. He says: 'I asked the Chief of Staff to give a judgement of Solomon and he ruled against me. "Everything at headquarters is held in common," he said. "When you've asked me for an aeroplane, it's been an American aeroplane I've given you, and without question. The BBC owns the transmitter, but while it's here it's common property." I went back very crestfallen and we tossed for it.'

Gillard won. At the release time of 6 p.m., he went straight into the news bulletin, live. Three hours later, *War Report* led with the dispatch, followed by messages from Churchill, Truman and Stalin. 'It was the climax of my war,' Gillard says.

East meets West in one of the historic moments of the war. The first American and Soviet troops shake hands on the wrecked bridge at Torgau. The date: 25 April 1945.

THE MAN WITH THE WHITE FLAG

Two weeks later, on 12 May, Gillard made a broadcast which he would have given anything not to have made and about which he is still emotional:

Last December we were looking for a British soldier to speak from Germany in the BBC's big, round-the-world Christmas afternoon programme, a Tommy to speak immediately before His Majesty the King gave his Christmas message.

In the end we found the very man we wanted, a Londoner, Corporal R.B. Pass of the First-Fifth Queen's Royal Regiment. He'd seen as much of the war as any man in the British Forces. In 1939-40 he fought in France. Then he went out to the Middle East to do the commando raids there. He went through the desert campaign, crossed the Mediterranean for the fighting in Italy, and then returned to England for the final campaign in north-west Europe. That was his record. We remember his broadcast.

Today, I received a letter from Pass's commanding officer, written just before the termination of hostilities in Europe. He says: 'Early yesterday morning, a German soldier approached our forward positions carrying a white flag, showing that he wished to surrender. Corporal Pass and four men went out to bring him in. When our men were well out into the open, concealed Hun opened up on them with machine-guns, killing three, including Corporal Pass, and wounding the remaining two. The man with the white flag got away ...'

WAR REPORT'S WAR

War Report lasted from D-Day until 5 May 1945, the day after the Germans surrendered. It was suspended from 4 February 1945 until the crossing of the Rhine on 23–24 March, while the Allies gathered their strength for the final assault. Twenty-seven BBC correspondents contributed to it from the Western Front, six from Italy, one each from the Balkans and Burma. Other dispatches were carried from the pick of the American and Dominion reporters and from Service observers with the talent for the job. One of these was Flight-Lieutenant Caverhill of the RAF – in fact, an ex-BBC features producer, otherwise known as the writer and wit Alan Melville.

Somewhere in Holland Stanley Maxted (with mike) makes use of a US Army Signals transmitter.

Two BBC correspondents died: Kent Stevenson was killed on a raid over north-west Germany in an RAF Lancaster on 22 June 1944, two weeks after D-Day; Guy Byam was killed on a daylight raid with the Eighth US Air Force over Berlin on 3 February 1945. Stanley Maxted was wounded when his Hamilcar glider landed in the Allies' push across the Rhine at the end of March 1945, but carried on reporting:

There was an explosion that appeared to be inside my head. The smell of burnt cordite. I went down on one knee. Something hot and sickly was dripping over my right eye and off my chin and all over my clothes.... I saw my pal, Peter Cattell, lying on one elbow, with blood making a spiderweb over his face. One of the men was on the floor, staring fixedly at nothing, as one of his legs, rigid in front of him, was quivering in convulsions.

All told, there were 235 War Reports, comprising about 1500–2000 dispatches. Some were significant, some less so; all were produced without time to think or to polish. And yet they amount to an oral history, a testimony, which was studded through with anger and compassion and even some humour, as well as a wealth of observation.

A solitary peasant harrowing his field behind his horse near the D-Day battle-front, 'looking nowhere but before him at the soil'; a dead paratroop 'laid out on a bed in the best bedroom, covered from head to foot with local flowers'; the chaffinches in the branches as Montgomery read the lesson at an outdoor service; the people in Chartres cathedral singing through their tears; the Dutch, lacking wood, 'making paper coffins and stacking them in churches'; the Nazi flag laid on the deliberately narrowed road into Dieppe so that the Allies were 'obliged to drive right over the Swastika and trampled it in the dust' – *War Report* teemed with a thousand transient moments captured in the BBC Sound Archive for all time.

It would be impossible to make a brief selection of dispatches that truly represented *War Report*. But here are nine, chosen because each is the work of a different correspondent and because each says something different about the final phase of the Second World War or, at least, its European theatre.

12 AUGUST 1944

Pierre Lefèvre of the BBC French section visited a town where he had relatives:

When I got into Granville, I drove down towards the harbour where an uncle of mine had a ship's chandler's shop. I enquired about it from the people on the corner as I waited in the traffic queue. 'You've been away four years, haven't you, my boy?' said a woman, her eyes filling with tears. 'Well, your uncle died a year ago; and your cousin – he died in an air-raid by the RAF only last week.' As I went round the town, gay and happy to be free, the same sad tale of death met me everywhere. My father's cousins – four of them – had all died. They were getting on in years, but privations and worry had hastened their deaths. Many of the young people I'd known were not back from Germany, they were still in the Stalags. Others had been deported to Germany in the past two years, slaves for the German war machine. The leader of the Resistance movement, a quiet, philosophical old professor of English at the local school, had been found cudgelled and full of Tommy-gun bullets in a field seven days before the liberation he'd worked so hard to bring about.

I found an aunt of mine in the street. She wept with joy, took me home, and after all the excitement and kissing was over, she still had to cook on a little fire of charcoal in the backyard – they'd been blitzed out of their house some weeks ago. My uncle still had to count the slices before he cut the bread, still they had no electricity, no gas, no candles either; but they don't worry about these things any longer. They think of the future; the conversation turns continually to the subject of rebuilding, of reorganizing. The main topic is the prisoners – do they know their fathers, their mothers, their wives, their children, are safe and free? Each family, remember, has a prisoner or deportee in Germany. They talk also of the people in the large towns – Paris, the industrial cities of the north, who write such pathetic letters asking always for food.

I asked: 'How's my cousin so-and-so?' 'Didn't you know?' they say. 'He was arrested six months ago and taken to Paris as a hostage. He's been shot.'

Yes, you see, when the great, deep joy of the first hours of liberation has passed, the hardships of war, both physical and moral, are still there.

21 AUGUST 1944

Frank Gillard, the backbone of the War Report team and probably the most prolific correspondent, witnessed the remnants of the German Seventh Army:

The road from Falaise to Argentan runs straight as a line across rolling country; driving down it this morning we came over the brow of a hill and there, stretched out before us, reaching right back out of sight, was an enormous column of prisoners, such a sight as I haven't seen since the last days in North Africa. They were marching, or, I should say, they were trudging, three abreast, packed tightly together with a few Bren carriers interspersed down the column carrying the wounded – the weary, tattered, unshaven remnants of the German Seventh Army, tramping back in the pouring rain towards the prisoners' camps, lugging their kit with them, and with their blankets draped over their heads and shoulders trying hard to keep dry.

Rear of the fighting line we met a rather harassed-looking officer doing his best to cope with battle and prisoners at the same time. 'I don't know what to do with them,' he said. 'They just keep coming in on us.' At a brigade headquarters we were told: 'Our brigade and a recce regiment took over 1100 yesterday. This morning at nine o'clock the recce telephoned to say they'd got 60 more; at twenty past nine they said it was 300; by half-past ten it was over 1000 again.'

I saw a list of the divisions from which these prisoners came. There were fifteen divisions named, infantry, para, Panzer and SS. What a mix-up! And what a revelation of the present disorganized and confused state of the German Seventh Army!

Five miles from Argentan we turned off the road north-east along a country lane. This had been one of the German escape lines through the gap; now it's just a graveyard of German equipment and troops. Bulldozers had to be used to sweep away the piled-up wreckage along this lane, and open it to our advancing infantry. It's an almost indescrib-

Frank Gillard records in the devastated centre of Kassel on VE-Day.

able scene; every conceivable kind of vehicle is there, German guns and tanks and trucks and armoured cars and staff cars and amphibious cars, and wooden carts loaded up with ammunition, with stores and with food, all utterly and completely smashed up. You could see where motor engines had been wrenched from their bearings by the force of the explosions and hurled 20 and 30 yards. Panther tanks had their turrets shorn clean off; the hull of the tank would be one side of the road and the turret on the other. That's what a rocket-firing Typhoon can do.

You can see how the Germans time and time again had desperately swerved off the road to avoid air attacks, seeking shelter under the trees in an orchard or under the thick hedge of a field. How on earth our pilots found them I don't know. Some had completely smothered themselves in greenery, yet they'd had their dose of trouble just the same.

Some of the most frightful slaughter of the whole of this war must have taken place up and down this road a few days ago.

I met some gunners along the lane looking at the results of their work, for they too had a very big share in the destruction of these trapped German forces. They told me that they'd called this area their killing ground. Scores of enemy vehicles had just been abandoned for lack of petrol; they'd been smashed up in some way and left. And through it all our own troops were going forward on foot to continue the chase. Greatly elated they were at the victory they'd won. Some of those I saw this morning had been fighting with scarcely any break since June. Today, they could see the results of their efforts. Many of them were singing, shouting, whistling, laughing, as they came down the road in the rain.

26 AUGUST 1944

Robert Reid, who on the day France surrendered in 1940, bounced into the canteen in Manchester throwing his arm around Wilfred Pickles' shoulder with the words, 'Well, we're in t'final!', reported from the great doors of Notre-Dame on the day after France was liberated. Inside, 40 000 people were gathered to cheer de Gaulle:

> The General's now turning to face the square and this huge crowd of Parisians (*machine-gun fire*).… He's being presented to people (*machine-gun fire*).… He's being received (*shouts of crowd, shots*).… Even while the General is marching (*sudden sharp outburst of continued fire, break on the recording*) …
>
> Well, that was one of the most dramatic scenes I've ever seen. Just as General de Gaulle was about to enter the cathedral of Notre-Dame, firing started all over the place. I'm afraid we couldn't get you the noise of that firing because I was overwhelmed by a rush of people who were trying to seek shelter, and my cable parted from my microphone. But I fell just near de Gaulle and I managed to pick myself up. He was trying to control the crowds rushing into the cathedral. He walked straight ahead in what appeared to me to be a hail of fire from somewhere inside the cathedral – somewhere from the galleries up near the vaulted roof. But he went straight ahead without hesitation, his shoulders flung back, and walked right down the central aisle, even while the bullets were pouring around him. It was the most extraordinary example of courage that I've ever seen. But what was to follow was horrible, because it happened inside Notre-Dame Cathedral. While the congregation were trying to take shelter lying flat on the ground under the chairs and behind the pillars, the firing continued at intervals; the police, the military and the Resistance movement, all these people came in and were trying to pick off the snipers. Some of the snipers had actually got on to the roof of the cathedral.
>
> … But Paris had come to celebrate the solemn *Te Deum* and it did; even while the firing was going on the people rose to their feet and stood there, with General de Gaulle at the head of them. And then, when it was all over, the General marched right down the aisle; heaven knows how they missed him, for they were firing the whole time; there

184

were blinding flashes inside the cathedral, there were pieces of stone ricocheting around the place.

… His exit was the scene for another attempt. There were bangs, flashes all around him, and yet he seemed to have an absolutely charmed life.… I don't mind saying that at the moment I'm just squatting cross-legged on the floor by the side of the cathedral making this recording. I thought it was rather a wise precaution to take. I didn't want to be too conspicuous standing up with the microphone in my hand.

27 SEPTEMBER 1944

Stanley Maxted, an ex-actor and the oldest correspondent of them all, was flown with Guy Byam to England after Arnhem and sat, dirty and shocked from the battle, speaking from a few notes:

About 5 kilometres [3 miles] to the west of Arnhem, in a space 1500 yards by 900, on the last day, I saw the dead and the living – those who fought a good fight and kept the faith with you at home, and those who still fought magnificently on. They were the last of the few.

I last saw them yesterday morning as they dribbled into Nijmegen. They had staggered and walked and waded all night from Arnhem about 10 miles north, and we were busy asking each other if this or that one had been seen. Everyone wondered what the final check-up would amount to. I walked up to one young lieutenant to ask him about his sergeant – a stout lad if there ever was one – and he started to explain what had happened and then turned away. Remember,

Stanley Maxted, who landed with the gliders at Arnhem, used his Midget throughout the battle, humping the machine from shellhole to shellhole.

all of these men have been practically ten days and ten nights under the most murderous concentrated fire I have seen in two wars. Then he turned again and said: 'It's hell to be pulled out when you haven't finished your job, isn't it?' That's the way they all felt. It doesn't occur to them that if they hadn't held the horde of enemy force at Arnhem, that force would have been down at Nijmegen upsetting the whole apple-cart.

Late on the afternoon before, we were told that the remnants of the First Airborne Division were going to pull out that night. The enemy was making it impossible for the elements of the Second Army to relieve us. BBC's Guy Byam, Alan Woods of the *Daily Express* and I were told by Major Roy Oliver of the Public Relations Division – who, incidentally, proved himself a great soldier as well – were told to destroy all our equipment with the exception of what would go into one haversack. We were told to muffle our boots with bits of blanket and be ready to move off at a certain time. When the various officers were told to transmit this news to that thin straggle of hard-pressed men around the pitifully small perimeter, a great silence seemed to come upon them even in the middle of the shelling – you see, day or night, the shelling and mortaring never stopped. The ones I saw just drew a deep breath and said: 'Very good, sir.' Then these staring eyes in the middle of black muddy masks saluted as they always would and faded away to crawl out on their stomachs and tell their men.

Perhaps I should remind you here that these were men of no ordinary calibre. They had been nine days in that little space I mentioned, being mortared and shelled, machine-gunned, and sniped from all around. When a tank or a self-propelled 88-gun broke through, two or three of them detached themselves and somehow or another had put it out of business. For the last three days they had had no water, very little but small-arms ammunition, and rations cut to one-sixth. Luckily, or unluckily, it rained and they caught the water in their capes and drank that. These last items were never mentioned – they were Airborne, weren't they? They were tough and knew it. All right, water and rations didn't matter – give them some Germans to kill and even one chance in ten and they'd get along somehow.

At two minutes past ten we clambered out of our slit trenches in an absolute din of bombardment – a great deal of it our own – and formed up in a single line.... We held the tail of the coat of the man in front and set off like a file of nebulous ghosts from our pock-marked and tree-strewn piece of ground. Obviously, since the enemy was all round us, we had to go through him to get to the River Rhine.

After about 200 yards of silent trekking we knew we were among the enemy. It was difficult not to throw yourself flat when machine-gun tracers skinned your head or the scream of a shell or mortar-bomb sounded very close. But the order was to keep going. Anybody hit was to be picked up by the man behind him. Major Oliver had reconnoitred the route earlier on with a headquarters' officer and had it memorized. The back of my neck was prickling for that whole interminable march. I couldn't see the man ahead of me – all I knew was that I had hold of a coat-tail and for the first time in my life was grateful for the downpour of rain that made a patter on the leaves of the trees and covered up any little noises we were making.... I felt as naked as if I were in Piccadilly Circus in my pyjamas, because of the glow from fires across the river. The machine-gun and general bombardment had never let up.

We lay down flat in the mud and rain and stayed that way for two hours.... After what seemed a nightmare of an age we got our turn and slithered up and over on to some mud flats. There was the shadow of a little assault craft with an outboard motor on it. Several of these had been rushed up by a field company of Engineers. One or two of them were out of action already. We waded out in the Rhine ... and helped push the boat off into the swift Rhine current. With our heads down between our knees we waited for the bump on the far side – or what might come before. It didn't come. We clambered out and followed what had been a white tape up over a dyke. We slid down the other side on our backsides, and sloshed through mud for four miles and a half – me thinking, 'Gosh! I'm alive, how did it happen?' In a barn there was a blessed hot mug of tea with rum in it and a blanket over our shoulders. Then we walked again – all night. After daylight we got to a dressing-station near Nijmegen and then we were put in trucks and ... that's how the last of the few got out to go and fight in some future battle.

27 SEPTEMBER 1944

Guy Byam, another witness at Arnhem, who swam the Neder Rhine with his recorded discs held above the water, reported:

They came out because they had got nothing left to fight with except their bare hands, maybe. All day, as for six days before that, the tanks and the mortars and the flame-throwers had smashed at the positions.... Every brick, every wall, every house was a part of the battle that ebbed to and fro, a yard here and a yard there. And those men who climbed out of their foxholes and slit trenches weren't beaten, mind you; no, they had to get out because of events the other side of the river. No, the German soldier never really beat them; their tanks could come in and they could shell us from a distance, hour after hour of it, but when the SS troops were sent in against our men they got murdered, and they hated every minute of it.

In the morning of the day that we came out I was asked as a non-combatant to go through the lines to contact the enemy, to enable us to evacuate our wounded. As I was making my way back to the area where we were dug in, after having seen a German medical officer, I was stopped by an SS lieutenant who said I was his prisoner, this despite the fact that I carried a Red Cross flag. I managed to get away, however, and soon got back to our own lines in a jeep going to fetch some more wounded. I must admit it was with dread that, in the morning sun, I came back to my lines …

At about ten o'clock we slowly groped our way through the woods … and crept in long lines down to the Rhine. The mortars were bursting in what seemed like a spray of sparks, almost amongst us now, and we lay on the ground, pressing our faces into the wet grass. It was then that I decided to have a go at swimming the river. The men themselves patiently waited their turn to get in a boat, and if a man floundering in the dark got ahead of somebody else, there would be a quiet 'Come on, chum, take your turn'. And the boat-loads got over the Rhine and, swept down by the current, I at last managed to reach the other bank. The hell was behind us. But not all of them got across, for as it got light the last ones were still left patiently waiting their turn. Not all of them could swim. And the Germans, seeing them, poured machine-gun fire into the men who huddled against the hedges and lay on the causeway …

16 APRIL 1945

Chester Wilmot, a trained historian who later wrote the classic analysis of the European war, *The Struggle for Europe* – and who lived through the war only to die when the peacetime Comet in which he was a passenger exploded over Elba – was there when two of the Stalags were broken open:

Twenty thousand Allied prisoners of war gained their freedom today when British tanks liberated two large prison camps, Stalag Eleven B and Stalag 357. More than 10 000 of them were British or American, and the British troops included 600 men of the First Airborne Division captured at Arnhem last year, and many more who were taken at Dunkirk.

This morning, when tanks of the Eighth Hussars reached these two camps near Fallingbostel, 35 miles south-east of Bremen, they found that our troops (the prisoners) had already taken charge of the camp and interned their German guards. An Airborne sergeant-major, an ex-Guardsman, was in command, and the British guards were as spick and span as any parade-ground troops. Their boots were polished, their trousers pressed, and their belts and gaiters Blancoed. The British troops had taken over the German offices, and their liberators found clerks busy typing out nominal rolls on German typewriters …

This afternoon, at Stalag Eleven B, I saw some of the 20 000 and learned from padres, doctors and NCOs how they'd been treated. They told me that in this camp there were 4256 British troops and 2428 Americans. Of these 6700, more than 1000 are in hospital suffering from wounds, injuries or starvation, and I saw several thousand more suffering from starvation who should have been in hospital in any civilized country.

Here in this camp I saw clear evidence of the German neglect and wanton disregard for the lives and health of their prisoners. Of the 4250 British, some 2500 have come into the camp in the last three weeks. The Germans have marched them from Poland, lest they should be set free by the Russian advance. Ten days ago in this camp there were 3000 other British and American prisoners who had made this terrible trek from Poland; but when the Second Army crossed the Weser, the Germans put these 3000 on the road again, and sent them marching back towards the Russians. They were determined to stop them being liberated, because they were airmen and paratroops.

How far they'll be able to march I don't know, for I saw today the pitiable condition of those who have already made the nightmare journey from Poland. They certainly were exhausted at the end of that journey. I saw them in hospital – drawn, haggard, starved – starved beyond description – limbs like matchsticks, bodies shrunken till their bones stood out like knuckles.

The doctor in charge of them said to me: 'Nothing has kept these men alive except Red Cross parcels and their own spirit.' But on that journey from Poland they had very few Red Cross parcels, and some got none …

An Australian gunner who'd been captured in Crete had marched even farther in far worse conditions – he'd come 500 miles from the other side of Breslau in two months. They'd started in January with snow on the ground and had been made to sleep in barns and unheated barracks, and one night he said they'd slept in the open. 'Men with dysentery or pneumonia,' he went on, 'had to keep marching. If they fell out they were either shot or left to die by the roadside. In the end,' he added, 'we managed to get some farm carts and we carried the worst cases in these.'

I wish those people who think the Germans should be treated lightly had seen what I saw today. But I saw also something that was inspiring and encouraging. All this German oppression and brutality and starvation hadn't been able to kill the spirit and self-respect of these men of Arnhem, men of Crete, of Dunkirk and Calais, men of Bomber Command and the Eighth Air Force. They'd managed to rise above their sordid environment. And this afternoon they had the supreme pleasure of watching their German guards being marched away to our prison cage; and, as they watched, they cheered.

19 APRIL 1945

Richard Dimbleby, who had been on more than twenty bombing operations over Germany and, as liaison with Bomber Command, brought many airmen to the *War Report* studio, went to the charnel house of Belsen, on what he described 'as the most horrible day of my life'. His dispatch ran to fourteen minutes. *War Report* could not carry it all, but it was broadcast in full later:

… There are 40 000 men, women and children in the camp, German and half a dozen other nationalities, thousands of them Jews.… In the last few months alone, 30 000 prisoners have been killed off or allowed to die.… I wish with all my heart that everyone fighting in this war, and above all those whose duty it is to direct the war from Britain and America, could have come with me through the barbed wire fence that leads to the inner compound.… I've seen many terrible sights in the last five years but nothing, nothing approaching the dreadful interior of this hut at Belsen. The dead and the dying lay close together. I picked my way over corpse after corpse in the gloom until I heard one voice that rose above the gentle, undulating moaning. I found a girl, she was a living skeleton, impossible to gauge her age for she had practically no hair left on her head and her face was a yellow parchment sheet with two holes in it for eyes. She was stretching out her stick of an arm and gasping something. It was "English, English, medicine, medicine", and she was trying to cry but had not enough strength. And beyond her down the passage, there were the convulsive movements of dying people too weak to raise themselves from the floor.

In the shade of some trees lay a great collection of bodies. I walked among them trying to count. There were perhaps 150 flung down on each other, all naked, all so

Richard Dimbleby outside Hitler's underground shelter in Berlin. The Russian major who is in charge of the Chancellery is on his left.

thin that their yellow skin glistened like stretched rubber on their bones. Some of the poor starved creatures whose bodies were there looked so utterly unreal and inhuman that I could have imagined that they had never lived at all. They were like polished skeletons, the skeletons that medical students like to play practical jokes with.

At one end of the pile a cluster of men and women were gathered round a fire; they were using rags and old shoes taken from the bodies to keep it alight, and they were heating soup over it. And close by was the enclosure where 500 children between the ages of five and twelve were kept. They were not so hungry as the rest, for the women had sacrificed themselves to keep them alive. Babies were born at Belsen, some of them shrunken, wizened little things that could not live, because their mothers could not feed them.

One woman, distraught to the point of madness, flung herself at a British soldier who was on guard at the camp on the night that it was reached by the Eleventh Armoured Division; she begged him to give her some milk for the tiny baby she held in her arms. She laid the mite on the ground and threw herself at the sentry's feet and kissed his boots. And when, in his distress, he asked her to get up, she put the baby in his arms and ran off crying that she would find milk for it because there was no milk in her breast. And when the soldier opened the bundle of rags to look at the child, he found that it had been dead for days.

Here in Belsen we were seeing people, many of them lawyers and doctors and chemists, musicians, authors, who'd long since ceased to care about the conventions and the customs of normal life. There had been no privacy of any kind. Women stood naked at the side of the track, washing in cupfuls of water taken from British Army water trucks. Others squatted while they searched themselves for lice, and examined each other's hair. Sufferers from dysentery leaned against the huts, straining helplessly, and all around and about them was this awful drifting tide of exhausted people, neither caring nor watching. Just a few held out their withered hands to us as we passed by, and blessed the doctor whom they knew had become the camp commander in place of the brutal Kramer.

We were on our way down to the crematorium where the Germans had burned alive thousands of men and women in a single fire. The furnace was in a hut about the size of a single garage. A little Pole whose prison number was tattooed on the inside of his forearm, as it was on all the others, told me how they burned the people. They brought them into the stockade, walked them in, and then an SS guard hit them on the back of the neck with a club and stunned them. And then they were fed straight into the fire, three at a time, two men, one woman. The opening was not big enough for three men and that I verified by measuring it …

Those officers and men who have seen these things have gone back to the Second Army moved to an anger such as I have never seen before.

The obscenity of Belsen. Richard Dimbleby who witnessed it, wrote: 'No briefing had prepared me for this'.

20 APRIL 1945

Edward Ward returned to reporting for the last month of the war, as if his last three years in prisoner-of-war camps had not happened:

I went up a shattered stairway to the upper floors of Leipzig's town hall. Many rooms were damaged by shells, others almost untouched. I went with two American soldiers who carried Tommy-guns at the ready, since we were the first to explore the inside of the building. In one room, which had been the *Ober-Bürgermeister's* council room, was a grisly spectacle. Three *Volkssturmers* lay sprawled, dead, over tables, with pools of blood on the floor – they had committed suicide. By the side of one was a bottle of cognac and a half-empty glass. He'd evidently needed courage. Most papers had already been removed, but otherwise all furniture in the rooms not hit by shells were intact and normal.

After exploring the town hall, I went into the neighbouring building. In an air-raid shelter I found a small group of Germans who staff the town hall restaurant. They told me that the *Ober-Burgermeister* and his wife and daughter had also committed suicide. Among these Germans was the caretaker of the town hall. He had the keys of the whole building. I took him over to the *Rathaus*, and asked which was the *Ober-Bürgermeister's* office. He took me upstairs to some doors which I'd found locked. He took a bunch of keys and opened the door. I shouted, "Anyone there?" No reply. I went into a luxuriously furnished, oak-panelled room. Seated at a large desk was *Ober-Bürgermeister* Freyberg, his hands on the table, his shaved head tilted back. Opposite, in the armchair, sat his wife; beside her, in the other armchair, sat his daughter, a flaxen haired twenty-year-old, wearing spectacles. On the desk was a phial, with its stopper lying beside it. They were all dead. The caretaker said he thought they'd committed suicide yesterday, or perhaps the day before. He told me Freyberg had been *Bürgermeister* for about nine years, and though he'd been a party member, he'd wanted to declare Leipzig an open town, but had been overruled. On the wall, opposite the dead man, was a large oil-painting of Hitler. There was another locked door, leading out of this room – the caretaker opened it. Here Chief City Treasurer Doktor Lisso lay slumped on his desk. On a sofa, opposite, lay his daughter, wearing hospital nurse's uniform. In an armchair sat Lisso's wife. Once again, on the table was an empty, unlabelled phial. By Lisso's side were two automatic pistols but he had chosen poison.

In an anteroom a dead *Volkssturmer* lay on the floor with twenty- and fifty-mark notes scattered round him – he, too, had poisoned himself. The caretaker seemed entirely unmoved by this terrible spectacle. We ordered the caretaker to lock up the doors again, and walked downstairs.

4 MAY 1945

Wynford Vaughan Thomas neatly closed the circle:

> This is Germany calling. Calling for the last time from Station Hamburg, and tonight you will not hear views on the news by William Joyce, for Mr Joyce – Lord Haw-Haw to most of us in Britain – has been most unfortunately interrupted in his broadcasting career, and at present has left rather hurriedly for a vacation, an extremely short vacation if the Second British Army has anything to do with it, maybe to Denmark and other points north. And in his place this is the BBC calling all the long-suffering listeners in Britain who for six years have had to put up with the acid tones of Mr Joyce speaking over the same wavelength that I'm using to talk to you now.
>
> I'm seated in front of Lord Haw-Haw's own microphone, or rather the microphone he used in the last three weeks of his somewhat chequered career; and I wonder what Lord Haw-Haw's views on the news are now? For Hamburg, the city he made notorious, is this evening under the control of the British Forces, and we found a completely and utterly bomb-ruined city.
>
> We thought Bremen was bad, but Hamburg is devastated. Whole quarters have disintegrated under air attacks. There are miles upon miles of blackened

Wynford Vaughan Thomas records interviews in the centre of Marseilles – with hand-to-hand fighting going on elsewhere in the city. 'You can have a drink in a bar in one street, but it's death to put your nose around the corner,' he reported.

walls and utterly burnt-out streets, and in the ruins there are still nearly a million people and 50 000 foreign workers living in the cellars and air-raid shelters. Today you don't see a single civilian on the streets; as soon as we came in we imposed a forty-eight-hour curfew, and there's a Sunday quiet over the whole city; all that stirs in the streets is a British jeep or an armoured car, or a patrol of British Tommies watching that the curfew is strictly enforced.

The docks are even more devastated than the town, the great shipyards of Bloem and Voss are a wilderness of tangled girders, and in the middle of this chaos fourteen unfinished U-boats still stand rusting on the slipways. Work on them finally stopped two months ago; after that date Hamburg was a dead city.

Rummaging through Lord Haw-Haw's desk we found a revealing timetable he drew up for his work, for 10 April 1945, and at the end of it is the glorious item: '1450-1510 hours, a pause to collect my wits.' Well he and the citizens of Hamburg have now got plenty of time to collect their wits, for tonight the sturdy soldiers of the Devons, the famous Desert Rats, are on guard over Haw-Haw's studios, the Allied military authorities are now running his programme, and instead of 'Germany Calling' the colonel in charge gives you the new call-sign of 'Station Hamburg'. This is Radio Hamburg, a station of the Allied Military Government. (*Same announcement in German.*) And from Hamburg we take you back to London.

TRIUMPH AND DISASTER COMBINED

War Report ended when the fighting in Europe stopped, but not before it had achieved both its greatest triumph and its greatest moment of disaster. On 4 May 1945, Chester Wilmot exclusively witnessed the German surrender inside Montgomery's tent on the wild Lüneberg Heath near the River Elbe, and his recorded dispatch was played into the programme. He had just said: 'It's now twenty minutes past six, the discussions have been short and to the point,' and Montgomery's sharp voice had begun: 'Now we're assembled here today to accept the surrender terms which have been made with the delegation from the German Army' – when the line went dead.

John Snagge, *War Report*'s usual announcer, was not on duty that night and his stand-in panicked. He should have apologized, said every effort was being made to re-establish contact. Instead he said, 'That is the end of tonight's *War Report.*' Almost immediately, the line came back, but it was too late. The BBC was besieged with calls. What had happened? Had Montgomery been assassinated? *War Report* asked for a break-in to programmes and an hour later the dispatch went out in its entirety.

The following night, when he went on-air, Snagge concluded: 'That is the end of tonight's *War Report*, and the end of *War Report*. The war goes on, the BBC correspondents will be in the field until victory is won. But with the conclusion of the campaign

195

4 May 1945: the German plenipotentiaries who will sign the instrument of surrender have come to Field Marshal Montgomery's tent on the hill at Lüneberg Heath.

on the Western Front, *War Report* completes its task.'

Off the air, the team sat in the office in an empty silence. The big blackboard in the middle of the room on which so many names had been scrawled day after day had been wiped clean. As they lingered, a cleaner in a brown coat came in hesitantly and asked, 'You haven't got a bit of chalk for the darts, have you?' Somebody got up and looked. There were two pieces. The cleaner accepted them gratefully. 'It's not like you'll be needing them now, is it?' he said.

A POSTSCRIPT

Unreliable and clumsy as it was, The Midget recorder had punched its weight across Europe. And yet, the correspondents knew from listening to German radio that their counterparts had something much better: quarter-inch tape. The Germans had had a portable machine since 1940.

At the end of the war, when he was seconded from his regiment to the Control Commission that was established to detoxify German broadcasting of Nazism, Dennis Main Wilson retrieved a machine from Radio Hamburg and put it on an RAF Transport Command Dakota addressed to: Engineering Department, BBC, Maida Vale, London. Six years later, in 1951, he found himself recording the first series of *The Goon Show* on acetate discs. '"Oi," I said, "come on. Six years ago I sent back a tape-recorder from Germany. Why can't I have one like that?" And you know what I was told? "Our chaps are still evaluating it."'

CHAPTER
10

WHAT DID YOU DO IN THE WAR, AUNTIE?

Flags were on sale in London from the middle of April 1945 and everyone waited to break out the bunting, but there was no clean, swift end to the war in Europe.

THE LONG WAIT

On 1 May, the BBC announced Hitler's suicide. At 7 p.m. the following day, programmes were interrupted to report the surrender of the Germans in Italy. There was another news flash at 10.30 p.m.: Berlin had fallen. On 4 May, the German troops in Denmark surrendered. But still the final curtain did not come down. On Monday 7 May, tension in the country was almost palpable and crowds, shouting without success for the King, gathered outside Buckingham Palace, the façade of which still bore the scars of enemy action. Hour by hour people listened to the BBC, expecting to hear that the war was over, but the announcement did not come. Just as on D-Day, the BBC was reporting only what its defeated enemies were saying; the Government, 'with barely credible stupidity', or at least with a lack of sensitivity for the feelings of its people, had promised not to make the announcement until a time which suited both the Russians and the Americans.

At 6 p.m. the BBC told the nation that Churchill would not be broadcasting that night; in Bedford, the Religious department, which had gathered together 1000 troops from outlying camps for a special service – and kept them waiting for three hours – stood them down until the following day. Then, confusingly, at 7.40 p.m., programmes were interrupted to say that the following day would be celebrated as Victory in Europe Day and that, 'in accordance with arrangements between the three great powers', Churchill would broadcast in the afternoon.

The kind of picture that *is* worth a thousand words:
London celebrates VE Day.

VICTORY AT LAST

It was an uninspired and messy way to bring nearly six years of war to a close. But VE Day came (with organ music, as in September 1939) and Churchill's long-awaited statement went out to the Empire at 1 p.m. GMT, three o'clock British Double Summer Time, spoken from the same room at Number Ten where Chamberlain had made his fateful declaration at the outbreak of war:

> Yesterday morning at 2.41 a.m., at General Eisenhower's headquarters, the representative of the German High Command … signed the act of unconditional surrender of all German land, sea and air forces in Europe to the Allied Expeditionary Force. Hostilities will end officially at one minute after midnight tonight … but in the interests of saving lives, the cease-fire began yesterday to be sounded all along the front. The German war is therefore at an end… We may allow ourselves a brief period of rejoicing, but let us not forget for a moment the toils and efforts that lie ahead. Japan, with all her treachery and greed, remains unsubdued.… Advance Britannia! Long live the cause of freedom! God save the King!

The BBC switched at once to plans for a ten-day victory celebration; seven different advance schedules had been prepared to allow for VE Day falling on any day of the week. A huge nightly retrospective of the war, under the title *Their Finest Hour*, began, with victory versions of all the main variety programmes. This was, the *BBC Handbook* of 1946 noted, 'perhaps the most star-spangled ten days of entertainment the BBC has ever produced'. On Sunday 13 May, Vaughan Williams' *Victory Anthem* was heard in a studio service in which the sermon was preached by the Archbishop of Canterbury, the prayer read by the Moderator of the Federal Free Church Council, and the lesson read by a US chaplain. At noon, Pontifical High Mass was broadcast from Westminster Cathedral and in the afternoon a thanksgiving service, which was attended by the King and Queen, came from St Paul's.

THE VE DAY CELEBRATIONS

It is fairly doubtful that anyone listened to much of what the BBC broadcast on the night of VE Day itself. Across the country, where in most places Churchill's speech had been broadcast over the loudspeakers rigged up at the local town hall, people threw themselves into wild rejoicing. There were fancy dress parades, street parties, bonfires. Central London was thronged and a Naval officer used his telescope to conduct the crowds singing outside Buckingham Palace as they waited for the King and his family to come out on to the balcony, which was draped in gold-fringed crimson cloth.

In an interview made forty years later, Queen Elizabeth told Godfrey Talbot:

> I think we went on the balcony nearly every hour, six times. And then when the excitement of the floodlights being switched on got through to us, my sister and I realized that we couldn't see what the crowds were enjoying … so we asked my parents if we could go out and see for ourselves.
>
> I remember we were terrified of being recognized, so I pulled my uniform cap well down over my eyes. A Grenadier officer amongst our party of about fifteen people said, 'We refuse to be seen in the company of another officer improperly dressed.' So I had to put my cap on normally.
>
> We cheered the King and Queen on the balcony and then walked miles through the streets. I remember lines of unknown people linking arms and walking down Whitehall, all of us just swept along on a tide of happiness and relief. I remember the amazement of my cousin, just back after four-and-a-half years in a prisoner-of-war camp, walking freely with his family in the frenzied throng.… I think it was one of the most memorable nights of my life.

Princess Elizabeth, who registered for national service on her 16th birthday, had been commissioned in the Auxiliary Territorial Service for two months.

Broadcasting House was also floodlit, for the first time since the Coronation in May 1937. The Stars and Stripes, the Russian flag and the Union Jack fluttered gaily above the entrance: the side of the building was alive with the flags of twenty-two Allied nations. But it was a changed Broadcasting House on which the light fell. Eight years earlier, its stones had gleamed white and pristine; now they were dark and muddy grey, pocked and disfigured by bomb damage. The BBC which operated from within the building was very much changed, too. It, however, had been enhanced by the war.

THE NEW BBC

In 1939, the BBC was regarded as an aloof and impenetrable organization, out of touch with the mass of its listeners; its news operation was vestigial and its reputation abroad virtually non-existent. Yet by 1945 it had so reinvented itself that it was an indispensable part of British national life, woven into the very fabric of everybody's everyday existence; and outside Britain the scale and authority of its news – in English and forty-five other languages – had made it the world's unrivalled international broadcaster.

Some of the factors which forged the new BBC were fortuitous, the most significant being the influx of newcomers who nearly doubled the pre-war staff. They turned what Lord Weidenfeld likens to 'a medieval order, an élite' into 'a professional, largely conscript army'. This was an army which accepted the tenets of faith 'to inform, educate and entertain' but which was unshackled from Reith's messianic vision of broadcasting. In whatever capacity the newcomers arrived, they were here to help win the war: journalists, dons, actors, ex-Army officers, businessmen, novelists, poets and, among the maverick spirits displaced from Europe who fetched up in Bush House, an even greater diversification of peacetime occupations.

The flood of journalists, many of whose newspapers had folded because of the war, in particular wrought the sea-change. They may have lowered the tone, but they brought their news values with them and they injected a sense of urgency which those journalists who were already in the BBC, like Dimbleby and Gardner, were too few to impose. The old BBC had not really cared for the breed. Even in the middle of the war, Sir Cecil Graves, Reith's pre-war deputy who suddenly found himself elevated to joint director-general on Ogilvie's departure, wrote a personal report on a member of staff in whose presence he always felt uncomfortable because he 'seemed to belong more to the world of journalism and commerce than to the BBC'.

Frank Gillard, who entered the BBC from school-teaching, says: 'The BBC had been a very respectable, rigid institution, run on Civil Service lines. All the new people who came had new ideas. We kicked out the stuffiness – we'd no room or time for that.'

Another factor which worked in the BBC's favour was the profound sociological upheaval which war induced, throwing the classes together, hugger-mugger, and throwing out the artificial middle-class niceties. Before the war, convention had decreed not only that a woman had to tender her resignation when she got married, but that she always wore a hat and gloves; and that while a man could take off his jacket in his office, he should never show his braces in the corridor. When Mary Lewis joined the BBC as a checking clerk in Duplicating she was told 'that I must not expect my boss to acknowledge me outside the office'. Such conventions simply disappeared once war began: they hardly made sense when men and women of whatever station were bedding down together in Broadcasting House's concert hall.

People began to use each other's Christian names up, as well as down, the pecking order (the BBC prides itself today on being a 'first-name' organization); and if what the broadcasting commentator Peter Black has described as 'the BBC's sultanesque attitude to women' did not end, the circumstances of war induced, if not the beginning of the end, at least the end of the beginning. 'What everyone remembers is how friendly the country as a whole became in the war,' Lewis says. 'It was the same in the BBC.' A sign of the times was that in 1940, after eighteen 'dry' years, Broadcasting House got a licence which allowed alcohol, the great social equalizer, to be sold on the premises.

War changed the work ethic, too. In peacetime, those employed in the BBC regarded it as 'an agreeable, comfortable, cultured, leisured place, remote from the world of business and struggle'. Wilfred Pickles, a jobbing actor rather than the announcer (and then newsreader) he briefly became, could not credit the attitude of at least some of the pre-war staff. He wrote about 'their leisurely, lazy outlook, an attitude of mind which grows on so many who work for the BBC. The corporation is the worst of all places for young people to start their working lives; the easy-going ways they pick up makes them totally unfitted for the bustling, get-things-done atmosphere of the commercial world, if they have to leave.'

There was precious little comfort, or leisure, in the wartime BBC, where sixteen-hour days were commonly worked, and without complaint. The driving force, self-evidently, was that programme-making was an essential contribution to the war effort. But the programme-makers had another reason for enjoying what they did: they were working with a freedom they had not experienced in peacetime. That, according to the announcer/commentator John Snagge, was because 'the Admin. cohorts' who up until September 1939 had ruled the roost, had disappeared into the Ministries as liaison officers. In *Those Vintage Years of Radio*, Snagge wrote dismissively of their 'bright dead alien eyes' (a quote from G.K. Chesterton's *The Secret People* which begins 'They fight by shuffling papers'). Shaking off their dead hand, he said, was 'the liberation which allowed great programmes to be born'. The playwright, poet and BBC producer, Louis MacNeice, once wrote that 'with ingenuity and a little luck a creative person can persuade (or fool) some of the administrators some of the time'. Hugh Carlton Greene could not be bothered playing games. When one of the dwindled band 'descended on Bush House we tended to regard him as a strange thing from outer space'.

RADICAL INNOVATIONS

Until the war, the BBC had shied away from innovation. It was a diffuser of information and entertainment rather than an originator of it. In Gillard's words: 'It built upon the old traditions of the pulpit and the lecture theatre and the concert hall and the variety house, but it didn't use the radio medium as a new method of communication.'

War required more: and the BBC delivered it, after a shaky start, helping the country to bear the strain and making it believe that there was a future worth fighting for. It tapped the rich seam of ordinary people, who in peacetime had got nowhere near a microphone, and relaxed the pre-war practice of scripting every word ('What was natural had first to become artificial before it could sound natural again'), letting the sound-bite captured on the fly give radio a spontaneity it had never had before. It injected news comment into its output, which was a radical departure. Ultimately, having learnt from its experience, it created *War Report*, the forerunner of modern broadcast journalism, which led in the immediate post-war period to the appointment of the corporation's first foreign correspondents. *War Report* enhanced the BBC's reputation, if it needed enhancing: for the vast majority of people the BBC had been 'their' BBC from the time of the hardships and dangers of the Blitz four years earlier.

War Report was the culmination of the BBC's war, but it owed a great deal to a programme that Britain did not begin to hear until 1945: *Radio News Reel*. This fast-moving nightly compendium of political commentaries, eye-witness accounts and short talks by servicemen, taught the BBC a great deal about projecting the immediacy of war, just as the North American Service, on which it first went out, taught the BBC a great deal about broadcasting professionalism. The pre-war practice had been to allow programmes to overrun. If a programme fell a little short, a pause would follow. If the gap until the next item was sufficiently long, it was filled by playing records. That would have been an untenable policy in taking on the slick, transatlantic commercial stations, which were geared to precise timing – and on which the BBC needed to be rebroadcast because there was no Stateside habit of short-wave listening. The BBC had to tighten up its presentation to compete and it did. The knock-on effect back home was the introduction of 'continuity', so disliked by Bruce Belfrage.

A BREATH OF FRESH AIR

If America liked the BBC – and by the autumn of 1942, 285 medium-wave stations were rebroadcasting it for a total of nearly 350 hours a week – then Europe's feelings bordered on idolatry. In his first year as German Chancellor in 1933, Hitler had declared: 'Artillery preparations before an attack, as during the First World War, will be replaced in the future war by the psychological dislocation of the enemy through revolutionary propaganda. The enemy must be demoralized and driven to passivity. Our strategy is to destroy the enemy from within, to conquer him through himself. Mental confusion, contradictions of feeling, indecision, panic – these are our weapons.' How well these weapons were applied as his Army marched across the map: the Nazis were not conquerors, they were liberators. 'After your heroic struggle, you have been liberated today,' German propaganda told the Belgians after their capitulation. 'You have not suffered defeat. On the contrary, you have conquered – conquered the dark powers that brought you to the edge of the precipice.'

History was rewritten in Holland with even more blatant overtones of *1984*: 'We are now in Amsterdam. In front of the royal palace there is a veritable concert of bicycle bells, and the cyclists perform amazing acrobatics in the traffic.... We go on to Haarlem, where the people greet us as old friends.... We reach the Hague, but have no time to look at the many buildings because we are making for the sea.... Only now do the Dutch soldiers feel free and safe. They know that over there in England lives the enemy of the world.' In countries suffocating under such a propaganda onslaught which spouted from the radio, the cinema, loudspeakers in the street and which plastered the posters and the newspapers, the words, 'This is London calling', heralding a BBC news broadcast, must have seemed like a breath of fresh air.

BOUQUETS ...

The historian G.M. Young, writing in *The Sunday Times* in 1943, said that the BBC's news output had given it 'a standing without rival on the European Continent'. He went on: 'What they say goes, and is whispered and copied and carried by men and women and children at the risk often of their lives and the lives of their families, from the Arctic to the Aegean. That is a great victory – I am not sure, if it is followed up, that [the year] 2043 will not regard it as our greatest victory.' The following year, George Orwell wrote: '"I heard it on the BBC" is now almost the equivalent of saying "I know it must be true".'

Were the BBC's reports truthful? By and large they were. Certainly the BBC broadcast what it believed the truth to be, within the bounds of censorship. Its scrupulousness extended beyond the verbal to the aural: no sound was ever dubbed on a *War Report* to make it that little bit more exciting. The BBC did not get everything right (for example, the discovery, after the war, that it had been used by the Yugoslav government-in-exile to read out names of Tito's Partisans whom the pro-government leader of the Chetniks, General Mihailovic, wanted assassinated, was profoundly shocking), but it broadcast nothing that it knew to be untrue. 'It may sound negative, but the BBC was committed to the avoidance of the propaganda lie,' says Desmond Hawkins. 'You can't ask more of people in war than that.'

... AND BRICKBATS

Not everyone ascribed to that view. There were allegations that the BBC was over-cautious in reporting the Holocaust or even that it deliberately played it down. That is not supported by those who did the broadcasting.

'I think it is a very destructive myth,' says Martin Esslin. 'The Establishment was worried lest, internally, the German propaganda line, that the war was being fought on behalf of the Jews, would have resonance among people with right-wing, Fascist and nationalist views. So the BBC was careful. But the BBC broadcast any information as soon as it became available.'

Adds Leonard Miall: 'We were very careful to try and avoid giving currency to rumours which might not be true and which would then jeopardize our general credibility. We broadcast a great deal about people being sent off to these camps. But what actually happened when they got there was not provable.'

It is sometimes cited as a proof of the BBC's 'playing down' that it held up Richard Dimbleby's Belsen report for over a day before broadcasting it. Dimbleby actually phoned the BBC to say that if it was not aired he would never broadcast again in his life and later wrote: 'When they heard it, some people wondered if Dimbleby had gone off his head.' But the argument is unfounded, and misses the obvious point: the scale of Jewish extermination was so horrific that the human mind had difficulty in encompassing it. Ed Murrow, broadcasting from Belsen, asked his American audience: 'I pray you to believe what I have told you about this place. I only

Between April and May 1943, the remaining 40 000 of 500 000 Jews in the Warsaw ghetto, largely unarmed, resisted the German deportation order against troops armed with flame throwers, armoured cars and tanks. The reaction of the outside world was incredulity.

reported what I saw and heard, but only a part of it. For the rest, I have no words.'

A question mark – perhaps – hangs over whether the BBC could have done more after December 1942, when Churchill made a Parliamentary statement about the fate of the Jews and the House of Commons stood in silence. Would it have had any effect if the BBC had issued warnings that anyone participating in atrocities would stand trial after the war? Lord Bullock finds 'it hard to believe'. Vovo Rubenstein believes otherwise and Lord Weidenfeld says: 'I cannot disagree. But that comes in the same category as saying that the Pope could have ex-communicated anybody in the German armed Forces who had anything to do with these things. It is conjecture.' As the war progressed, attempts were made to persuade the BBC to broadcast lists of known guards and officials in the extermination and labour camps. The BBC worried that if individuals were named others, equally culpable, would believe that they were safe and so continue in their excesses, while those named, knowing that their behaviour was made public, would have no reason to change. Who is to say that the BBC was wrong?

'I don't think the BBC could have done more, without the British Government issuing formal statements and warnings,' says Konrad Syrop, who worked in the Polish section and was later a war correspondent in Normandy. 'No such statements were issued. The BBC could only reflect what the Government was saying. It wasn't autonomous.'

AN INDEPENDENT SERVICE?

To what extent the BBC was independent, rather than autonomous, is less a matter of conjecture than of semantics. Perhaps Desmond Hawkins sums it up best when he says: 'The BBC couldn't, in wartime, be independent; it would be childish to think that there were not ultimate sanctions that the nation had to reserve to itself. But nor was the BBC dependent. It stood on a declared and understood position. It was its own man, on the terms that were possible.'

In early 1940, the BBC clearly felt that the degree of imposition on its freedom was relatively slight. That year's *Handbook* acknowledged the necessity of censorship on the BBC, as on the newspapers, but added: 'This, in effect, is the only small diminution of its peacetime liberties that the BBC has suffered.' In December 1943, during the BBC's twenty-first anniversary celebrations, the Minister of Information, Brendan Bracken, backed the BBC's view:

> At the beginning of this war, the Government was given power to interfere in the affairs
> of every institution in this country including the BBC. And though I am always willing
> to take responsibility for all the BBC's doings, I have refused to interfere in the policies of
> the corporation. The governors and many members of the staff often consult with the

Ministry of Information and sometimes they condescend to ask us for our advice and we give it for what it is worth. But I can say from my own personal experience that no attempt has ever been made by the Government to influence the news-giving or any other programme of the BBC.

Between these statements, however, had come the two black years during which the war was being lost and Churchill had come within an ace of taking over the BBC. Desperate in the face of defeat, the Government had blamed the messenger for the message; the temptation was to turn off the broadcasters and replace their constant truth with something more reassuring. The likely consequence of that – certainly if defeat had not turned to salvation – would have been ever cruder propaganda, suppression and even falsification. As it was, the tide did turn, the BBC rode out the storm and went on to triumph. As Lord Bullock says with shrewd humour: 'When you're winning, your propaganda is good, if you're losing, it's lousy. If we had lost the war, the BBC would have been blamed for a good deal of it.'

The BBC deserves great credit for fighting its corner and holding out for objectivity, integrity – and sanity. But it might well have lost the argument if Churchill had not appointed Brendan Bracken, who appointed Patrick Ryan and Ivone Kirkpatrick as the Government's internal advisers. There was irony in this, as Harman Grisewood testified: 'The legend is of some glorious resistance by the BBC to the incursion of these outside people. It reminds me of the *Iliad*, these gallant Trojans inside the BBC, fighting the wicked Greeks, which was how the Government was thought of. The skill with which Ryan and Kirkpatrick overcame these feelings has never been sufficiently recognized … both of them became what could properly be called BBC patriots.'

The BBC was less fortunate in the men who led it for most of the war. Frederick Ogilvie, who replaced Reith as director-general in 1938, was a high-minded man with no stomach for leading the BBC in wartime. Who was he, except vice-chancellor of Queen's University, Belfast?' John Snagge wrote. 'The men and women putting out the programmes never knew, and scarcely cared … there was about to be a war, and then it would be every programme for itself.' Ogilvie lasted until 1942, when he was replaced by 'a double-headed DG, consisting of Robert Foot ("Who's he?" asked the staff) and Cecil Graves ("Oh, him"). It made no difference either way. The BBC had, as someone put it, one foot in the graves.' It was only when the long-serving Graves stood down through ill health and Foot (the former general manager of the Gas, Light and Coke Company who had originally come into the BBC to sort out its finances) left to become chairman of the Mining Association of Great Britain, that a man who measured up to the job finally filled it. By then – March 1944 – the war was already in its endgame. The role of William Haley, the BBC's editor-in-chief for only four months before his elevation, was to rebuilt the corporation for peace.

ALL CHANGE!

For most of the population, VE Day was the end of it: only those with men fighting in the Far East were interested in the campaign against the Japanese. People began to pick up the pieces of their lives as they continued to contend with shortages and rationing and concentrated on the first General Election for ten years.

Churchill had wanted to hold the coalition government together until the war was won outright. But national unity was at an end, the coalition was dissolved on 23 May and a Conservative caretaker administration was put in place while campaigning began. For the four successive weeks before polling on 5 July, from Monday to Friday, both the Home Service and the General Forces Programme carried twenty- or thirty-minute election addresses from the party leaders. Listening figures were enormous, averaging 45 per cent of the adult population. A leftward shift in public opinion had been evident since 1942, but Churchill's ill-advised 'Socialism means Gestapo in Britain' broadcast was a big factor in Labour's landslide, which was announced on 26 July.

The BBC had begun to lay its peacetime plans as early as 1943; and in a speech in 1944, Haley promised

July 1946: the war was over but austerity continued. People queue on the last day before bread rationing is introduced. Clothing remained rationed until 1949, petrol until 1950 and other food until 1954.

listeners that there would be a choice of three full radio networks – with a revival of regional broadcasting. On 29 July 1945, the Light Programme replaced the General Forces Programme. Its brief was to entertain, and to interest while not ceasing to entertain, and to compete with the Home Service, which essentially remained what it had been throughout the war: the mirror of the life of the whole community. (The final building brick, the Third Programme, the network of artistic value and serious purpose, was not to appear until September the following year, three months after the return of television.) The change signalled another: the news on the two networks was now broadcast at different times, read by different voices, and standardized to a length of ten minutes, with the exception of the nine o'clock bulletin, which was fifteen minutes long. The number of bulletins had been increased to eleven daily.

On 1 August, in co-operation with the British Forces Network in Germany (run by Army Welfare), the Light Programme introduced what was to become one of radio's best-loved programmes, *Family Favourites*. There was cricket on the Home Service: a

Polling day 1945: the result was delayed three weeks for the forces' vote to arrive. Labour's majority was 146. Had a candidtate stood against Churchill, he might have lost his seat.

scratch Australian XI was playing England, and Howard Marshall was back in the commentary box. The fifty-first Promenade Concerts were also being broadcast, one of them graced by the Spanish cellist Pablo Casals (who had chosen to remain in retirement in the eastern Pyrénées during the Nazi occupation of France), playing with the BBC Symphony Orchestra. Night after night the Albert Hall was packed from floor to roof; all attendance records were broken.

The 'business as usual' sign belied the fact that the BBC was strapped for cash and was still struggling with the problems of resettling staff returning from the Services, of absorbing those in the foreign language and monitoring sections whom it wanted to retain, and helping those who were going home. The *BBC Handbook* of 1946 said:

> Like everything else in Britain, broadcasting is suffering from the effects of the lean hard years of the war. Studios have been damaged and cannot immediately be replaced: staff has wasted away and has not been able to renew itself as in normal years: life itself lost most of its liveliest colour and broadcasting was equivalently circumscribed. Now life is flowing back to us. There are colourful scenes and occasions to report with whatever added distinction the practice of war-reporting has taught: there are all too many problems of vital concern to each one of us to be discussed freely and fairly without seeking controversy for controversy's sake: there is great need for laughter and for the deepened understanding which great music and great drama of the past and of today can give; and great need for recording soberly, truthfully and honestly the events which are making history day by day.

THE FALL OF JAPAN

By July the war against Japan had entered its final phase. The decisive battle at Okinawa which had begun in March had been won, opening the way to the invasion of the Japanese home islands. On 26 July, the Allies issued an ultimatum seeking immediate, unconditional surrender. This was rejected. On 6 August, Frank Phillips read the news:

> Scientists, British and American, have made the atomic bomb at last. The first one was dropped on a Japanese city this morning. It was designed for a detonation equal to 20 000 tons of high explosives, that is 2000 times the power of one of the RAF's 10-ton bombs of orthodox design. President Truman gave the news this afternoon in a statement from the White House.... This atomic bomb, the President added, is a harnessing of the basic powers of the universe. The force from which the sun draws its power has been loosed against those who brought war to the Far East. This actual harnessing of atomic energy may in the future supplement coal, oil and hydro-electric plants as sources of power.

The atomic bomb precipitated the end of the war. The first destroyed four square miles of Hiroshima and caused 70 000 deaths; the second on Nagasaki killed 39 000 people.

On 9 August, the bomb dropped on Hiroshima was followed by a second, on Nagasaki. Group Captain Leonard Cheshire recorded an eye-witness account for broadcast:

At the time of the explosion, we were wearing Polaroid welder's glasses. They were so dark that even the tropical sun showed through them as nothing more than a vague pinpoint of light. Even then, the explosion … was so bright that it had the same effect as if night had turned into day.

A few seconds later, when it was safe to take off our glasses, we looked out towards the target and saw a vast ball of fire. It was about 2000 feet in the air, and half a mile in diameter. This fire, which generated almost ten million degrees of heat, began rocketing up into the heavens at a speed of something like 20 000 feet per minute…. Even at a range of 20 miles we could see the dust from the earth being sucked up into the air like a vortex …

Stuart Hibberd, who had put out the news of Russia's declaration of war on Japan at the end of that evening's Prom on 8 August, came through Oxford Circus Underground two days later, after the 1 o'clock news had announced that Japan had asked for an armistice. He wrote in his diary: 'I thought everyone had gone mad. ATS and Wrens were standing on the top of Peter Robinson's building showering down paper on people's heads below, and holding long paper streamers, which billowed out in the wind …'

On Tuesday 14 August, Japan surrendered. Again there was an unnecessary delay in making the announcement and it was not until 11.45 p.m., when most of the country was in bed, that the BBC warned listeners to stand by. At midnight, the voice of Clement Attlee, the new Prime Minister, brought the story to a close.

VJ Day, Wednesday 15 August, was not quite a repeat of the celebrations which had taken place three months earlier; this time, there was a sense of anti-climax. At 9 p.m. the King broadcast to his people:

The war is over. You know, I think, that those four words have for the Queen and myself the same significance, simple yet immense, that they have for you.… There is not one of us who has experienced this terrible war who does not realize that we shall feel its inevitable consequences long after we have all forgotten our rejoicings of today.… From the bottom of my heart, I thank my peoples for all they have done, not only for themselves, but for mankind.

And that was that.

A BRIEF CHRONOLOGY OF THE SECOND WORLD WAR

1939

31 March	BBC staff numbers 5100
1 September	BBC Home Service, on 391.1 and 449.1 metres, replaces National and Regional Programmes at 8.15 p.m. BST; television service closed down. Germany invades Poland
3 September	Prime Minister Neville Chamberlain announces the outbreak of war from 10 Downing Street at 11.15 a.m.; King George VI's message to Britain and the Empire broadcast at 6 p.m.
5 September	Board of governors reduced by Order in Council to two; recorded broadcast from survivors of the *Athenia* in the news
21 September	Petrol rationing begins
30 September	Start of *The Home Front*, describing aspects of wartime life in Britain
1 October	First wartime broadcast by Winston Churchill, First Lord of the Admiralty
13 October	First report from Richard Dimbleby with the BEF in France
16 October	Eye-witness account from Edinburgh of the German air-raid on the Firth of Forth
17 October	Names of German prisoners-of-war included in BBC German news bulletins for the first time
29 October	Introduction of *Children's Hour* on Sundays
1 November	First public appearance in wartime of BBC Symphony Orchestra, at Colston Hall, Bristol
10 November	*The Shadow of the Swastika* is broadcast, the first of a series of dramas about the the Nazi party. *Garrison Theatre* begins
11 November	Broadcast of the Queen's message to the women of the Empire
15 November	Gracie Fields broadcasts from 'somewhere in France'
4 December	First broadcast of *Lift Up Your Hearts*, daily early morning prayers, and *Up In The Morning Early*, daily physical exercises

1940

7 January	Start of the Forces Programme
8 January	Food rationing begins
9 February	Norman Birkett anonymously counters Lord Haw-Haw in *Once A Week*, later renamed *Postscript*
31 March	BBC staff numbers 6445
9 April	Germany invades Denmark and Norway
10 May	Germany invades the Low Countries; Neville Chamberlain comes to the microphone to announce his resignation
19 May	Churchill's first broadcast as Prime Minister of a National Government

17 May	German troops enter Brussels
26 May	*Hi, Gang!* begins
27 May	Evacuation of British and Allied troops from Dunkirk begins
28 May	Brussels surrenders
5 June	J.B. Priestley's first *Postscript* broadcast
10 June	Italy declares war on Britain and France
14 June	German troops enter Paris
18 June	Broadcast of Churchill's 'This was their finest hour' speech; General de Gaulle's first broadcast to France
22 June	The French sign an armistice with Germany
23 June	*Music While You Work* begins
7 July	*Radio News Reel* begins in the Empire Service
10 July	Start of Battle of Britain; full-scale air attack on south-east England
7 September	Start of the Blitz on London
10 September	Dig for Victory campaign launched
15 September	RAF effectively wins the Battle of Britain
25 September	St George's Hall gutted by incendiary bombs, BBC theatre organ destroyed
13 October	Princess Elizabeth, aged 14, broadcasts a message in *Children's Hour* to children of the Empire – her first broadcast; Princess Margaret adds a good night
14 October	Tatsfield Receiving Station bombed; both 110-foot masts brought down
15 October	Delayed action bomb explodes in Broadcasting House during 9 p.m. news; seven staff killed
19 November	Adderley Park transmitter in Birmingham totally destroyed; staff in nearby shelter killed
8 December	Land-mine causes severe damage to Broadcasting House; European Service evacuated to Maida Vale
1941	
1 January	*Any Questions?* (later renamed *The Brains Trust*) begins
14 January	Start of V campaign in Belgian Service
21 February	BBC premises in Swansea destroyed by incendiary bombs
March	The Battle of the Atlantic begins
17 March	European Service moves into Bush House
31 March	BBC staff numbers 10 504
16 April	All premises on the eastern half of the Broadcasting House island site totally destroyed by high-explosive bombs; fatalities include one member of BBC staff
24 April	Board of governors increased to six members
10 May	Queen's Hall demolished by bombing; Maida Vale studios receives a direct hit by high-explosive bomb; one member of BBC killed; Bedford College in London (Overseas Service) severely damaged by fire; Rudolph Hess lands by parachute in Scotland
31 May	*Workers' Playtime* begins

2 June	Clothes rationing begins
6 June	First of weekly talks by 'Colonel Britton' to the Fifth Army of Europe
22 June	Germany invades Russia; Churchill offers all possible aid in a world-wide broadcast
13 July	Announcement broadcast simultaneously from London and Moscow of the signing of the Anglo-Russian Agreement
22 July	Board of governors restored to pre-war number
10 August	Broadcast by the Queen to the women of the USA
9 November	Start of Vera Lynn's show *Sincerely Yours*
6 December	Japan attacks Pearl Harbour; USA enters the war
8 December	Churchill broadcasts on Japan's entry into the war
21 December	First episode of *The Man Born To Be King* broadcast; broadcast of concert in honour of Stalin's 62nd birthday
25 December	Hong Kong surrenders to the Japanese

1942

January	The war in the Pacific begins
27 January	F.W. Ogilvie resigns as BBC director-general; R.W. Foot and Sir Cecil Graves become joint BBC directors-general
29 January	*Desert Island Discs* begins
1 February	First daily broadcast of *America Calling Europe*, in German, Italian and French, recorded from USA by radio-telephone and rebroadcast by BBC to Europe
15 February	Broadcast by Churchill announcing the fall of Singapore
22 March	First broadcast of a daily news bulletin in Morse code in certain European languages
31 March	BBC staff numbers 11 849
21 April	Command performance of *ITMA* at Windsor Castle on Princess Elizabeth's sixteenth birthday
6 May	First broadcast by the Radio Doctor
10 May	Churchill broadcasts survey of first two years of his premiership
30 May	First thousand-bomber raid, by the RAF, on Cologne
22 June	First performance in Britain of Shostakovich's *Leningrad Symphony*, broadcast on the first anniversary of Germany's invasion of Russia
7 October	First of a weekly fifteen-minute newsletter broadcast to Russia with co-operation of TASS (discontinued 26 May 1943)
23 October	Second Battle of El Alamein begins
4 November	Axis Forces in retreat at El Alamein
7 November	Broadcast in celebration of the twenty-fifth anniversary of the Russian Revolution
8 November	Sunday *Postscript* broadcast by Mrs Eleanor Roosevelt
23 November	Germans encircled at Stalingrad
6 December	Sunday *Postscript* broadcast by General Smuts, recorded in South Africa

1943

18 January	First BBC correspondent, Richard Dimbleby, accompanies RAF bomber crew on a raid on Berlin
2 February	German Army at Stalingrad surrenders
28 February– 6 March	Sixty programmes broadcast about the British Army
April	Record level of German U-boats operates in the Atlantic
1 April	*RAF Night*, a sequence of programmes in praise of the Royal Air Force
3 April	Start of *Saturday Night Theatre*
5 April	First broadcast of Yehudi Menuhin playing with the BBC Symphony Orchestra
16 May	Peals of bells broadcast in celebration of victory in North Africa
13 June	Overseas Forces Programmes becomes the General Overseas Service; the Empire Service becomes the Overseas Services (Pacific, African, North American, Eastern, Latin American)
July	Turning point in the Battle of the Atlantic
4 July	Inauguration of a radio service for the American Forces in Britain, in collaboration with the BBC
10 July	Allies invade Sicily
12 July	Introduction of a special news service for editors of clandestine newspapers in occupied Europe
25 July	Mussolini overthrown
1 September	R.W. Foot made sole BBC director-general; W.J. Haley made first editor-in-chief
4 September	Broadcast of recordings made by Wynford Vaughan Thomas and Reginald Pidsley in a Lancaster bomber over Berlin the previous night
8 September	Recording of General Eisenhower's broadcast from Algiers announcing the surrender of Italy
10 September	German troops enter Rome
13 October	Italy declares war on Germany
8 November	Broadcast of *In Honour of Russia*, a sequence of programmes the day after the twenty-sixth anniversary of the Russian Revolution
14 November	Programmes broadcast to commemorate the twenty-first anniversary of the BBC

1944

1 January	Simultaneous transmission of *Atlantic Spotlight* – joint venture of BBC and NBC – in America and Britain; second anniversary of *Shipmates Ashore*
27 February	First day of the new GFP preceded on 26 February by *Home Is On The Air*, intended to show British Forces overseas what the new network means; *Variety Bandbox* begins
31 March	W.J. Haley made BBC director-general; BBC staff numbers 11 657

26 April	6 p.m. news announces the new service, ABSIE, will start on 30 April, broadcasting to Europe by US Office of War Information, to be auxiliary to BBC services
18 May	Monte Cassino taken
22 May	One-hundredth edition of *Can I Help You?*
4 June	Fall of Rome announced on midnight news
6 June	D-Day: 8 a.m. news of invasion of France; the King broadcasts at 9 p.m.; announcement that new network, the AEFP, will start the following day; first *War Report* follows the news after the King's speech
10 June	Opening night of jubilee Proms
13 June	V1 (flying bomb) attacks on London begin
16 June	GFP interrupted at 11.15 a.m. for Herbert Morrison, speaking from the House of Commons, to announce that Germany is using pilot-less planes (V2s)
23 June	Fourth anniversary of *Music While You Work* – 3615th edition; at the time it was the longest run of any broadcast series
30 June	Flying bomb lands in the Aldwych outside Bush House; several European Service staff severely injured
25 August	News of liberation of Paris announced in the French Service at 12.30 p.m.; the flag of the French Forces of the Interior flown at Broadcasting House
3 September	The liberation of Brussels is announced
8 September	First V2 ballistic rockets fall on London
9 September	Actual chimes of Big Ben broadcast again for the first time since 16 June; broadcast celebrating the liberation of Luxembourg
17 September	Allied Airborne troops land behind German lines at Arnhem; 8 a.m. news announces the lessening of the black-out and the end of fire-guard duties and some Civil Defence duties in certain areas
24 September	Dobson and Young begin a fortnightly series of *Music With a Smile*
27 September	Allied defeat at Arnhem
4 October	Fourth anniversary programme of *Works Wonders*
13 October	Broadcast celebrating the liberation of Athens
21 October	Broadcast celebrating the liberation of Belgrade
22 October	Final broadcast of *Les Français Parlent aux Français*
8 November	250th edition of *War Commentary*
3 December	Stand-down of Home Guard
4 December	*Jobs For All, Number One* and *Full Employment* begin
1945	
27 January	Auschwitz extermination camp is captured by the Russians
March	BBC staff numbers 10 727
28 April	Mussolini and his mistress executed by partisans
30 April	Hitler marries mistress Eva Braun and then commits suicide
5 May	German forces surrender unconditionally to Field Marshal Montgomery

8 May	VE Day; broadcasts by Churchill and the King; special programmes relayed to all parts of the world
5 July	General Election day
26 July	General Election results announced; Labour is elected, with Clement Attlee as Prime Minister
29 July	Regional broadcasting resumes; the Light Programme begins
1 August	*Family Favourites* begins
6 August	Atomic bomb dropped on Hiroshima
8 August	Russia declares war on Japan
9 August	Atomic bomb dropped on Nagasaki
14 August	Japan surrenders unconditionally
15 August	VJ Day

INDEX